The Duchess of Berry and the Revolution of 1830

Imbert de Saint-Amand

BIBLIOLIFE

THE

DUCHESS OF BERRY

AND THE REVOLUTION OF 1830

BY

IMBERT DE SAINT–AMAND

TRANSLATED BY

ELIZABETH GILBERT MARTIN

WITH PORTRAIT

NEW YORK
CHARLES SCRIBNER'S SONS
1893

CONTENTS

THE DUCHESS OF BERRY

AND THE

REVOLUTION OF 1830

THE DUCHESS OF BERRY AND THE REVOLUTION OF 1830

I

THE COMMENCEMENT OF 1830

A T the Tuileries, the year 1830 opened with the same ceremonial, the same protestations of devotion as its predecessors. The first of January was both a national solemnity and a family festival. Charles X. was far enough from dreaming that it was the last New Year's Day he would spend in the palace of his fathers, and even his most relentless adversaries did not believe that his downfall was so near. Seated on his throne and receiving the homage of the great departments of State, he still possessed the full prestige of a sovereignty which seemed above all attacks from the Revolution; for, since the Charter, the ministers alone were responsible, the King not at all. At this time the old monarch persuaded himself that he would have no need of *coups d'État* to maintain his throne. "You are very right, gentlemen," said he to the members of the municipal council, " in

1

declaring that the welfare of kings and that of peoples are inseparable; one of them cannot be destroyed without the other. I hope that with the aid of Providence, all will occur as we could desire, and as all Frenchmen ought to desire. We shall be sensible of the intimate union existing between the maintenance of the throne and that of public liberties. The happiness of France depends thereupon."

According to an ancient usage, a deputation from the towns of Pontoise and Beauvais were admitted to present a sheep to the sovereign. The court jewellers displayed to him the trinkets and articles of silver-plate offered as gifts to the Dauphiness, the Duchess of Berry, the Duke of Bordeaux, and Mademoiselle. M. Giroux offered him various New Year's presents from the Children of France. The gardeners of the royal gardens presented the fruits of their industry, and the chief huntsmen the products of the chase.

On January 5, there was a family dinner at the Tuileries. The Twelfth-night cake was cut, and the bean fell to the Duke of Bordeaux. Who was chosen as queen by the little Prince? Madame the Duchess of Orleans. He did not suspect that she would be queen in reality before the year was out.

Already there was more than one legitimist who unconsciously, and possibly against his will, was getting ready for this new royalty. Like Thiers and Odilon Barrot in 1848, Chateaubriand in 1830 was causing a revolution without knowing it. He thought himself working simply for the overthrow of a ministry, and in reality he was accomplishing the downfall of a throne. At the time when Prince de Polignac came into power, he had sent in his resignation as ambassador of France at Rome, and perhaps he was beginning to repent of it. "When the moment approaches for the swallows to depart," he has said in his *Mémoires d'Outre-tombe*, "there is one that goes first, to announce the approaching journey of the others; mine was the pinion that anticipated the last flight of legitimacy. Was I charmed with the eulogies heaped upon me by the journals? Not the least in the world. . . . In the depths of my conscience I had a certain fear of having already pushed the Opposition too far; I was about to become unwillingly its link, arm, and centre; I was afraid of it, and this fear increased my regrets for the tranquil asylum that I had lost."

Ought not the author of the *Génie du Christianisme* to have perceived that his royalism was getting out of gear when he received, January 1, 1830, the following letter from M. Thiers, that systematic and relentless enemy of Charles X.? "Sir: not knowing whether a newly started journal will be promptly delivered, I forward you the first number of the *National*. All my collaborators join me in begging that you will kindly consider yourself, not as a subscriber, but as our benevolent reader. If, in this first article, which has been a source of great anxiety to me, I have succeeded in expressing opinions you approve, I shall feel reassured and certain of finding myself in a right path. Receive, sir, my respects."

And yet M. Chateaubriand's sympathy with the new sheet was by no means lively; for, after citing this letter, he adds: " The patron of the *National*, Prince Talleyrand, did not contribute a sou to its treasury; he merely fouled the spirit of the journal by casting his contingent of treason and rottenness into the common fund. . . . I will tell how I knew the editors; but, from this moment, I should set M. Carrel apart; superior to MM. Thiers and Mignet, he was simple enough, at the time when I became acquainted with him, to consider himself as inferior to the writers whom he surpassed; he maintained by his sword the opinions broached by these scribblers."

From the first days of 1830, there had been uneasiness in the air; but though political passions were keen and journalistic polemics heated, no one yet believed that a revolution was at hand.

The ministry was generally supposed to be in danger, and the prophets awarded it but a few months, or, perhaps, even a few weeks, of life, but the throne still appeared firm. The royal decree convoking the Chambers for March 2d was published January 7th in the *Moniteur*, and appeared to defer, if not to banish, all ulterior schemes for a *coup d'État*. The republicans had not yet begun to raise their heads, and the Bonapartists knew that the Austrian government was in nowise disposed to surrender to them the *son of man*, as the Duke of Reichstadt was styled by the poet Barthélemy. Nevertheless, shrewd spectators began to perceive that the imperial glories were again coming into fashion in all classes of society. The fact might be verified in the salon of the Countess de Flahaut. Her house, situated on the corner of the Champs-Élysées and the street which, after bearing successively the names of Angoulême, La Charte, and De Morny, is now called La Boëtie, was the rendezvous of the most prominent persons in society.

In his book entitled *Ma Jeunesse*, Count d'Haussonville has said: "Madame de Flahaut was English, the daughter of Admiral Keith. She had fallen in love, in 1815, with the brilliant Count de Flahaut, one of the Emperor Napoleon's aides-de-camp, at the time of the battle of Waterloo, where he had fought like a hero. As a foreigner, it was permissible for her to attract persons to her house who would not be met so naturally elsewhere. Invitations to the concerts and balls which, thanks to her large fortune, she frequently gave, were much sought after. The faubourg Saint-Germain was far from severe towards her. M. de Flahaut, in spite of his imperialist past and his existing connection with the Lafayette and Casimir Périer group, was justly esteemed a very well-bred man and a most agreeable host. He willingly assembled young people from every camp around him, and gave entertainments at which he paid particular attentions to the Duke of Chartres, eldest son of the Duke of Orleans."

There was a little gathering of dandies at General de Flahaut's house, who prided themselves on setting

the fashions; among the rest, the Montebello brothers, and MM. Charles Laffitte, Achille Fould, Walewski and De Moray.   Concerning the two latter,
Count d'Haussonville has said: " They were always
very attentive and amiable towards me. The manners of both were gracious and distinguished. They
were devoid of affectation and had a *comme il faut*
air which in them seemed like a gift of nature."
The effect produced on the greatest ladies of the
faubourg Saint-Germain by the young Count Walewski was one of the signs of the times. No great
nobleman of high legitimate society was more in the
fashion during the winter of 1829–1830.

Listen again while M. d'Haussonville describes the
worldly beginnings of the man who, twenty-six years
later, was to be Minister of Foreign Affairs to Napoleon III. and president of the Congress of Paris:
" Count Walewski's entrance into society took place,
oddly enough, under the auspices of all that was
most exclusive and pure in the aristocratic circles of
Paris.   One might call it a settled thing among the
most courted ladies of the faubourg Saint-Germain
to offer the most cordial reception to a young man
whose features recalled in a striking manner, though
with a pleasing and mild expression, those of the
celebrated mask. M. Walewski, to his credit, remained perfectly modest in face of all this feminine
alacrity to please him. Without becoming in the
least conceited, he allowed the most artful of them,
those who were entitled to consider themselves

the prettiest or the wittiest, to spare no pains or expense on his account, whether for brilliant toilettes or for wit, each employing the means of attraction which became her best. Every evening, in the most fashionable salons, he ran a real steeple-chase between a learned marquise who affected to speak to every ambassador in his native language, and a beautiful duchess who was then the type of sovereign elegance in Paris. Every one was betting on these two ladies, and the chances seemed doubtful, Walewski being careful to share his discreet attentions evenly between them."

In spite of political preoccupations and the extreme severity of an exceptionally cold winter, there was great animation in the salons and theatres. At the Tuileries, where she occupied the Pavilion of Marsan, the Duchess of Berry gave soirées twice a week which Charles X. honored by his presence, and which had all the more social prestige because the invitations to them were not numerous. It must be recognized that, although the charming Princess was grace, politeness, and kindliness itself, yet the wealthy middle class, proud of their riches, had a grudge against her for surrounding herself so exclusively with the heads of the aristocracy. The society of the *little palace*, as the Pavilion of Marsan was called then, aroused angry passions like those that had been enkindled in the days of Marie Antoinette, by the society of the Little Trianon. Nothing is so implacable as feminine vanity. The fashionable

women of the Chaussée-d'Antin were exasperated at
seeing themselves excluded from the faubourg Saint-
Germain and the court. How heartbreaking for these
ladies not to have been invited to the famous masked
ball of 1829, where the Duchess of Berry appeared
as Mary Stuart! The women of the upper middle
class, and especially the wives of leading capitalists,
could not accustom themselves to the superiority of
the great ladies. It is true that those among them
who, thanks to their wealth, had married men bearing great names, sometimes showed themselves more
infatuated with an escutcheon to which they were
unaccustomed, than women who belonged by birth
and marriage to the most illustrious families of the
French nobility. One can hardly imagine the extent to which the most liberal persons, and even the
most revolutionary, still permitted themselves to be
fascinated by the splendor of titles. The position of
eldest son to a peer of France was still a unique one,
even in 1830, and there was not a notary in Paris
who had not some banker's daughter, with an immense *dot*, to offer to the inheritor of a seat in the
Chamber of Peers.

In reality the liberals, so jealous of the ancient
families, were bitter against the old aristocracy only
because they hoped to construct a new aristocracy to
their own advantage. Was it the democratic sentiment, the great principle of equality, which impelled
them to revolution? No; it was personal interest, it
was vanity above all. Did they treat their inferiors,

their tradesmen, their domestics, in a politer, more humane, more Christian fashion than the great nobles did? Were they, after their triumph, to show themselves more generous, benevolent, and just toward the poorer classes than the nobility had done to the Third Estate? Not at all. What especially displeased the fine ladies of the Chaussée-d'Antin in the reign of Charles X. was the thought that they could not occupy the first rank. In their view, no Government would be suitable but one in which they should be received at court, and their husbands could don the fine uniform of officers of the National Guard. While awaiting the realization of this dream, they amused themselves as best they could in their own society, which did not fail to be animated and even brilliant. They made themselves especially noticeable at the great charity festivals. No winter having been more severe, people sought to alleviate the sufferings of the poor by combining almsgiving and pleasure. But even at the charity ball given at the Opéra on February 15, there were evident signs of the jealousies which were to be one of the principal causes of the approaching Revolution.

The King had defrayed the costs of the ball. Desiring that the subscribers' money should all go to the poor, he had undertaken to pay all the expenses. The musicians of the Fifth Regiment, who executed the fanfares at the entrance, had refused all remuneration, and so had the firemen and the detachments

of the royal guard and the gendarmes who were on
duty. Servants constantly circulated through the
hall, carrying trays loaded with ices and other re-
freshments, which they offered gratuitously to everybody. It was the King who paid for them. And
yet, in spite of the advice of the Viscount Sosthène
de La Rochefoucauld, he abstained from appearing
at this ball, where he would have received an ova-
tion, and opposite his box, which remained empty
throughout the evening, that of the Orleans family
attracted general attention.

The ball was magnificent. The King having placed
the decorations of the Menus-Plaisirs at the disposal
of the commissioners, the hall and its approaches
presented a fairy-like aspect. At the entrance, stairs
covered with carpets; on each side, shrubs and flowers; on the first landing, mirrors garlanded with ver-
dure; in the hall and the greenroom, candelabras
and sconces. Read the account given in the *Journal
des Débats:* "From the boxes, the aspect of the
parterre was curious. There was an inexpressible
diversity and movement. Quadrilles of ladies, prom-
enaders, spectators, everybody, was mixed up: peers
of France, deputies, officers, civilians, Englishmen,
Russians, Germans; representatives of every order
in the State and of every language in Europe were
there. Some young Egyptians in rich Oriental costumes promenaded in the midst of all that crowd
in frock coats and narrow pantaloons; they seemed
greatly astonished by this fête, and, in fact, I think

they could nowhere see anything more beautiful, unless in the Arabian tales."

The commissioners and lady patronesses had been chosen both from the high aristocracy and from liberal social circles, charity belonging to no party. At this eclectic entertainment, the Duke of Chartres selected as dancing partners the Duchess de Guiche, Madame Alphée de Vatry, the Princess de Beauffremont, and Mademoiselle Munster, the daughter of a diamond merchant. Mademoiselle Delphine Gay, afterwards Madame Émile de Girardin, composed some verses on this ball, in which she expressed her belief and hope that it heralded the cessation of disputes and greater accord between parties and classes. The naïve young girl was completely mistaken. Never had the blending of different social classes been farther off. Do not the accents of their rivalries pierce even through the account given by the *Journal des Débats?* "Some persons," said this sheet, "pretend to have noticed that the higher society preferred to remain in the boxes, leaving the pit and the dancing to the second rank in this assembly of the social *élite*. For our part, we judge of quality at a ball by grace and elegance, and we remarked no difference between the boxes and the pit. Certain refusals of admission are also talked of. We disbelieve in them. In an assembly of four or five thousand persons there is hardly room to play at aristocracy and etiquette. . . . At half-past one in the morning the orchestra played several gallopades.

The spectators, drawing back, left a passage, a sort
of long corridor, down the whole extent of the
saloon, where the gallopade was in full swing. The
Duke of Chartres was one of the dancers." A very
elegant and very handsome youth, the young Prince
was a great success. One might have thought that
the beauties of the Chaussée-d'Antin had a presentiment that he would give balls that would take
the place of those of the Duchess of Berry, and that
they would have the happiness of being invited to
them.

Five days after the charity ball at the Opéra, a
Chapter of the Order of the Holy Spirit was held
by the Dauphin at the Tuileries, after Mass. The
Duke of Nemours, having reached his fifteenth year,
was proclaimed a knight of the order. In the evening he was present, with the Duchess of Berry, the
Duke of Chartres, and the eldest daughter of the
Duke of Orleans, at a ball given by the Duke du
Duras, First Gentleman of the Chamber. There
was a ball to which the fair ladies of the Chaussée-
d'Antin would like to have been invited!

The time was near for the session of the Chambers
to open. A great contrast existed between the surface and the depths, the appearance and the reality
of things. M. Guizot has described it as a fermen-
tation beneath immobility. Nothing was done; everything was expected. People saw calm weather, and
predicted a storm. "Nobody acted," he adds, "and
everybody made ready for unknown opportunities.

We led our ordinary life, and felt ourselves on the
verge of chaos. No one conspired, no one rose, there
were no tumultuous gatherings; but we prepared for
anything. In Brittany, Normandy, Burgundy, Lor-
raine, and Paris associations were publicly formed
to refuse the payment of taxes if the Government
should attempt to collect them without a legal vote.
The ministry remained timid and inactive."

Political anxieties were hourly on the increase, and
yet neither charitable, fashionable, nor theatrical affairs were hampered in the least at Paris. When the
extraordinary representation was given at the Opéra,
for the benefit of the poor, the actors generously par-
ticipated in the public eagerness by refusing all in-
demnity for their assistance. "It pleases one," said
the *Moniteur*, "to see those who cultivate the arts,
honor themselves by a disinterestedness worthy of
praise, and to find estimable qualities in such accord
with talent."

At the Opéra they were playing *Guillaume Tell* and
La Muette with great success. At the *Italiens*, two
admirable singers, Mademoiselle Sontag and Madame Malibran, excited transports of enthusiasm,
the Duchess of Berry giving the signal for the applause. In the morning of February 25, she was
present, with the Duchess of Angoulême, at the
church of Saint Thomas Aquinas, where there was
a charitable meeting for the insane poor. The ser-
mon was preached by the Abbé Deguerry, chaplain
of the royal guard. A great literary event occurred

the same evening at the Théâtre Français: the
first representation of *Hernani*. Two days later the
Moniteur said: "Let it suffice to-day to avow the *stunning* success of a work mounted with admirable care,
a great wealth of decorations and costumes, and one
which ought to excite great curiosity. The delightful acting of Firmin in the rôle of Hernani, his admirable conception of the character, the incomparable
talent of Mademoiselle Mars (*Doña Sol*) in the fifth
act, Joanny's intelligence and energy in the rôle of the
Duke, guarantee for this work a long course of most
productive representations." The *Moniteur* was justified in calling it a *stunning* success, for it produced
a real tumult, a sort of boisterous and bitter quarrel
between the romanticists and classicists. This literary strife was like a prelude to the political struggle
which, from the beginning of the session, was about
to break out between the friends and enemies of the
King.

II

THE royal session of the opening of the Chambers was to take place March 2. On the day before that ceremony, Charles X. went from the Tuileries to Notre Dame to be present there at the Mass of the Holy Ghost. Two squadrons of chasseurs, two squadrons of body-guards with their bands, the heralds at arms, and pages preceded his carriage, in which the Dauphiness sat on his left, and the Dauphin and the Duchess of Berry occupied the front seat. Marshal Oudinot, Duke de Reggio, and the Duke de Mouchy were on horseback, one at the right and the other at the left side of the sovereign's carriage. A squadron of grenadiers and gendarmes closed the march. Many of the deputies absented themselves from Mass. The benches of the Left were empty, those of the Centre very scantily filled, those of the Right alone were almost completely occupied. To credit the ministerial journals, Charles X. excited the enthusiasm of the population as he went to and fro between the palace and the cathedral. In reality, he had been received much more coldly than usual.

The *Constitutionnel* published this article: " The

Mass of the Holy Ghost was celebrated to-day according to usage. Religion has been called on to consecrate by the éclat of its ceremonies the opening of the most important legislative session, thus far, in our parliamentary annals, for it is about to decide the very nature of the Government. Hence a visible anxiety was depicted on the faces of those who witnessed the pageantry of the day. . . . To-morrow, a ministry odious to an immense majority of Frenchmen is about to face that parliamentary majority which its organs have been insulting in such a cowardly manner for the last six months. To-morrow, the lie which it engendered in an evil day will betray itself. The faction has said: There is but one *royalist* ministry — which signifies in its language one counter-revolutionary ministry — that can be in a majority in both Chambers. The heads of the faction spoke with such assurance, they appeared so convinced, that they have carried conviction into the counsels of the throne. Thus was brought forth the Polignac Ministry, the disastrous result of vain fears and underhand trickery. Very well! they have lied."

The opening session, which was to be the last one of the reign, took place at the Louvre, in the *Salle des États*, on March 2. At one o'clock a salvo of artillery from the guns of the Invalides announced that Charles X. had started from the Tuileries. Accompanied by the princes of his family, he crossed the great Louvre Gallery, the *Salon Carré*, the Gal-

lery of Apollo, and stopped for some minutes in the hall
leading to that of the Guards of Henri IV., to receive
the homage of two grand deputations of twelve
members of the Chamber of Peers and twenty-five from
the Chamber of Deputies. These deputations were
led to the King by the Marquis de Dreux-Brézé,
grand master of ceremonies. The Dauphiness, the
Duchess of Berry, and the Duchess of Orleans had
already repaired to their tribune, whither the Duke
of Bordeaux in the uniform of a cuirassier was
brought by his tutor, General Baron de Damas; Mademoiselle his sister was also present, accompanied by
her governess, the Duchess de Gontaut. "The precocious intelligence of these august children," said
the *Journal des Débats*, "the interest they seem to
take each year in this imposing ceremony, are not
its least attractions to many spectators." The Chancellor of France, Marquis de Pastoret, took his stand
in front of his armchair; Prince Talleyrand, Grand
Chamberlain, had his own chair covered with corn-
colored velvet fringed with gold. The ministers
were on the benches at each side of the throne. At
the forcibly pronounced words: "The King!" there
was a general movement; everybody spontaneously
arose, and Charles X. was seen to enter, wearing the
uniform of a general officer, and followed by the
princes of his family. He was received with unanimous applause. One might have thought his ancient
popularity had returned. He seated himself on his
throne, with the Dauphin and the Duke of Chartres

on his right, and the Dukes of Orleans and Nemours
on his left. The princes wore the costume of peers
of France, and were decorated with the great collar
of the Order of the Holy Spirit.

The expression of the old King's face was as benevolent and kindly as ever, but it had an air of solemn
gravity and sorrowful resolution. The sovereign
read his discourse in the midst of profound silence.
He announced that the peace of Europe was consolidated, and that independent Greece was about
to be reborn from its ruins. "In the midst of the
serious events with which Europe was occupied,"
continued Charles X., "I was obliged to suspend the
effects of my resentment against a barbarous power;
but I can no longer permit the insult offered to my
flag to go unpunished. The signal reparation I shall
obtain, while satisfying the honor of France, will
turn, with the aid of the Almighty, to the profit of
Christianity." He afterwards announced that the
Budget was balanced by an excess of receipts over
expenditures, and closed his discourse as follows:
" Gentlemen, my first care is to see France, happy
and respected, developing all the riches of her soil
and manufactures, and peacefully enjoying the institutions whose welfare I have firmly resolved to
assure. The Charter has placed the public liberties
under the protection of the rights of my crown.
These rights are sacred; my duty towards my people
is to transmit them intact to my successors.

"Peers of France and deputies of departments, I

doubt not I shall have your assistance in accomplishing the good I wish to do. You will repel the perfidious insinuations which malice seeks to propagate. If culpable manœuvres stir up obstacles against my Government, which I do not wish to anticipate, I shall find strength to overcome them in my resolve to maintain the public peace, the just confidence of the French people, and the love they have always manifested for their Kings."

The Assembly was vividly impressed by this language. The Right and the Centre burst into acclamations. There were even members of the Left who applauded this swan-song of legitimate royalty. M. Guizot, who had just been elected deputy for the first time, and who was present at this royal session, has said of it: "The attitude of the King was, as usual, noble and benevolent, but he showed traces of repressed agitation and embarrassment. He read his speech with some precipitation, although quietly, as if in haste to get through with it, and when he came to the phrase which contained a royal menace under a temperate form, he accented it with more affectation than energy. In laying his hand upon it he let his hat fall, which the Duke of Orleans picked up and returned to him, kneeling."

The throne speech ended, the Chancellor, after receiving orders from Charles X., announced that the King permitted the Duke de Nemours, prince of the blood, and peer of France by right of birth, to take in his presence the oath prescribed to all the

peers of the realm. The Chancellor read the formula
of the oath, which was thus expressed: "I swear to
be faithful to the King, to obey the Constitutional
Charter and the laws of the Kingdom, and to com-
port myself in all things as beseems a good and loyal
prince of the blood and peer of France." It was
noticed with what an energetic accent the young
Prince, then fifteen years old and as handsome as the
day, responded: "I swear it!"

Hardly had Charles X. quitted the Assembly, than
a lively discussion on the subject of his discourse
ensued between the Right and the Left. The first
praised it to the skies, the others saw in it a declaration of war. There was no agitation among the
masses, nor in the streets; but in the political world
there was a very keen one. In the Chamber of
Deputies the discussion of the address was very
animated.

If M. de Chateaubriand's partisans had voted with
the Ministry, it would have had a majority. But
those royalists who, like this illustrious writer, were
making a revolution without knowing it, made a
coalition with the Left, and the chamber passed, by
a vote of two hundred and twenty-one against one
hundred and eighty-one, the famous address destined
to become so famous under the title of Address of
the Two hundred and twenty-one, which under a
respectful and courteous form, contained as a résumé
a menace against the King's policy, and which may
indeed be called the first cause of the revolution of

1830. It had been discussed in secret committee on
the 15th and 16th of March, in the vast hall, empty
of spectators. " M. de Polignac," says M. Guizot, an
eyewitness, " was in his seat, immovable and scantily
surrounded by friends, and looking like a man
bewildered and surprised, thrown among a circle
which he does not know very well, and where he is
unwelcome, and charged with a delicate mission
whose result he awaits with inert and powerless dignity. . . . Evidently, when they performed bold acts
of volition, neither the King nor his minister was
at his ease ; there was in the expression as well as in
the soul of both these persons, a mixture of resolution and feebleness, confidence and anxiety, which
testified at once to blindness of mind and the foreboding of misfortune."

The *Gazette de France*, as if it had already foreseen
the approaching catastrophe, wrote : " Two hundred
and twenty-one men, having taken an oath of fidelity
to the King, have sanctioned the first manifesto of
the revolution of 1830. They will have to answer
to the King, who has not yet been deprived of his
authority, and who, surrounded by a devoted army,
leaning on a faithful peerage, and defended by the
love of all his people, will demand, with severity, an
account of his attacked prerogative and the violated
Charter." Thus it was that the two parties mutually
accused each other of attacking the Charter.

Listen again to M. Guizot : " Two days after the
Address had been voted, March 18, 1830," says he,

"we repaired to the Tuileries to take it to the King. Only twenty-one deputies were added to the bureau and the great deputation of the Chamber. We were but forty-six in all. We waited for some time in the Salon de la Paix until the King should return from Mass. There we were, standing, and in silence. Opposite us, in the embrasures of the windows, were the King's pages and some people belonging to the court who were designedly inattentive and almost impolite. Madame the Dauphiness crossed the salon to go to the chapel, hastily and without looking at us. She might have been colder yet without my feeling that I had any right to be surprised or to complain. There are crimes, the memory of which silences all other thoughts, and misfortunes before which one bows with a respect that is very like repentance, as if one had caused them himself."

Charles X. had received communion at the Mass, as was his custom in all solemn or difficult circumstances of his reign. On returning from the chapel he had stopped in the Throne Room, where, surrounded by the princes and princesses, the ministers, and the great officers of the crown, he admitted the deputies to his presence. M. Royer-Collard, President of the Chamber of Deputies, read the Address, which was already but too well known to the King. In this document there were perfectly respectful passages; this, for example: "Hastening at your voice from all quarters of your realm, we bear you, Sire, from every side, the homage of a faithful people, still affected

by having found you the most beneficent of all in
the midst of universal beneficence, and revering in
you the accomplished model of the most touching
virtues. Sire, this people cherishes and respects your
authority. Fifteen years of peace and liberty, which
it owes to your august brother and yourself, have
rooted profoundly in its heart the gratitude which
attaches it to your royal family. Its reason, ripened
by experience and by liberty of discussion, tells it
that it is above all in matters of authority that
antiquity of possession is the most sacred of titles,
and that it is no less for its welfare than for your
glory that the ages have placed your throne in a
region inaccessible to storms. Hence its conviction
agrees with its duty in offering it the sacred rights
of your throne as the surest guarantee of its liberties, and the integrity of your prerogatives as necessary to the preservation of its rights."

M. Royer-Collard read with satisfaction this passage, so respectful, almost obsequious, to the sovereign. But he was troubled and embarrassed when
he came to this other passage, which provoked such
profound resentment at the Tuileries: "Sire, the
Charter which we owe to the wisdom of your august
predecessor, and whose advantages Your Majesty
firmly intends to consolidate, consecrates as a right
the intervention of the country in the deliberation of
public interests. This intervention should be, and
in fact is, indirect, wisely circumspect, circumscribed
within exact limits which we shall not permit any

one to dare to pass; but it is positive in its results,
for it effects a permanent co-operation between the
political views of your Government and the wishes
of your people, the indispensable condition of the
regular progress of public affairs. Sire, our loyalty,
our devotion, condemns us to say to you that this
co-operation no longer exists."

When he had to utter this final sentence, which
Charles X. considered as insulting, M. Royer-Collard,
far from displaying arrogance, softened the tone of
his voice, as if he were grieved to address such language to the sovereign.

A few days later, the Viscount Sosthène de La
Rochefoucauld was to write, in a report addressed to
Charles X., March 24, 1830 : " 'Never,' said Royer-
Collard to me within a day or two, 'has the King
been so fine, so dignified, so much a king, as on the
day when we took him the Address : sad without ill-
temper, severe without anger; I was affected to tears.
He will bear me a grudge, I said to myself, but for
my part I am convinced that I have done him an
immense service ; the session had become impossible
with the existing ministry, and yet the King could
make no changes in it in presence of the Chambers.
At present the King is on his feet; it is his business
to do what is right, for he is still master; later on
he would not be so, and events would march more
quickly than men's wishes. In spite of everything,
I pity him from the bottom of my heart, and both his
dignity and his sadness have touched me profoundly.

I hope, at any rate, that he was pleased with the respectful tone in which I read him the Address; that was my duty.' "

Charles X. made his reply in a sonorous voice, but one that betrayed keen emotion. " Gentlemen," said he, " I have listened to the Address you present me in the name of the Chamber of Deputies. I have a right to count on the concurrence of the two Chambers to accomplish all the good I meditate. It saddens my heart to find the deputies of the departments declaring that, on their side, this concurrence does not exist. Gentlemen, I declared my intentions in my speech at the opening of the session ; these resolutions are immovable ; the welfare of my people forbids me to depart from them. My ministers will acquaint you with my resolutions."

They say that on leaving the palace of the Tuileries, M. Royer-Collard exclaimed: " What a truly great and imposing thing a king is on his throne ! I never was so struck with it as I am to-day." He is reported to have said later: " I thought the King would yield; if I had foreseen his resistance, I would not have voted the Address."

March 19, 1830, the day after the Address had been presented to the sovereign, the ministers carried to the Chamber the royal decree, proroguing it until September 3, a prorogation which was the signal of a dissolution. The deputies divided at once. Some cried: " Long live the King ! " Others responded: " Long live the Charter ! " Some one in a tribune cried:

"Long live the Constitution!" A deputy of the Right asked the President to have the tribunes emptied. M. Royer-Collard contented himself with replying: "Sir, there is no longer a Chamber." The last parliamentary session of the reign of Charles X. was at an end.

III

PUBLIC OPINION

IN view of the conflict that had supervened between the crown and the Two hundred and twenty-one, there was anxiety in both camps concerning the probable verdict of public opinion. The partisans of Charles X. were in nowise discouraged. Order prevailed throughout the realm. Not only was there no financial panic, but public funds rose perceptibly — a fact mentioned with lively satisfaction by the royalist journals. In its issue of March 20, the *Gazette de France* said: "It ought never to be lost sight of that nothing but a revolution could bring about a triumph of the democracy, and hence that all calculations based on this triumph are so much the more empty because people would lose a thousand times more than they could gain by it. The admirable instinct of self-interest has correctly divined this high political verity, for everything that has happened in the liberal direction has lowered the funds, while every manifestation of the royal strength has raised them. It is a remarkable thing that the discussions on the Address caused stocks to fall for several days, while the King's reply has sent them

27

up. For a long time facts like this have made
people say that the *ecus* are royalists. When one
thinks of the many illusions of the liberal party for
these two years past, he cannot help seeing that it
has a bandage over its eyes."

On its side, the *Constitutionnel* wrote : —

" It is they who deepen the shadows around the
throne, who would like to confine truth to the threshold of the palace, who by infamous impostures cal-
umniate a generous people, submissive to the laws,
inimical to perjury and faithful to its duties; it is
these men, covered with the mask of a hypocritical
devotion, who disturb the harmony of the powers of
state."

To believe the ministerial journals, there was nothing grave in the situation. We read in the *Gazette
de France* of March 21: " Agitation prevails only at
the surface, the froth bubbles, but the depths of society remain tranquil. The revolutionary journals
make a noise, and those of the third party make still
more. Certain loungers in cafés are disturbed about
it at a fixed hour every morning, so as to forget it
altogether until the same hour next morning. Are
these cries and sarcasms, this factitious tumult, this
intentional scandal, the opinion of an entire people?"

At the Tuileries, etiquette was observed in the
calmest and most regular way. Charles X. seemed
tranquil and even joyous. On Sunday, March 21,
he received after Mass a remarkably numerous throng
of courtiers. The *Constitutionnel* said on the 24th:

"Our adversaries are losing their heads. Good fortune inebriates them. The hundred deputies who appeared at the Tuileries on Sunday, the carriages that filled the court, are an admirable text to turn to a lying advantage, in order to thicken the bandage on eyes that are most interested in seeing clearly. Well! these carriages, supposing there were a thousand of them, have set down twelve or fifteen hundred courtiers under the Pavilion of the Horloge. What does that prove? Madame de Sévigné said in the old days that all France was there. Perhaps that was true under Louis XIV.; but France is somewhere else to-day; she is in the electors, the tax-payers and their families; and all these look with pity at a ministry which thinks itself strong because it is foolhardy, and which is throwing itself headlong into an abyss whose depth it has not sounded."

Meanwhile, the opposition was organizing resistance with a daily increasing boldness: it offered a banquet at Paris to the Two hundred and twenty-one voters of the Address; it arranged triumphal receptions for them in their departments; it sought every means of conciliating public opinion. The *National*, M. Thiers's journal, emboldened by the impunity of its attacks, used increasingly violent and revolutionary language. It never ceased recalling, as an ominous date, the year 1688, which is that of the fall of the Stuarts. "James II.," it remarked, "had understood the incompatibility between himself and the new ideas of the English

people. He fled without any one pursuing him;
his departure left the throne vacant, and the English
were then so little inclined to revolution that they
offered the crown to the nearest relative of the fugitive King."

On seeing M. Thiers throw off his mask, and advo-
cating the candidacy of the Duke of Orleans to the
throne of France as early as February, 1830, the
men who were in opposition, but a dynastic opposition, should have made some salutary reflections.
They persisted none the less in their bitter attacks
on the ministry. Nevertheless, they protested against
the date of 1688, which had become the programme
of the *National.* " What is a change of dynasty,"
we read in the *Débats* of February 21, " since at
last, after fifteen years of Restoration, we have
arrived at that question, thanks to the ministry of
August 8? Is it a revolution? Yes; and of the
most dangerous sort. What did the revolution of
1688 cost the English people? Sixty years of excep-
tional laws and legal despotism, sixty years during
which all opposition was either suspected of being
Jacobite or forced to be so, and hence was powerless
to defend liberty; Prince Edward's civil war, the
Scotch agitation; a pretender ever ready to rally
the discontented and to lend the color of justice to
their cause; more than a century of opposition to
Catholics and the enslavement of Ireland — that is
what the revolution of 1688 cost the liberty and
stability of England."

The conclusion of the article of the *Journal des Débats* was as follows: "A change of dynasty is as impossible in France as the abolition of the Charter. In 1688, England found glory and genius in the usurpation. William of Nassau was there. In 1830, though we should look all over Europe, we should nowhere find a William of Nassau. In 1688, Europe was so disposed that all its wishes called William to the throne of England, and the usurper arrived in London with the alliance of all kings. In 1830, Europe is so disposed that an usurper would enter the Tuileries, as Bonaparte did on March 20, with the armed enmity of all Europe."

When M. de Lamartine delivered his discourse of reception at the French Academy, April 1, 1830, this future founder of the Second Republic spoke of monarchy in general, and of Charles X. in particular, in language that was a veritable dithyramb. "This century," said the orator-poet, "will date from our double restoration; the restoration of liberty by the throne, and of the throne by liberty. It will bear the name either of that kingly legislator who consecrated the progress of the times in the Charter, or of this honest King whose oath is a charter and who will maintain for his posterity this perpetual gift of his family. . . . History tells us that peoples personify themselves, so to say, in certain royal races, in dynasties which represent them; that they decline when these races decline; that they revive when they are regenerated; that they perish when these succumb;

and that certain families of kings are like those domestic gods who could not be carried away from the thresholds of our ancestors unless the hearthplace itself were ravaged or destroyed."

How was this passage of the discourse received? An auditor shall inform us. In a report addressed to Charles X., April 7, 1830, the Viscount Sosthène de La Rochefoucauld writes: "The King will not repel an important observation which I made the other day at M. de Lamartine's reception at the Academy, and which is due to him from my entire devotion. The *élite* of the capital were gathered there. In eulogizing Louis XVIII., the orator spoke of the Charter as one of his benefits. A murmur of gratitude was heard. Passing to the eulogy of Charles X., he spoke of the confidence which his oaths should inspire. People looked at each other mechanically. This suspicion, however unjust it may be, unfortunate if well-founded, still more unfortunate if it be not, explains the general uneasiness that prevails."

Speaking as a friend, not as a courtier, the Viscount de La Rochefoucauld did not spare warnings to his King. He had written to him, March 17, 1830: "Sire, over the very tomb of Louis XVIII. in the name of his oaths, in the name of our France, that France so fair, so flourishing, and so strong, in the name of your dynasty, in the name of your august heir, I dare supplicate you not to compromise beyond recall the heritage which your august brother

left to you in a state so prosperous and tranquil. . . .
Louis XVIII., Sire, had foreseen all that has happened; take care not to realize his sad predictions!
No; it is in vain that one thinks himself able to
trifle with public opinion ; it is a dangerous torrent
to which dikes must be set, but which it is utterly
impossible to force back to its source. Kings are
men, Sire: it costs them something to say they have
been wrong. Be more than a man, more than a
king, and have the courage to pause before the
abyss dug beneath the steps of your throne."

There is reason to remark that a good number of
persons belonging to the greatest families in the
kingdom showed hostility to Prince de Polignac.
Thus, as has been observed by Count d'Haussonville,
in his book entitled *Ma Jeunesse*, several of the most
ancient and devoted adherents of King Charles X.,
such, for example, as the Duke de Fitz-James, other
considerable personages occupying the highest positions at court, and even the Duke de Polignac, eldest brother of the president of the council, made no
mystery of their disapprobation. "I remember,"
adds M. d'Haussonville, "that in the very salon of
the Duchess de Guiche, I have several times heard
her husband, first gentleman to the Duke of Angoulême, let fall expressions which gave me to understand that the Dauphin himself, whose attitude in
political matters was always so correct, was rather
displeased with the excessive zeal and the purposes
of a man whom the King, his father, on account of

an ancient friendship of his youth, had had the imprudence to place at the head of public affairs."

Meanwhile, the more the opposition increased, the more calmness and serenity did Charles X. display. During Holy Week, he fulfilled his duties as the Most Christian King, with complete tranquillity of heart and mind. On Holy Thursday, April 8, 1830, the ceremony of Washing the Feet took place in the Tuileries, in the Gallery of Diana. Charles X. washed the feet of thirteen children representing the apostles. He gave each of them a little bag containing thirteen five-franc pieces, served them with thirteen dishes, a loaf weighing a pound, and a jug of wine. The Dauphin and the great dignitaries assisted the King in this pious ceremony, at which the Dauphiness, the Duchess of Berry, the ministers, the ambassadors and their wives, and the ladies of the princesses were present.

April 15, Charles X. reviewed, on the Champ de Mars, the troops of the garrison of Paris. The Dauphin, the Dauphiness, and the Duchess of Berry were present at this review, which was very fine. The discipline and the spirit of the troops seemed excellent to the sovereign. He thought himself sure of the army, and did not doubt the final success of his policy. The two most moderate of the ministers, MM. Courvoisier and de Chabrol, having refused their concurrence in the hypothesis of extreme measures, both left the council. The most audacious member of the Villèle Cabinet, M. de Peyronnet, became Minister of the Interior. "What has always been lacking," said the monarch, proud of his choice, "is the boldness to raise one's standard. Well! the very name of Peyronnet is a standard which I raise." The Chamber was dissolved May 16, and the opening of the new Chamber, which was to be elected in July, was fixed for August 3. The royal fleet, carrying a whole army under the command of General Count de Bourmont, was about to sail for Algeria in a few days; and Charles X., awaiting the future with confidence, counted on both an electoral and a military triumph when he should receive at his court the visit of the King and Queen of Naples.

IV

THE PALAIS-ROYAL BALL

THE King of Naples, having conducted to Madrid his daughter Marie Christine, — now become the Queen of Spain, — did not wish to return to his dominions without visiting the King of France, the head of the House of Bourbon. He arrived at Saint-Cloud, with the Queen his wife, May 15, 1830. Born August 19, 1777, widowed of Marie Clémentine, Archduchess of Austria, the mother of the Duchess of Berry, November 15, 1801; remarried October 6, 1802, to the Infanta of Spain, Marie Isabelle, born July 6, 1789, François I. had reigned over the Two Sicilies since January 3, 1825. He was delighted to see his daughter, the Duchess of Berry, and his sister, the Duchess of Orleans, once more. France was like a second native land to him, and he found himself at home there. After resting for an hour at the palace of Saint-Cloud, he left it with Charles X., who brought him to the Élysée palace at Paris. Acting in character as head of the House of Bourbon, the King of France took the back seat of the carriage and placed the Queen of Naples at his right; the King of Naples was on

the front seat, with the Duchess of Berry at his right.
Charles X. and Their Sicilian Majesties were received
at the Élysée by the Prince of Salerno, the Duke of
Orleans, the ministers and ambassadors of Spain and
the Two Sicilies. The Duke de Blacas had been
appointed governor of the Élysée palace during the
whole time the King and Queen of Naples should
reside there.

The political situation was at this time in a very
disturbed condition. The coming elections, the relentless party strifes, and anxieties about the Algerian expedition, agitated men's minds extensively.
Incendiary fires were daily devastating the departments of La Manche and Calvados. The Government
was compelled to send troops to the localities thus
ravaged, and each party accused the other of being
the author of these crimes. There was general
uneasiness at Paris, and all clear-sighted persons
predicted approaching catastrophes. These apprehensions contrasted with the numerous fêtes given in
honor of Their Sicilian Majesties and the brilliant
exhibition of all the enchantments united at the
capital by the theatres and the arts.

May 16, the King and Queen of Naples, the Prince
of Salerno, the Duke of Orleans and his family, dined
at the Tuileries with the Duchess of Berry. May
19, the Vicount Sosthène de La Rochefoucauld (afterwards Duke of Doudeauville), superintendent of
amusements, addressed a report to Charles X., in
which he said: " The King of Naples seems con-

tented with the state in which he found the manufactory of Sèvres. Their Sicilian Majesties were
very gracious with me. The performance of the
previous evening had greatly impressed them. They
complimented me in an amiable manner on the un-
precedented perfection which French singing had
attained. Five years ago people of taste fled from
the opera; the highest receipts, which were three
thousand francs then, now frequently amount to six
or seven thousand. The coulisses have been closed,
in spite of the wrath of the courtiers, and by that
means many disorders have been abolished. Hence
the possessors of shares in the *Figaro* torment me
about it continually."

Political preoccupations mingled with those of art.
In the same report, the noble Viscount said: " To
come to more serious matters, I decline to believe the
news which has been told me as certain; the consequences would be too frightful, because all that has
been said would then be justified. The King would
then be involved in a terrible way. In that case he
would be forced, sooner or later, to draw back. To-
day it would suffice for him to inform himself and to
resolve. . . . It is a coterie which is seizing power,
and will have it on any terms, in spite of the certain danger to which it exposes the monarchy."

Meanwhile the festivities continued to be more
and more brilliant. May 23, the Duchess of Berry
gave a ball at the Tuileries to the King and Queen
of Naples. She went with Their Sicilian Majesties

to the palace of Compiègne, May 25, and on the 28th to Chantilly, where she breakfasted and dined with the Duke of Bourbon. She did the honors of her pretty chateau of Rosny to her crowned visitors, where she arranged a fête of exquisite elegance.

If the King of Naples were a perspicacious observer he could have divined, by more than one symptom, the latent antagonism already existing between the situation of his daughter, the Duchess of Berry, and that of his brother-in-law, the Duke of Orleans. There was a performance at the palace of Saint-Cloud, and Charles X. permitted his grandchildren to be present at it.

Listen to the account of the Duchess de Gontaut: " We passed through the Orangery to go to the playhouse. Charles X. gave his arm to the Queen of Naples, and said to the Duke of Bordeaux, ' Follow us.' The young prince entered the Orangery. Finding himself abreast with the Duke of Orleans, he halted respectfully. Baron de Damas gave him a push thereupon, and said aloud, ' Pass on, Monsieur. The King so wills it.' Mademoiselle, in her pretty, childish way, approached her uncle and took his hand. When we reached the theatre," adds the Duchess de Gontaut, " the Duke of Orleans seated himself near me, lamented the incident which had just occurred, and seemed to be wounded by the lesson he pretended to have received. I assured him that the intention of the Baron de Damas was simply to notify the Duke of Bordeaux that the King was waiting for him. He was slow to believe it."

The ball given by the Duke of Orleans, May 31,
in honor of the King and Queen of Naples, was of
extraordinary brilliancy. Charles X. was present,
and to judge from the evidences of profound deference lavished upon him by his cousin, one could
scarcely have suspected the secret rivalry that had
existed for so many years between the two branches
of the House of Bourbon. The Palais-Royal, of revolutionary memory, was resplendent. The Duke of
Orleans had done things in grand style. Terraces
covered with orange trees and flowers of all varieties
seemed to continue the salons by a suite of hanging
gardens. The decorations were magnificent; one
would have called it an enchanted palace. There
was no less animation outside than within the apartments. From seven in the evening an immense
throng occupied the garden and blocked up the streets
through which Charles X. was to pass.

The King, the Dauphin and Dauphiness, accompanied by the great officers of their households and
an escort of body-guards, arrived at a quarter past
nine, and were received at the foot of the grand staircase by the Duke of Orleans and his two sons, the
Dukes of Chartres and Nemours. All the prominent
persons in Parisian society were present at the fête ;
great nobles and civilians, capitalists and soldiers,
artists and literary men. All parties were represented. The former heads of the Emigration elbowed
the chiefs of the revolutionary opposition. The
Palais-Royal was a neutral ground where the bitter-

est adversaries met for a ball. Charles X., whose
benevolent and optimistic nature was easily prone to
illusion, naïvely imagined that he had not a single
enemy in all this crowd, and that the monarchical
principle was beyond all dispute. Joy and confidence beamed on the sovereign's face. He found
the Duchess of Orleans at the head of the grand
staircase, offered her his arm, and passed through
the first salons, addressing gracious remarks to the
ladies who formed a double line at either side of him.

A few minutes later, the King and Queen of Naples
arrived, with the Duchess of Berry and the Prince of
Salerno. Charles X. interrupted his progress to go
several steps to meet the Queen, and stopped to chat
with her. According to the *Moniteur*, he seemed to
be making very flattering remarks, judging from the
expression of happiness on her face. Charles X.
went through all the apartments, the luxury of
which dazzled him. Turning toward the Duke of
Orleans, who followed him respectfully: "Oh, come,
Monsieur," said he, smiling; "do you know you are
undertaking to be better lodged than I am?" He
continued his progress, keeping the King and Queen
of Naples always at his side, which did not prevent
his chatting graciously with the ladies who crowded
round him. Having passed through all the apartments, he advanced toward the border of the terrace
looking on the garden. It was lighted up with lamps
of every hue. The moon and stars rivalled the brilliancy of the illuminations. When Charles X. ap-

peared on the terrace, shouts arose from the immense
crowd filling the garden, which, as it seemed to the
monarch, were nothing and could be nothing but
cries of joy and love. During this time the bands
belonging to several regiments of the royal guard
played the airs so dear to the Bourbons: "*Vive
Henri IV.! Charmante Gabrielle!*" In the midst of
this atmosphere of harmony, lights, and flowers, the
King began to think of his fleet, crossing the seas
to conquer a barbaric realm. "Gentlemen," said he,
looking at the clear sky, "this is very fine weather
for my Algerian fleet!"

The friends of Charles X., however, seeing him
surrounded by the whole opposition, considered the
fête an unlucky omen. They said the demonstrations of respect made by the liberals toward the
King were hypocritical, and were aware of something mysterious and disquieting in the atmosphere
which veiled conspiracy under the appearance of
pleasure. The joyous sounds of the orchestra hardly
drowned the serious conversations of men who were
talking politics and predicting near catastrophes.
"This is a real Neapolitan fête," exclaimed M. de
Salvandy, "for we are dancing over a volcano."

Noises from outside reached the very doors of the
glittering salons, like the signs that herald a storm.
Several times the crowd which the Duke of Orleans,
through love of popularity, had been so imprudent as
to let into the garden, threw down the gates which
separated them from the inclosure into which none

but the invited guests were admitted. The police
and the guard could not keep them back. Orators,
mounted on improvised platforms, excited them.
They tore down bushes, piled up chairs, and set
them on fire. The old people among them bethought
themselves of the beginning of the Revolution, July
12, 1789, the day when, in this very garden of the
Palais-Royal, the home of insurrection, Camille Des-
moulins, pistol in hand, stood up on a chair and
shouted: "Citizens, there is not a moment to lose.
The dismission of Necker is the tocsin for a Saint
Bartholomew of patriots. This very evening foreign
battalions will issue from the Champ-de-Mars to cut
our throats. But one resource is left us, — to rush to
arms." "To arms!" shouted the crowd in reply,
seizing the busts of Necker and of Philippe-Égalité,
and bearing them in triumph through the most populous streets. Two days later, the Bastille was taken.

Did Charles X. recall these souvenirs during the
brilliant festivity where friends and enemies lavished
on him such obsequious homage? did he foresee that
before two months were over the Palais-Royal would
give the signal for another cataclysm? We do not
believe it. Good care was taken not to let him know
that malice had set fire to the chairs that were flam-
ing in the garden. He thought it a mere accident,
the beginnings of a fire almost immediately extinguished.

The Duchess de Gontaut thus describes the affair
in her Memoirs: "The fête was splendid. All was

joy and pleasure when a cry of 'Fire!' was heard
from the garden. Flames rising as high as the windows were perceived; chairs piled up to a prodig-
ious height were burning; illumination-lamps were
flying through the air, thrown by unknown hands.
There was a general fright. The authors of this
disaster were unknown; several arrests were made.
The Duke of Orleans, as one may fancy, was in
despair. The King smilingly reassured the dismayed
dancers. Serenity was soon restored and the ball
began again. My daughter Charlotte was there,
and so was her husband. From Saint-Cloud we
could plainly see this conflagration improvised by
malice: I was alarmed for the very dear persons
whom I knew at the ball. I wrote to the King,
asking for orders, but in reality, I confess, as a
means of knowing the extent of this occurrence.
The King wrote back to me in pencil on my own
note: 'All is over. Go to bed and sleep; your
daughter is dancing.'"

People were reassured. Charles X. had, as ever, a
smile on his lips, and the ball went on. Let us permit an ocular witness to speak, Arsène Houssaye, who
on that evening made his entrance into society, and
who thus relates, in his interesting and charming *Confessions*, the impression produced upon him
by the ball: "What struck me in the first place was
that no one seemed gay. I had ingenuously believed
that people came to balls with festive countenances;
but with the exception of Charles X., who always

smiled, even at ill-fortune; Madame the Duchess of
Berry, who had preserved a nameless ray of Naples
sunshine; the Duke of Chartres and the Duke of
Nemours, as handsome as the princes in fairy tales,
all these court faces resembled the faces of actors
who are giving the hundred-and-first representation.
They were playing their parts without enthusiasm,
as if they no longer believed in the comedy. And
yet, if any one thought the end of the piece was near
for the Bourbons, it certainly was not Charles X. and
the courtiers. At court they imagined France had
had enough of revolutions. Who then would dare
to arm anew against this royalty by right divine?"

It is certain that Charles X. was convinced that his
throne could not be shaken. And how could he
avoid illusions at this moment when the chiefs of the
opposition were testifying the same respect, the same
enthusiasm, for his person as the former *émigrés?*
The tactics of the day were to separate the King
from his ministers, to flatter the sovereign and hurl
invectives at his ministry. Read the account given
of the ball in the *Journal des Débats*, which was then
relentlessly attacking the Cabinet presided over by the
Prince de Polignac. The Chamber of Deputies had
been dissolved May 16, and the opening of the new
Chamber was set for August 3. "By a touching
sentiment of delicacy," says the *Débats*, "nearly all
the members of the defunct Chamber, which is
speedily to be reborn, had received invitations. One
might have said they were still deputies of France.

. . . But the most affecting thing of all in this
reunion, so spontaneous and so unhoped-for, of men
of every shade of opinion, was the King, the King of
France, in the midst of his subjects, with a kindly
word for every one, a great king who concerns himself in nowise about our unhappy dissensions. It
was happiness to see him happy at this fête, to
behold that head so calm and smiling, to listen to his
lightest words. . . . The King of France was the king
of the fête. . . . For an instant one saw only him, one
saw nothing but the King coming, in spite of old-time
etiquette, into the palace of a subject, among his
subjects. The King left the Palais-Royal at half-
past twelve, later than he supposed. At one in the
morning, His Majesty had arrived at Saint-Cloud,
not suspecting, doubtless, how many people he had
made happy."

The King and Queen of Naples, as well as the
Dauphin and Dauphiness, had left almost at the
same time as Charles X. But the Duchess of Berry,
who was very fond of dancing, did not leave until
half-past five in the morning. The ball, which so
long as the crowned heads were present had preserved an official and slightly constrained appearance, now became joyous and noisy. There was an
orchestra in each of the five principal salons. Besides these five orchestras, a sixth was heard in the
intervals between the dances, which was placed in
the centre of the glass gallery. This was the band
of the royal guard which was playing fanfares for

those outside. "The ball was as animated as a
bourgeois fête," says the account in the *Débats*.
"The Duchess of Berry, Mesdemoiselles d'Orléans
and their brothers, set the example. For a rarity in
these State balls there was a great deal of dancing,
and that without too much ceremony. One could
see at the house of the Duke of Orleans, more than
anywhere else, what unskilful dancers we are. A
courtier of the old *régime* would have had difficulty
in recognizing now that dance so perfect and so
much appreciated in its graces which was of strict
etiquette in the best days of the Great King. But
this is a small misfortune for which even the court
is easily consoled. We all have something else to
think about."

At two in the morning the ball was interrupted
by a supper at which people sat down. The Valois
Gallery was opened, where eight hundred women
placed themselves at table. The Duke of Chartres,
who was nineteen, and the Duke of Nemours, who
was fifteen, were both of them charming, one as a
colonel of hussars and the other as a colonel of
chasseurs, and they did the honors of this magnificent repast with extreme courtesy. Supper over,
the ball recommenced. Everything had been renewed, — flowers, candles, music. It was as if there
were a second fête, less thronged, but more animated
than the first. The gallopade was danced, led by
the son of Count Apponyi, Austrian ambassador, in
rich Hungarian costume; and it was a curious thing,

by way of contrast, to see these young nobles, friends
of the white flag, passing to and fro in the gallery
where the bust of Horace Vernet had represented
the victories of the tricolor. At six in the morning
they were still dancing, and the symbolic fête ended
like a triumph of the Parisian middle classes.

After the departure of all the guests, the crowd
was in the garden, looking at the broken chairs and
the remains of the extinguished fête. The account
given in the *Moniteur* announced that the King had
given marks of his satisfaction, and had not even
mentioned the sort of riot which had saddened the
fête. As to the *Journal des Débats*, observe how it
described this revolutionary symptom: "A single
accident, very slight, to which nothing but malevo-
lence could give importance, somewhat disturbed the
general happiness. The facts are as follows: As one
may fancy, the crush was great in the garden of the
Palais-Royal. People crowded, pushed; the whole
city was there. The idea of getting a little more room
occurred to some of them, and they leaped over the
garden walls. It was the old story of Panurge's
sheep; everybody leaped over. One disorder brought
on another; children threw the garden chairs at each
other's heads in sign of joy. Soon after they built
them into a scaffolding, which they afterwards took
the notion of setting on fire. The thing was done;
so many torches were there all ready! The armed
force thought it was its duty to arrest several persons on this account. The most unfortunate thing

about it is that all the flowers in the garden are
ruined, and that the pedestal of the statue of Apollo
is burnt to a cinder." This incident, apparently so
slight, was a grave presage. Panurge's sheep, of
which the journal spoke, were to come again in the
month of July. People had begun by burning chairs;
they were going to end by upsetting a throne.

V

THE TAKING OF ALGIERS

THE greatest evil of party spirit is that it not only obliterates the notion of justice, but also the sentiment of patriotism. What occurred at Paris in the month of July, 1830, affords the proof of this melancholy verity. In all the history of France there is not a more glorious feat of arms, a more brilliant service rendered to Christianity and civilization, than the taking of Algiers. Well, politics had so deteriorated the national character that the tidings of this magnificent victory which at other epochs would have aroused unanimous transports of joy and enthusiasm, was received with indifference, not to say hostility, by the enemies of the Polignac Ministry. And yet Charles X., in his magnanimous enterprise, had just succeeded better than Charles V., better than Louis XIV. It was for him that the prediction of Bossuet had been accomplished: " Thou shalt yield, or thou shalt fall under that victor, Algiers, rich with the spoils of Christianity. Thou sayest in thine avaricious heart: I hold the sea beneath my laws, and the nations are my prey. The lightness of thy vessels gives thee confidence, but thou shalt see thyself attacked within thy walls like a ravenous bird among its rocks and in its nest, where it is dividing its booty among its young."

In spite of the pusillanimous counsels of the opposition, which prophesied nothing but defeats and disasters, in spite of the jealousy of England, whose threats the French government had haughtily defied, the King's fleet had sailed from Toulon, May 25, 1830, carrying on its vessels, along with the veterans of the imperial epic, young officers destined to win great names in military annals: Pélissier, Lamoricière, Changarnier, MacMahon. Never had a fleet gone to sea in more magnificent array. "Our marine, resuscitated from the fight of Navarino," said Chateaubriand, "set out from these ports of France, but lately so abandoned. The roadstead was covered with ships which saluted the land as they departed. Steamboats, the new discovery of man's genius, went and came, bearing orders from one division to another, like sirens, or like aides-de-camp of the admiral. The Dauphin remained upon the strand, whither all the inhabitants of the city and the mountains had descended. Could he who, after having torn his relative, the King of Spain, from the hands of revolution, saw the dawning of the day by which Christianity was to be delivered, have believed that his own night was so near?"

As if he had had a presentiment of the approaching revolution, the Dauphin did not allow himself to be intoxicated by the resounding acclamations. Accustomed for more than a year to the coldness of Parisian

crowds, he was extremely moved by these cries of
devotion and joy. But he did not exaggerate their
importance. "Alas!" he exclaimed, "I suspect there
are not many electors among those who are shouting
thus." And, in fact, among the patriots who noisily
expressed their good will toward the army and the
fleet of France, there were not many who paid three
hundred francs of taxes.

Could one believe it? During this glorious expedition, the opposition was on the side of the Moors.
As has been remarked in his Memoirs by Duke Ambroise de La Rochefoucauld-Doudeauville: "Many of
the opposition journals forewarned the Dey of all the
preparations, and thus doubled the difficulties of the
attack; a great number of generals were even alarmed
by the temper of the marine and doubted its concurrence."

The expedition had begun. All hearts in France
should have throbbed for the triumph of the French
standard. All political quarrels should have been
forgotten, so that but one memory should remain:
that of the country. Listen to Count d'Haussonville:
"All minds," he says in his book entitled *Ma Jeunesse,*
"were bent on this Algerian expedition. Men
awaited the result with, it must be owned, very different feelings. The Government which had long ago
conceived and prepared for it with great skill, hoped
to win great advantages therefrom for the triumph of
its policy. The opposition, on the contrary, showed
alarm, affected to doubt its prudence and utility, and

willingly predicted a failure. Such was the theme developed in a brochure that had just been published by Count Alexandre de Laborde."

M. d'Haussonville was under the spell of the Count's three daughters, the eldest of whom was Mademoiselle Gabrielle Delessert; of the two younger, one married M. Bocher afterward, and the other M. Odier. July 9, 1830, he saw them all three at the Opera, in the same box with their father. He went to them between the acts. But let him tell it: "I began," says he, "for the sake of winning M. de Laborde's good will, to talk about his recent brochure. Alas! it was to be feared that he was only too much in the right, and that, unluckily for us, the enterprise whose difficulties he had so well explained, would result badly; and, as I was warming up on this subject, perhaps excessively, so as to please my fair listeners, the curtain suddenly rose. The manager made his three bows to the audience, approached the prompter's place, and read the despatch announcing the taking of Algiers. I had chosen my time badly. I decamped from the box with all speed, and am running still."

Here is the despatch which the manager read before the scenes: "Vice-Admiral Dampierre to His Excellency the Minister of Marine and the Colonies: — Before Algiers, July 6, 1830. — The army of the King has triumphed; the fate of Algiers has been decided since yesterday; the King's flag is floating over all the forts, and above the palace of the Dey.

The European question, agitated for centuries, is
settled."

The next day, July 10, might be read in the
Journal des Débats: "The cannons are booming in
Paris. This warlike sound has something in it that
charms our ears; it recalls glorious souvenirs and
it bequeaths others to posterity. The Restoration
solidifies and consecrates itself by victories; this idea
should add to the glory of royalists. . . . France
to-day is proud of finding herself again victorious,
and the King is proud of this glory of his people. It
is a new bond between them; this day of unalloyed
glory and majesty granted to the old age of Charles
X. will be hailed by the acclamations of the entire
nation." It was the patriot speaking there. Now
see how, in the same article, the partisan expresses
himself: "We shall not permit M. de Bourmont,
under a constitutional monarchy, to perform an act
of despotic monarchy. We shall demand a reck-
oning for the illegality of the war while thanking
God for the victory. Military fanfaronades serve
no purpose in the tribune; he will have to answer
and to satisfy the law. These are our sentiments at
the sound of the cannon of Algiers: joy for the victory, gratitude to the army, and felicitations to the
King; and along with all this, rigorous inquiry and
suitable punishment for the illegality of the war.
On the subject of Algiers we have two things to
do which are better than replying to the impotent
rhodomontade of our adversaries; the first is to

examine what our ministers are going to do with
their conquest, and the second is to accuse them of
having made war illegally, without credits voted by
the Chambers. Accuse the ministers! What! after
a victory? Yes; for Algiers is conquered, but not
by the Charter, not by the laws of the State. . . .
Our adversaries must see that this triumph does not
afflict us, does not depress us; affliction would be
contemptible, depression would be stupid. That
would be to forget both what France is, and that it
is the King, not the ministry, that has conquered."

Nevertheless, it was very fine, this victory on which
the adversaries of the Polignac Ministry congratulated themselves with such reserve. At dawn on
June 13, after a violent tempest, the sky had suddenly cleared. Algiers had appeared to the astonished eyes of our sailors and soldiers, with its ranks
of terraces, all white against a background of dull
green. Then the fleet passed in front of the city to
gain the peninsula of Sidi-Ferruch, which it reached
some hours later. Admiral Duperré calculated that
it would take not less than twenty-seven days to dis-
embark the army. This pessimistic prevision received
an eminent refutation on June 14: eight hours had
been enough to effect the landing. The marine and
the army rivalled each other in courage. June 24,
Lieutenant Amédée de Bourmont, second of the four
sons the general had taken with him, was mortally
wounded on the field of honor. July 5, his father,
overcoming grief by heroism, took Algiers. The

Dey's envoy had said to the victor: "When the Algerians are at war with the King of France, they ought not to say their night prayers before concluding peace."

M. Ernest Daudet has said in his concise and admirable *Histoire de la Restauration:* "There are here great and sorrowful memories which one knows not how to evoke without paying homage to them and repairing the injustice which has enveloped them so long. Time, in passing over them, permits us, moreover, to judge them with more equity than did their contemporaries. To-day generous hearts take pleasure in drawing nearer to the last days of the reign of Charles X., so tragic and so fatal. They place impartially in juxtaposition the imprudent conduct of the old King and that glorious conquest of Algiers which is an honor to his memory, and of which one can say with more justice than it has been said of the decrees of July, that it constitutes the veritable testament of the government of the Restoration."

The news of the taking of Algiers had reached Paris July 9. M. d'Haussez, Minister of Marine, was the first to receive it, and he made haste to bear it to the sovereign. Charles X. trembled with joy, and as his minister bent to kiss his hand, "To-day men embrace each other," cried the old monarch, and he pressed M. d'Haussez to his heart.

Two days later, July 11, there was a *Te Deum* of thanksgiving at Notre Dame, at which Charles X. and the royal family were present.

The King, coming from Saint-Cloud, arrived at the Tuileries at eleven in the morning. At noon he heard Mass in the palace chapel. After Mass, the chancellor, ministers, great dignitaries, great referendary of the Chamber of Peers, the Papal Nuncio, the marshals, peers of France, ambassadors of Spain and of Naples, ministers of state, and a great many generals, had the honor of paying him their court. After the reception he presided at the council of ministers, at which the Dauphin was present. At half-past three, a salvo of artillery announced that the sovereign and his train were leaving the palace of the Tuileries to repair to Notre Dame. The cortège started in the following order: gendarmes; staffs of the first military division and of the place of Paris; a carriage belonging to the Dauphin, and one belonging to the Duchess of Berry, containing the great officers of the crown; bands and body-guards, heralds-at-arms, a numerous staff, and the carriage of the King.

In this carriage, which was that used at the coronation, Charles X. had the Dauphin and the Duchess of Berry with him. Marshal Marmont, Duke of Ragusa, and the Duke of Luxembourg were on horseback at either side of it. A detachment of body-guards marched in a double line on both sides of the royal carriage. A detachment of mounted body-guards, a carriage belonging to the Duchess of Berry, in which were the Princess's ladies, a squadron of cuirassiers, closed the march. The royal guard and

the troops of the line formed a double line along the
whole length of the route taken by the cortège. A
salvo of artillery announced its arrival at the Metro-
politan Church. Beneath the cathedral porch, the
Archbishop of Paris said to the King: "The hand
of the Almighty is with you, Sire. Fortify your
great heart yet more, and your confidence in Divine
assistance and the protection of Mary will not be in
vain. May Your Majesty soon receive an additional reward. May he soon come again to thank the
Lord after other marvels, not less pleasant, not less
brilliant!"

Charles X. responded: "Monsieur the Archbishop,
we had implored the aid of the Almighty for an
expedition which was to be at once so glorious for
France and so useful to humanity. The Lord has
blessed our arms. It was my duty and that of each
of my subjects to render Him at once solemn thanks-
givings. This signal benefit has made me experience a happiness such as I have not felt in very
many years. I come to prostrate myself at the feet
of the Most High, to offer Him the homage of my
lively and profound gratitude. I solicit from Him the
grace to devote the remainder of my powers to rendering my people happy, and I desire ardently that
Frenchmen may understand that I breathe but for
their welfare."

The sovereign was afterwards conducted processionally under a canopy to the choir, where an armchair and a *prie-Dieu* had been prepared for him.

Then the *Te Deum* was intoned. A woman of feeling, patriotic in soul, the Duchess of Berry was profoundly affected. The resounding religious chants recalled those of her marriage, celebrated fourteen years earlier in the same sanctuary, and it seemed to her that her husband was contemplating the triumph of the King and of France from the heights of heaven.

On his return to the Tuileries, Charles X. was saluted by repeated cheering from the crowds thronging his passage. He re-entered the palace at a quarter-past five, and started for Saint-Cloud half an hour later. He went with a joyful heart, not suspecting that he would never again appear within the walls of Paris.

The Duchess of Berry wished to associate her children with the national gaiety. The following day, July 12, they gave a collation at the Trocadéro, Saint-Cloud. The gay festivity was terminated by fireworks. They were the last discharged in honor of the elder branch. The Revolution would allow itself to be moved neither by the prestige of victory, nor the grace and innocence of the Duke of Bordeaux and his sister.

VI

THE CHILDREN OF FRANCE

THE Duchess of Berry was a happy mother. The two children whom she cherished, and who had the strongest affection for each other, increased daily in grace and intelligence. The Duke of Bordeaux was receiving a military and Christian education that was producing the best results. He was brought up in the love of God, of country, and of honor. It was hoped to make of him a religious and valiant king. Besides his governor, under-governor, tutor, and under-tutor, he had also a first valet-de-chambre, the Chevalier de La Villatte, who never left him, and who loved him *maternally* (the word is Chateau briand's), while giving him at the same time an energetic and virile education. Captain de La Villatte was a noble character. Under the Terror he had taken his father's place in the prison of the condemned, and had thus saved him from the scaffold. He was one of the first in the intrenchments of the Trocadéro, in Spain. This brave soldier, faithful dog of the monarchy, as Chateaubriand again styles him, treated the young prince as a veteran treats a child of the regiment; he taught him to rise early, to bear heat and cold and fatigue. No fire was made in the child's bedroom unless the thermometer was below the freezing point. He went out in all weathers, climbed trees, so as to become, as he said, tall and strong like his friend La Villatte, took pleasure in the manual exercise, and went through the drill wonderfully well. A little regiment composed of his young comrades had been formed for him, — the three Gramonts, the two Bourbon-Bussets, Damas, Brissac, Rivière, Darfort, Sinety, Blacas, Meffray, Locmaria, Bouillé, Nicolay, etc., who were called the Bordeaux regiment, and who wore the uniform of the infantry of the royal guard. The little prince was never happier than when he bivouacked at Bagatelle or in the Élysée garden with his infantine troop, and made over a campaign fire a soldier's soup, which Charles X. tasted and always found excellent.

September 29, 1827, his birthday, the Duke of Bordeaux put his regiment through the drill; he had his knapsack on his back like his little soldiers, and wore like them the uniform of the third infantry of the guard, on duty that day at Saint-Cloud.

Two years later, September 29, 1829, the young prince was fêted — for the last time at Saint-Cloud — by the body-guards. One of them, M. Choquart, had composed a cantata in his honor, two of whose stanzas we subjoin : —

"Jeté sur l'océan des âges
En sommeillant dans ton berceau,
Tu conjuras tous les orages
Qui couvraient encore un tombeau.
Ce berceau, comme une arche sainte
Calmant une auguste douleur,
A reçu sa dernière plainte
Et nos premier chants de bonheur.

"Viellis avec le blanc panache,
Nos cheveux prendront sa couleur;
Mais, quand ta bannière sans tache
Ira flotter un champ d'honneur,
Ceux qui l'auront toujours suivie,
Fier de mourir à ton côté,
Donneront un reste de vie
Pour ta jeune immortalité." [1]

The King said to the author: "Your verses are
charming, sir; they were dictated by a ·generous
heart."

The little prince had military instincts already.
At the commencement of the Algerian expedition, as
his grandfather, who had received no tidings for two
days, seemed uneasy, he asked an audience of him
without explaining his motive. Brought to the King,

[1] Cast upon the ocean of time — While slumbering in thy cradle,
— Thou didst charm away all storms — That still covered a tomb.
— This cradle, like a sacred ark, — Soothing an august anguish, —
Has received its last plaint — And our first songs of joy.
  Grown old with the white plume — Our hair will assume its
color; — But, when thy spotless banner — Shall float above the
field of honor, — Those who shall always have followed it, — Proud
to die beside thee, — Will give a remnant of life — For thy young
immortality.

he kneeled down and said: "Sire, I am too young to fight yet; but let me go to Algiers; I am sure that our soldiers will be still braver when they see me."

Notwithstanding the too frequent adulations addressed to him in that atmosphere of enthusiastic royalism in which he lived, he already knew how to guard against flattery. One day, while playing, he accidentally struck a courtier with his whip, and the man immediately thanked him for his clumsiness as if it were a favor. The young prince turned toward Captain La Villatte and said in an undertone, alluding to La Fontaine's fable: "That is a flatterer. Well, he won't get my cheese."

The Duke of Bordeaux had been taught to love both soldiers and the poor. He had no greater joy than that of giving alms. On his fête day, Saint Henry's, July 15, he spent his little savings in clothing a certain number of children and old people. Usually he spent his money very quickly and very willingly. All of a sudden he became economical and denied himself the gratification of the least whim. The cause of this sudden change was sought for, and after a while the mystery was cleared up. Captain de La Villatte had spoken of a bazaar for the Sisters of Charity whom he wanted to establish in his own village of Plauzat, and as funds were lacking, the little prince began to hoard, so as to be able to provide for the good sisters in whom the captain was interested.

The Duke of Bordeaux had his own poor as he had

his own regiment. He called the indigent children
brought up at the establishment of Saint Nicolas his
little boys. He made parties for playing prisoner's
base with them in the park of Bagalette, and when
any one gave him a new toy, they doubled his pleasure if they promised to give one like it to his *little
boys.* His childhood was passing happily, and one
would have said then that the future smiled upon him.
Old Parisians all remember the sympathy he inspired
in the multitude, and the salutes which greeted him,
and which he and little Mademoiselle returned so
gracefully and prettily. The people, who are good,
love children, and they shared in the maternal joys
of the widow of the Duke of Berry.

There is nothing more touching than the mutual
affection between a brother and sister of nearly the
same age, who receive the same education, and enter
life hand in hand. I have had the same happiness as
the Duke of Bordeaux. Like him, I was brought up
with a charming sister, born not long before me, who
was the companion of my entire childhood. Alas! I
lost her, and the memory of her constantly returns
when I think of the early years of the two children
of the Duchess of Berry; for, poor or rich, obscure
or illustrious, private individuals or princes, we all
have a community of joys, and still more a community of sufferings.

Mademoiselle, who was just a year older than her
brother, — she was born September 21, 1819, and he
September 29, 1820, — showed from her tenderest

infancy qualities of mind and heart which were to
make an elect lady of her. No princess was more
worthy of happiness, and yet what afflictions, what
calamities, Providence had in store for her! She was
but eight years old when the horrible tragedy of her
father's death was described to her in detail. It was
at the chateau of Rosny that her governess, the
Duchess de Gontaut, told her this startling story. In
the early days of her marriage, the Duchess of Berry
wishing to spend a few weeks in the country during
the fine weather, in order to be free from etiquette
and recover from the fatigues of her life as princess,
her husband had bought the estate of Rosny, where
they both lived as private persons, and where the happiest moments of their existence were spent. After
the assassination of the Prince, his widow became more
attached than ever to a dwelling which recalled such
affecting souvenirs. She founded an asylum there for
the widows and old men of the village, a school for
poor children, and caused a church to be built, with
a chapel, in which was placed her husband's heart.
A service of masses and prayers was maintained for
the repose of the soul of the prince whose death had
caused so many tears. Four gray nuns were attached
to the charitable establishments created by the princess. She was fond of visiting them, and taking
part in the light tasks of the dispensary, the children's
lessons, and the nursing of the sick. One might have
called her at this time the fifth gray nun of Rosny.

Listen to the Duchess de Gontaut: "Madame the

Duchess of Berry loved to inspect the different
establishments she had founded at Rosny, and often
went there accompanied by Madame the Dauphiness
and even by the King. Madame the Duchess of
Orleans visited them frequently. On one of these
visits Madame brought Mademoiselle along; I followed them. Mademoiselle, being then eight years
old, comprehended already the misfortune of being
an orphan.

"On reaching Rosny, I perceived from a distance,
and for the first time, the monument erected to
Monseigneur. I was affected by it, and begged
Madame's permission to acquaint Mademoiselle,
close to the precious remains of her father, with the
touching details of his last moments, his sublime
forgiveness of the assassin who had caused his death,
and the favor he never ceased but with his last
breath to entreat of the King. I wished also to
make this young heart understand the agony of her
mother's sufferings — so grand, so courageous —
who was able to the very last moment to give
strength and consolation to Monseigneur dying. . . .
Madame, moved by the sentiments I had just expressed to her, approved my intention. . . . The
next day, after Mass, Madame having retired,
Mademoiselle knelt beside the funeral monument
and listened to the sad story of her father's death.
Presently I saw her tears begin to flow; I saw her
stretch out her arms to that marble so close to the
noble heart which she could thenceforth appreciate.

Admirable little princess! She was touching, she was charming, then."

Mademoiselle had learned with her brother to practise charity. It had been settled that at lesson-time, and especially in the courses, counters should be given them as rewards for correct answers, and taken away again for faults of memory or judgment. At the end of each month the King and the Duchess of Berry redeemed these counters at an invariable rate, and the total was consecrated to good works — such as clothing the poor, women, old men, and children. These charities were generally reserved for the feast days of Saint Louis and Saint Henry. One day there were three hundred francs too little in the alms-bag. The little prince and his sister begged to double their tasks, and had soon earned the counters necessary to the sum intended for their poor.

Charles X. had granted his granddaughter a pension which would allow her to help misfortune, to be generous to her friends, and to show attentions to those around her. The young princess liked to give much better than to receive. Her great pleasure was to make New Year's presents. She was as generous and amiable as her mother.

The old King had a profound tenderness for his grandchildren. He saw them every day, and nothing charmed him more than the progress of their young intelligence.

It is a curious thing that the Duchess of Angou-

lême never gave New Year's presents to the Duke of
Bordeaux and Mademoiselle, and never omitted to
do so to the children of the Duke of Orleans. It
was only by accident that Charles X. learned this.
Affected by the tact of the young prince and his
sister, who had never remarked upon it, he resolved
to recompense them for it, and asked what they
would like as New Year's gifts. " Horses that I can
ride on," said the Duke of Bordeaux, with vivacity.
" A carriage, and even a little postilion," said Mademoiselle, very timidly. The King had a drawing
made of a little carriage, two horses, and a postilion,
and showing it to his grandchildren, he said: " That
is what you want, isn't it? " Mademoiselle answered
with a smile, " It is very pretty, but it is very
small." The good grandfather, charmed with her
good humor, embraced her; then he took the two
children to the window, whence they beheld in the
courtyard of the Tuileries, with as much gladness as
surprise, a little postilion, ponies, and an open carriage. " They both enjoyed it," says the Duchess de
Gontaut, " until the moment when they no longer
possessed anything."

On Saint Henry's day, Charles X. had given the
Duke of Bordeaux a superb plaything which pleased
him much. It was a marvel from the shops of
Giroux: a stormy sea in gold and silver, covered with
little boats which were set in motion by a spring to
the sound of a music box. Having received a fine
collection of butterflies and birds from the daughter

of the Emperor of Brazil, the Duke of Bordeaux,
wishing to thank the princess in a princely fashion,
sent her this toy with the permission of the King,
who remarked at the time to Madame de Gontaut:
" I have already noticed that Henry is not selfish;
it is the sign of a good heart."

The brother and sister had a precocious tact and
wit of which their mother was justly proud. Both
of them already played their part of prince and princess very well. The Duke of Bordeaux knew how
to speak to officers and soldiers. Little Mademoiselle presided at a court circle with the ease and
affability of a queen. At the very moment when the
revolution of July broke out, she was getting ready
to go to Dieppe without her mother to entertain her
young cousins, the sons and daughters of the Duke
of Orleans. At this epoch the Duchess of Berry
was intimately persuaded that if a riot ever should
occur, all that would be necessary to quiet the sedi-
tion would be for her to take her children by the
hand and show them to the crowd.

VII

THE LAST DAYS OF CALM

ON Sunday, July 11, 1830, Charles X., coming from Paris where he had spent a day worthy of the Most Christian King, had re-entered his palace of Saint-Cloud. Perhaps he had never prayed so heartily beneath the ancient arches of Notre Dame as on this beautiful day when he came to offer thanks to God for the victory of his troops and the taking of Algiers. He brought back from the cathedral a holy and patriotic impression. Possibly the acclamations that greeted him as he passed by were less numerous, less cordial, than usual; but the old monarch was a trifle hard of hearing, and doubtless had not observed the difference. In the evening, sitting down at table in the palace of Saint-Cloud, his favorite residence, he received the congratulations of his family, the members of his civil and military establishments, who were on duty near him. He regretted only the absence of the Duchess of Angoulême, who was then taking the waters of Vichy. The pious princess, a thorough Frenchwoman, would have been so rejoiced on this beautiful and glorious day! When night had come, from the roofs of Saint-Cloud the King saw the innumerable lights of Paris in the distance. Public edifices and private houses were illuminated. He who had triumphed in the morning would have been greatly astonished had some prophet of misfortune come to tell him that the Revolution would never again permit him to enter within those walls where a thousand lights were glittering to celebrate the victory of the royal arms.

From the results already obtained, Charles X. understood thoroughly that the elections would not be favorable to the ministry, but he did not afflict himself about it, because he thought the success of the opposition would be his opportunity to cut the Gordian knot once for all. He regarded the taking of Algiers as a fortunate omen. To his mind, it was the judgment of God pronounced in favor of the royal cause. Never had his face shown greater calmness, more good nature and serenity ; never had his manners been more amiable and gracious. He resembled a country gentleman who might have lived on his estates at the very extremity of France, never talking of politics, nor occupying himself with what was said and done at the capital. To judge by the conversations going on between the King and his courtiers, one might have supposed that the situation of the realm had never been more tranquil.

The Duchess of Berry, whose circle shared the sovereign's ideas and approved the policy of the Prince de Polignac, was full of liveliness and gaiety. The beautiful shades of the park of Saint-Cloud had

never seemed more agreeable to her. On the mountain of Montretout, in the most admirable position
and commanding the finest view, the garden called
Trocadéro had been laid out. It was intended for
the promenades of the Duke of Bordeaux, and was
connected with the second story of the palace of Saint-
Cloud, that in which the young prince was lodged,
by a light footbridge thrown across a large alley. As
to the Duchess of Berry, she occupied an apartment
on the ground floor which had been that of the King
of Rome under the Empire, and that of Charles X.
during the reign of Louis XVIII. The tranquillity
and radiance of nature caused the amiable Duchess
to forget the vain agitations of men. She peacefully
enjoyed the charm of the royal *villeggiatura*, and
Charles X., who felt himself beloved by his son, his
daughter-in-law, and his grandchildren, was as happy
as a family man as he was as king.

The court journals hardly mentioned anything but
the sovereign's hunting expeditions and some audiences given by him. July 13th he was shooting in
the park of Saint-Cloud with the Dauphin. The
15th was Saint Henry's day, the feast of the Duke of
Bordeaux. At nine in the morning the musicians
and drummers of the body-guards came to play beneath the windows of the young prince. The Duke
of Orleans with all his family paid him a visit.
Afterwards he received the congratulations of the
officers of the King's household and those of the
princes and princesses, the Pope's Nuncio, the ambas-

sadors of Spain and Naples. The market-women of
Paris, Versailles, and Saint-Cloud were admitted to
enjoy the honor of presenting him bouquets. At nine
o'clock the King and the Dauphin left the palace to
go shooting in the woods of Marly. Ten days later
the Ordinances were to be signed. The Viscount
Sosthène de La Rochefoucauld has written in his
Memoirs: "Ten days before the fatal Ordinances,
M. de Polignac said to the King in nearly these
words: 'Sire, there are no marks of devotion that I am
not disposed to give you; but the success of the
Ordinances does not appear to me sufficiently assured
to tempt me to risk my head for them.' 'Come,'
said the King, laughing and taking him by the ear,
'you will give it to me on the day when I ask for it,
and you will sign when I tell you to.'"

Before Mass on Sunday, July 18, the King received
at Saint-Cloud the deputations from the court of
cassation, the court of finances, and the royal council
of public instruction, who felicitated him on the success of the African expedition. He replied thus to
the address of Count Portalis, first president of the
court of cassation: —

"I confess this moment is one of the sweetest my
heart could experience. A Frenchman to the bottom
of my soul, how proud ought I not to be of the glory
acquired by our arms, solid glory for the interests
of France in the first place, and for those of all
Europe! I return a thousand thanks to God, who
has done more than I. I do not doubt that all

nations will participate in the glory of our arms, a sweet, a sacred glory, a glory which will reflect forever upon the heroes who have done nothing but obey my orders, and who, with almost inconceivable valor and vigor, have been able to conquer, and at the same time to gain the affection of a part of the population who fought against them."

After Mass, as he was passing through the Salon of Mars, the King received the homage of a deputation from the markets and wharves : the fisherwomen had the honor of presenting him with bouquets. The deputations carried fourteen flags and oriflammes.

The great fountains in the Saint-Cloud park were playing on this 18th of July, when Charles X. had all the semblance of a happy and victorious king. The court saw things in rose-color, and the populace was mirthful. The town, the palace, the park, the environs, wore a festive air. A large crowd admired the cascades framed in superb architecture, whence the waters, springing from ledge to ledge, sent up white foam and reflected the radiance of the sun.

The following day, July 19, the Government fully understood the result of the elections. It was a triumph for the opposition. It had 270 out of the 428 newly elected deputies, 202 of whom were numbered among the 221 voters of the Address. The ministry had not more than 145 supporters ; thirteen deputies were doubtful. If the defeated ministry had given place to a Casimir-Périer ministry, the monarchy might possibly have escaped from its critical position. But the King, the ministers, the court party, alike repelled the idea of such a concession. Charles X. was already decided on the Ordinances. But, veiling his resolutions in impenetrable mystery, he seemed to pay no attention whatever to what was happening so near him. Fancying that success depended on one thing only, secrecy before the undertaking, he told himself that the population, taken by surprise, and having neither arms nor ammunition, would be incapable of any resistance ; and that, since the disbanding of the National Guard, nothing was to be feared from the *bourgeoisie*. Like his grandfather Louis XV., and almost all the Bourbons, he had the talent of dissimulating well. To those who spoke to him of a *coup d'État*, he said: "I am tired of these calumnious insinuations"; and even to the members of his family he did not communicate his intentions. In official circles the order of the day was absolute tranquillity.

"When I go to the Ministry of Foreign Affairs," said the English ambassador, "I seem to be entering Milton's paradise of fools. These fools are in a deplorable situation, but they believe in themselves in a wonderful way."

Etiquette was maintained with imperturbable regularity, and the court bulletins were always in the same style. We read in the *Moniteur :* "Saint-Cloud, July 20. — Last evening, before the order, the King was at work with His Excellency, Prince de Poli-

gnac, President of the Council. To-day, at eleven
o'clock, the King heard Mass in the Chapel. The
King sent his condolences to Madame the Marshal
Countess de Bourmont, on the occasion of the death
of her son, M. Amédée de Bourmont. His Majesty
received the Baron Imbert de Saint-Amand, major of
the Lancers of the Guard, in private audience. At
noon the King and S. A. R. M. the Dauphin went
shooting in the park of Saint-Cloud; the Duke of
Luxembourg accompanied His Majesty. S. A. R.
Mgr. the Duke of Bordeaux, accompanied by Baron
de Damas, his governor, went to promenade .in the
park of Bagatelle."

In the evening of July 23, Prince Talleyrand came
to present his homage to Charles X., and after the
order, he had the honor of joining the sovereign's
card party.

The same evening, the Duke de Broglie wrote to a
member of his family: " The wind seems in the direction of a *coup d'État*, but one adjourned until after
the reunion of the Chambers and the follies that are
expected from the Chamber of Deputies. That is a
good deal, for after all it is permitted to hope that it
will commit no follies. In any case, I think that
the greatest would be the *coup d'État* itself. I am
convinced that in case of a *coup d'État* the refusal
to pay taxes would be prompt and universal, without
any disorder. I should much prefer, however, not to
come to that."

The secret of the King's plans had been scrupu-

lously kept. Nothing at court or in the city could
arouse the least suspicion. Prince de Polignac's
intention had been to concentrate at Paris all the
troops of the first military division; but this proposition was not accepted, because it was feared that it
would betray the plan whose speedy execution was
contemplated. In the session of the Ministerial
Council, held at the palace of Saint-Cloud July 24,
it was inquired what military measures had been
taken. M. de Polignac replied that he could assem-
ble eighteen thousand men at Paris within a few
hours. He sincerely believed he had to do with a
mere handful of journalists and *bourgeois;* that the
people would take no part in the affair; and that
there would be, at the utmost, nothing more than
trifling and ill-concerted skirmishes which a few
squads of policemen and gendarmes would instantly
repress.

Meanwhile, dissimulation was pushed so far that
it became, to tell the truth, the only means by which
the minister sought to assure the success of the
Ordinances. He was convinced that he had all the
chances of the game on his side, provided only that
the public should not know the Ordinances until
the very day when they were issued. "The Government played close," writes the Duke de Broglie in
his *Souvenirs.* "The session was to open August
3; it made a display of the preparations rendered
necessary by this solemnity. The journals were
inexhaustible on the already drawn-up projects, and

the reforms made or to be made; the King's letters
were despatched; I had mine, and I am very sorry
not to have kept it; several others did not receive
theirs until the very day after the catastrophe. No
military preparations; no movement of troops in
Paris or the environs; the titular Minister of War,
M. de Bourmont, was triumphing in Algeria, making
the last of the Barbarossas disgorge and vacate the
premises. His *alter ego ad interim*, M. de Cham-
pagny, knowing nothing at all, although he was the
Dauphin's favorite, was recreating himself in a
country house in the environs of the capital."

Even the Dauphiness, whose stay at the baths of
Vichy was not yet ended, had not been taken into
confidence. Assuredly, if the daughter of Louis
XVI. could have suspected what was going on she
would have felt obliged to be near him who was her
king, her uncle, and her father-in-law in the hour of
danger. Never could she have been persuaded to
remain at a distance from the spot where so great
a game was to be played. As to the Duchess of
Berry, she had not the least notion of an approaching catastrophe. She was thinking of nothing but
her plans for travel and for country life. The
Duchess de Gontaut relates in her unpublished
Memoirs that the princess, having to go to Rosny,
wished to send her daughter Mademoiselle to take some
sea-baths at Dieppe during her absence. Learning
that the Duchess of Orleans intended going to the
Chateau d'Eu with her daughters, she thought it

would be pleasant for them to go by way of Dieppe
and stop there for several days. She offered them
hospitality in the house she owned there, and which
she was not to occupy this year. Mademoiselle
would do the honors in her absence. The little
princess was very joyful at the idea of such a
mission. Her governess told her that the first thing
necessary was the sanction of the King. "Make
your plan," replied the good grandfather; "it will
amuse me, and if I find it suitable and reasonable I
will consent." Mademoiselle, enchanted, drew up
her programme at once: the usual reception, the
mayor at the head, speech in hand; young girls in
white, baskets of flowers, a gala dinner, a grand ball,
and in the evenings rural fêtes. All this required
considerable preparations. Having consulted M.
Charles Leduc, inspector of her household, the
young princess was a trifle disconcerted to learn
that she was far from possessing the necessary pro-
vision of silverware, linen, and china. She made her
destitution known to the King, and he promised to
aid her by giving her permission to borrow from the
civil list. Everything was arranged. Nothing remained to be done but to send the invitations.
"Mademoiselle," adds the Duchess de Gontaut,
" wrote the Duchess of Orleans a respectful, gracious,
and rather original letter which she laid before the
King; he approved it, was amused by it, and promised
to send it. The reply of the Duchess of Orleans to
the grand-niece whom she loved was affectionate and

amiable, accepting with pleasure, and terminating
with these words: "Never forget, my dear Louise,
that your aunt cannot find strength enough in her
heart to refuse what you ask of her; expect me and
your cousins also shortly at Dieppe." Orders were
then given to Charles Leduc to ask for what the
King had promised to borrow; he received silverware, linen, etc., from M. Singer, controller of the
civil list. The chests containing these articles were
placed at his disposal; he was to start for Dieppe on
Monday, July 26. Monday, July 26! That was
the very day on which the Ordinances would be
published in the *Moniteur*. They were to be signed
on Sunday, July 25, by the King and the ministers,
at the palace of Saint-Cloud.

VIII

THE ORDINANCES

A FEW days before the 25th of July, Count Pozzo di Borgo, the Russian ambassador, had found Charles X. sitting in front of his desk, with his eyes fixed on the Charter, opened at Article 14, which authorizes the sovereign to issue ordinances. The King was reading and re-reading this article, to seek in it conscientiously what he desired to find there. On this subject we read in the Memoirs of Duke Ambroise de Doudeauville : "Charles X. told me that he held greatly by the Charter and would always be faithful to it, in the first place because he had sworn to, and secondly because he had nothing to put in its place. But he saw that even this Charter was greatly menaced, and more than one speech, more than one writing, must have made him believe that he could utilize Article 14 to arrest the evil, and consolidate his brother's work. His plan, I cannot doubt, was to retrace his steps as soon as he should have defeated the plots of the conspirators who labored incessantly to overthrow the throne and the Charter itself, because it had been given by a Bourbon. He believed, and it was a grave mistake, that

he would not require heroic means for the execution
of these Ordinances, and the blindness of those who
counselled him was so great that not a single precau-
tionary measure was taken."

Possibly Charles X. deluded himself; but he was
in good faith at all events, and his conscience did not
reproach him.   To his mind, the preamble of the
Charter determined its true spirit.   In this preamble
Louis XVIII. had written: " While recognizing that
a free and monarchical Constitution ought to fulfil
the expectations of enlightened Europe, we · have
also been obliged to remember that our first duty
toward our people is to preserve for their own
interests the rights and prerogatives of our crown.
We have hoped that, taught by experience, they
would be convinced that the supreme authority alone
can give to the institutions which it founds, the force,
permanence, and majesty with which it is itself
invested; that thus, when the wisdom of kings freely
accords with the wish of peoples, a Constitutional
Charter may be of long duration; but that, when
violence wrests concessions from the feebleness of
government, public liberty is in no less danger than
the throne."

Charles X. was intimately convinced that in pro-
mulgating the Ordinances he would do nothing at
variance with his conscience, and that they were conformable not merely to the spirit, but to the letter of
the Charter.   He had meditated on this phrase in the
will of Louis XVI.: " I recommend my son, should he

have the misfortune to become king, to reflect that
he owes himself entirely to the welfare of his fellow-
citizens; that he should forget all hates and resent-
ments, and particularly those which spring from the
griefs and afflictions I experience; that he cannot
procure the welfare of his people except by reigning
in accordance with the laws; but, at the same time,
that a king cannot make them respected and accomplish the good he has it in his heart to do, except in
so far as he has the necessary authority, and that
otherwise, being constrained in his operations, and
inspiring no respect, he is more detrimental than
useful."

If the souvenir of Louis XVI. was not an excuse
for the errors of Charles X., it was at least an exten-
uating circumstance. Had not the Martyr King been
sufficiently reproached for his concessions and weak-
nesses? Had he not been sufficiently criticised for
abandoning the Girondist Ministry? Had it not been
said repeatedly that with a little more vigor he could
have put down easily all the dangers of his situation?
In the eyes of Charles X., the liberals of 1830 were
new Girondins, as much to be dreaded as those of
1792. To the counsellors who urged him to deliver
himself wholly into the power of a liberal ministry,
he replied: "I dont want to mount a cart like my
brother."

Persuaded that he was acting still more in the
interests of France than in his own, and that the
Ordinances he was about to sign that evening were

a work of safety and social conservation, the old
King doubted neither the legality nor the success of
his enterprise. He thought that all he had to do
to make it succeed was to keep the secret until the
next morning. Hence, during his last day of dissimulation, that of Sunday, July 25, 1830, he preserved an air of calmness and indifference which
baffled all suspicions.

The palace of Saint-Cloud wore the same aspect
as on previous Sundays. As usual, a certain number
of courtiers and political personages repaired thither
to present their homage to the sovereign after Mass.
At noon he entered the chapel with the Duchess of
Berry and the Dauphin. Large arches or bays united
the Gallery of Apollo with the chapel and the royal
tribune. From a hundred and fifty to two hundred
persons, grouped opposite these openings apparently
with the intention of hearing Mass there, were standing up and talking in almost loud voices of things
quite different from the divine office. A liberal his-
torian, M. de Vaulabelle, in describing this day of
July 25th has said: "The interior of the court of
Charles X. had in nowise the austere, almost monas-
tic aspect with which certain writers have endowed
it. In all the realm, Saint-Cloud and the Tuileries
were perhaps the places where clerical influence was
felt the least, if one could judge by external signs;
no prelate, no priest, enjoyed marked credit there;
the King's confessor was an obscure priest named
Jocard, without any sort of influence, and who remained completely obscure until his latest day."

The Mass being ended, the King crossed the Gallery of Apollo, addressing some benevolent remarks to those ranged on either side his path. Prince Paul of Würtemberg, the Chancellor of France, the ministers, marshals, grand officers of the crown, peers, deputies, the Papal Nuncio, the ambassadors of Spain and Naples, the prefects, and a great number of generals, paid him their court. Afterwards he received in special audience Lord Stuart de Rothesay, the English ambassador, the Archbishop of Besançon, and M. Dupré de Saint-Maur.

Among the functionaries who had come to the palace of Saint-Cloud was M. Mangin, prefect of police. Without telling him anything about what was preparing, the ministers asked him for information concerning the disposition of people at Paris. " I suspect," he answered them, "the motive which excites your solicitude ; but all I can tell you is that whatever you may do, Paris will not budge. Go ahead boldly ; I answer for Paris with my head."

The Council afterwards opened in the cabinet of the King, who had his son on his right hand and Prince de Polignac on his left. The session opened by the reading of a report from M. de Chantelauze, Minister of Justice, on the general situation. This report was to be published next day, as a prefix to the Ordinances. Charles X. gave it his full approbation. The Ordinances were then read. The first suspended liberty of the press. The second dissolved the Chamber of Deputies. The third created a new electoral system which reduced the number of representatives to two hundred and fifty-eight. The fourth convoked the electoral colleges for September 6 and 8, and the Chambers for the 28th of the same month.

The reading terminated, Prince de Polignac declared that he was in a position to repress any attempt at disturbance.

Charles X. then collected the opinions. The Dauphin, being first consulted, gave his adhesion by an inclination of the head. All the ministers did likewise. The King interrogated his conscience once more, and his conscience approved. He reminded himself of Article 14 of the Charter, which is thus worded: "The King is supreme chief of the State, commands the land and naval forces, declares war, makes treaties of peace, alliance, and of commerce, appoints to all places of public administration, and *makes the rules and ordinances necessary for the execution of the laws and the safety of the State.*"

As to what concerned the press, Charles X. thought it was covered by Article 8 of the Charter: "Frenchmen have the right to publish their opinions and cause them to be printed, *while conforming themselves to the laws, which should repress the abuses of this liberty.*" Before giving his signature, he declared, as if to reassure his royal conscience for the last time, that his resolutions did not exceed the limits set by the Charter to his power, and that it was his firm intention to return to the customary

·state of things as soon as the popular ebullition should have settled down. At the moment of signing he leaned his forehead on his two hands and remained pensive. Then, resuming the pen: "The more I reflect," said he, "the more I am convinced that it is impossible to do otherwise." And he signed. The ministers signed after him, each one bowing to him profoundly before affixing his name at the foot of the Ordinances. "Gentlemen," he exclaimed then, "these are grave measures. You may count on me, as I count on you. It is life and death between us now."

At the very moment when this scene was occurring at Saint-Cloud, the Duke of Orleans was leaving his chateau of Neuilly to go to Saint-Leu, to dine with the Duke of Bourbon, Prince of Condé, who was to do the honors of the repast with the Baroness de Feuchères. The English ambassador, the Swedish minister, and several members of the diplomatic corps figured among the guests, and also Baron de Vitrolles, who had been at Saint-Cloud that morning. Before dinner they strolled in the garden. The Duke of Orleans took the arm of M. de Vitrolles. "You were at Saint-Cloud this morning," said he. "What did you see there? What do you think?" And as the Baron did not conceal his fears of the possibility of a near determination which might bring about some grave changes, "But what do they want to do?" replied the Duke, with evident emotion. "They cannot dispense with the Chambers nor go outside of what is legal."

After dinner the salon was thinned out by the
departure of several of the guests, those who were
to take parts in the play announced to take place
in the little theatre of Saint-Leu. These were chiefly
persons belonging to the household of the Prince of
Condé, with the Baroness de Feuchères at their head.
Two pieces were played, one serious, the other comic.
During the *entr'acte*, the Duke of Orleans resumed
his conversation with the Baron de Vitrolles.

"But what can they want?" said he. "What are
they pretending to do? Ah! my God, what are they
getting ready for us?" Apropos of this conversation,
M. de Vitrolles has written in his Memoirs : "The
Duke of Orleans continued talking with me about
his apprehensions for a considerable length of time.
We left off with the vaguest suppositions, none of
which were reassuring, and I have remained entirely
convinced that at this moment the prince had neither
foreseen nor prepared the events which flung him in-
evitably into power. Prejudiced though I was against
his character and his underhand and timid opposition
throughout the entire Restoration, I could not perceive in our continual communications on that day,
either a guilty hope or even that evil smile which
must have played about his lips if he had foreseen the
misfortunes of the others and the advantages he would
be able to derive from them. He did not see through
the clouds, and they alarmed him."

At eleven in the evening, the very hour when all
subsided into silence at the palace of Saint-Cloud,

and when the Duke of Orleans was present at the society comedy being played at the Château Saint-Leu, the Minister of Justice, M. de Chantelauze, who had just summoned the editor-in-chief of the *Moniteur* to his ministry, handed him in a mysterious way the report of the Ordinances, intended to appear in the next day's issue. The editor, glancing through them, was unable to repress a movement of emotion. " Well? " asked another minister who was present, M. de Montbel. " God save the King and France ! " returned M. Sauvo. " We will hope for the best," replied the two ministers. The editor of the *Moniteur* made ready to depart. " Gentlemen," said he as he was leaving, " I am fifty-seven years old ; I have seen all the days of the Revolution, and I withdraw in profound terror."

IX

ON Monday, July 26, 1830, when those who dwelt in the palace of Saint-Cloud awoke, not one of them, with the exception of Charles X. and his son, had any notion of the Ordinances with which the morning *Moniteur* was speedily to acquaint them. The weather was fine. The King and the Dauphin were to go hunting in the forest of Rambouillet. The Duke of Bordeaux and his sister were to visit a manufactory at Versailles, and pass the rest of the day at the Little Trianon, where a dinner had been prepared for them and their entire households through the care of Baron de Damas. Before starting for the chase, Charles X. embraced his grandchildren, and made very little reply to the story of their plans for the day. He walked up and down, and seemed pre-occupied. The following conversation took place between him and the Duchess de Gontaut: —

"'Have you read the *Moniteur?*'

"'No, Sire; it is tiresome, and never tells anything.'

"'It will not tire you to-day, and may possibly surprise you. Read it; you will find there four Ordinances that I have signed.'

90

" And the King, counting them off on his fingers,
added: —

" 'Modification of the electoral law, suspension of
the constitutional régime, suppression of the liberty
of the press, dissolution of the Chamber.' "

The Duchess turned pale. The dialogue began
anew after an instant of silence.

" 'Well! what do you think about it?'

" 'Sire, we have arrived, then, at that dreadful
moment, a *coup d'État!*'

" 'You have a good heart. I have told you so a
hundred times; but you are too quick, you allow
yourself to get excited.'

" It was the King's words which, enlightening me,
alarmed me more than anything that could have been
told me. I asked him to permit me to remind him
of the dangers of the position which His Majesty was
almost jestingly making known to the young princes,
saying to them: 'Be good, be very good now, for I
have no more troops to bring you to your senses;
they are absent, disseminated throughout all France.
I have had to send them away to arrest the incendia-
ries and punish the spirit of anarchical revolt spread
in all parts of the kingdom.' . . .— 'That is only
too true. Alas! Sire, there is the trouble. Can I
help fearing the choice of this moment for a *coup
d'État?* I cannot doubt the good intentions of M. de
Polignac nor his attachment to the King; but if His
Majesty permits, it is my duty to tell him that the
absence of M. de Bourmont, who knows both the

strength and weakness of the army, is regretted here,
while M. de Polignac's presence in the Ministry of
War, far from reassuring, alarms and fills with consternation not merely those who surround His Majesty, but the entire body of royalists in France.
People talk of it at present without ill-will against
the minister, but with the terror inspired by the
moment.'"

Charles X. seemed displeased. Then, with clasped
hands, the Duchess de Gontaut begged him to allow
her one word, one possibly indiscreet question.

"Speak," he said to her; "I authorize you, I even
require it."

"Has not the King, in signing the Ordinances,
violated the Charter given by his august brother and
adopted by himself?"

"No; I swear it to you. On my word of honor,
I do not believe it; they have assured me that
Article 14 of that very Charter gives me sufficient
and positive authority to govern by Ordinances in
case of urgency."

"Urgency? Has the King come to that?"

"Can you doubt it? What do you think, for
example, of the periodical journals whose only ten-
dency is to inspire or justify anarchical acts? Disorganization is spread throughout the whole kingdom,
and you see, a decided stand must be taken in order
to put a stop to it. Calm yourself and enjoy this
fine day; I am going to spend it at Rambouillet. So,
you see I am perfectly tranquil about the results of

the measures I have just mentioned to you. I enjoin
you to send an usher to meet me on my return this
evening, merely to give me news of the children."
Then, embracing the Duke of Bordeaux and Mademoiselle, the old King advised them to be good,
promised to meet them next morning, and turning
toward the Duchess de Gontaut, said kindly:
" Adieu; all will go well; calm yourself."

While the sovereign was going from Saint-Cloud
to Rambouillet, the Parisians had learned the Ordinances from the *Moniteur.* The official journal had
appeared somewhat later than usual. It began thus:
" Saint-Cloud, July 25. — To-day, before Mass, His
Excellency Lord Stuart de Rothesay transmitted to
the King in special audience the letters by which
His Britannic Majesty confirms his appointment as
Ambassador Extraordinary at the court of France."

Then followed the ministerial report relative to
the Ordinances. This report, which occupied the
whole remainder of the first page and the first column
of the second, was signed: President of the Council
of Ministers, Prince de Polignac; Keeper of the
Seals of France, Minister of Justice, Chantelauze;
Minister Secretary of State of the Marine and the
Colonies, Baron d'Haussez; Minister Secretary of
State for the Interior, Count de Peyronnet; Minister
Secretary of State for Finances, Montbel; Minister
Secretary of State for Ecclesiastical Affairs and Pub-
lic Instruction, Count de Guernon-Ranville; Minis-
ter Secretary of State for Public Works, Baron

Capelle. Then followed the Ordinances, which filled two columns of the second page and a part of the third.

The *Moniteur* went hardly anywhere except among the high officials, the members of the two Chambers, and the other journals. Moreover, it was necessary to be well versed in political matters to appreciate the importance of the number which had just appeared. Hence there was at first but little excitement among the masses of the people. Only the middle classes seemed disturbed, and this disturbance was chiefly concentrated at the Bourse. Nothing announced a formidable insurrection. Public funds went down about four francs, which showed the displeasure of the wealthy middle class and the financiers, but did not indicate a popular rising. People went about their business or pleasures as usual; the cafés were full. There was a popular fête at La Villette, and people went there in crowds. Already the court party was chanting victory. Prince de Polignac repeated his oracle: "They will not budge." Charged with the Ministry of War during Marshal de Bourmont's absence, he tranquilly passed an adjudication in the house of this Ministry. After having read the Ordinances, Viscount Foucault, colonel of the Parisian gendarmerie, had repaired to the prefect of the police. " Here," said he, "are measures which are probably going to give us plenty to do; I am invited to dinner in the faubourg Saint Honoré, but I shall stay at home." " Why not go?" replied the prefect of police. "It will be enough for you to say where you can be found in case of need."

Marshal Marmont, Duke of Ragusa, who, according to the ministerial plan, was to repress the troubles in case any should arise, was at Saint-Cloud in the morning, where he was on duty as major-general of the royal guard. Not having been forewarned of anything by Charles X., he wished at least to read the *Moniteur* containing the Ordinances, and sent to ask for it from the Duke de Duras, First Gentleman of the Chamber. The Duke sent word that as the only copy that had reached Saint-Cloud was in the King's cabinet, he could not communicate it to anybody. "I went to Paris," the Marshal has written in his Memoirs. "Not having seen the *Moniteur* yet, I sent to ask for it from Baron de Fagel, minister from the Low Countries, whose house adjoined mine. My surprise in reading the Ordinances was all the greater because, in the night of Saturday and Sunday, M. de Polignac had given his word to the Russian ambassador, Pozzo di Borgo, that there would be no *coup d' État.*" It is true that, according to M. de Polignac, the Ordinances did not constitute a *coup d' État*, but a legal application of Article 14 of the Charter.

This was not the opinion of the opposition journals. Their editors assembled in the offices of the *National*, and deputed M. Thiers to draw up a protest which was signed by forty-four of their number, and in which they declared that the Government had lost that character of legality which commands obedience.

During this time Charles X. and the Dauphin continued their hunting in the forest of Rambouillet, without a word concerning politics. The chase was not good, and in the end the tracks of the stag were lost. The huntsman tried in vain to draw the King's attention to the broken branches which showed which way the animal had gone. Charles X., who was ordinarily attentive to these details of hunting with hounds, was now indifferent to them, and the members of his suite, knowing nothing about the Ordinances as yet, wondered why he seemed so abstracted.

At Paris, groups began to form in the streets and at the Palais-Royal towards five o'clock. Some outcries were made. As Prince de Polignac was returning to the Ministry of Foreign Affairs, on the boulevard des Capucines, stones were thrown at his carriage; but a charge made by the gendarmes stationed at the Ministry quickly dispersed the gathering. Informed of the lowering of public funds by the Bourse commissary of police, the Prince replied: " That is nothing; the funds will go up again; and if I had any capital at my disposal, I would not hesitate to buy into them."

All was quiet in the evening. There was dancing at the balls on the barriers. The theatres were full. Opposition showed itself only in the readiness of the public to applaud anything which could be construed as a hostile allusion to the Government. It was the reception day of several of the ministers. Their soirées were brilliant. Their numerous visitors, saluting them, fancied they beheld victors. Count de Guernon-Ranville has related that the very men whom he had until then considered very liberal, felicitated him on the stand taken by the Ministry and said plainly that it was the only way to have done with revolutionists.

At the same time, Charles X. and the Dauphin, returning from Rambouillet, re-entered the palace of Saint-Cloud. It wanted a quarter to eleven in the evening. On alighting from his carriage, the King said to Marshal Marmont: " Have you been at Paris? Is there anything new?" The Marshal responded: " A great alarm and depression, Sire, and an extraordinary fall in the funds." The Dauphin followed the King. He asked the Marshal how much the funds had fallen. He replied: " Monseigneur, four per cent." The Prince answered : " They will go up again."

When Charles X. entered the salon, he found there the Duchess of Berry, who threw herself into his arms and congratulated him upon being king at last. The sovereign did not even take the trouble to announce to Marshal Marmont that he proposed to confer on him the command of all the armed forces. He contented himself with giving him the watchword, as usual, and went tranquilly to bed, while every one retired in silence.

X

THE night of July 26–27 was the last moment of respite granted by Providence to the royal cause. If this night had been usefully employed, if military preparations had been vigorously made, if the police had seized the journals in press and prevented their publication, if the Parisians had found all the garrison under arms when they woke in the morning, Charles X. might still have triumphed. But nothing was done. The unfortunate sovereign, absolutely deceived about the situation, was the sport of

> "Cet esprit d'imprudence et d'erreur
> De la chute des rois funeste avant-coureur." [1]

Marshal Marmont, Duke of Ragusa, who had slept at Saint-Cloud, where he was on duty as major-general of the guard, did not even know on Tuesday morning, July 27, that the command of the troops had been reserved for him. Irritated at not having been put at the head of the Algerian expedition, which

---

[1] That spirit of imprudence and error, the dismal forerunner of the fall of kings.

he had passionately desired, he was dissatisfied with both men and things. "Discontented with what concerned me personally," he has written in his Memoirs, "and alarmed by the future, I dreamed of one thing only: my departure. Hence I was awaiting the end of my service with keen impatience. I was to be free the first of September. I had arranged everything for a long absence, and had determined to start for Italy in October. I expected to pass the winter and spring there. It was my intention to see once more the immortal battle-fields of my youth. There I would find souvenirs which would repay me for present annoyances; I should grow young again in recalling the keen sensations which had procured for me a brilliant glory, while remembering my early days in the most beautiful country of the world. If the upheaval of this poor France had occurred during my absence, imperative duties would not have linked my name to the catastrophe."

The Marshal spent every Tuesday at the country house of one of his friends, in the environs of Saint-Germain. He was getting ready to go as usual, when one of the King's footmen came to tell him that the King wished to speak with him after Mass, at half-past eleven. The Marshal waited until the office was over, and then entered the cabinet of the King. "It appears," said the sovereign, "that there are some anxieties about the tranquillity of Paris. Go there, take the command, and call first of all on Prince de Polignac. If all is orderly by evening, you can return to Saint Cloud."

Marshal Marmont started immediately for Paris. On his arrival he repaired to the Ministry of Foreign Affairs in the boulevard des Capucines, where Prince de Polignac acquainted him with a royal ordinance thus expressed : —

"Article 1: — Our cousin, the Marshal Duke of Ragusa is appointed to the superior command of the troops of the first military division.

"Article 2. — Our President of the Council, holding the portfolio of War during the interim, is charged with the execution of the present ordinance.

"Given at our palace of Saint-Cloud, July 27, of the year of grace 1830, and of our reign the sixth. *Signed :* CHARLES."

At one o'clock the Marshal installed himself at the headquarters of the guard, in the Place Carrousel. He found things in a deplorable state from the military point of view. The royal guard had been decreased by two regiments which had just been sent to Normandy, where for several months incendiary fires, attributed to political ill-will, had been occurring. The garrison of Paris, which Prince de Polignac had estimated at eighteen thousand men, amounted only to eleven thousand. The four commanders of the four divisions of the guard were absent. No precautions had been taken in view of a riot. The army was to be obliged to camp in the public places without ammunition or provisions. The fidelity of the regiments of the guard could be relied on, but it was not the same with the four regiments of line troops that were associated with them. No one had even taken care to confine the troops. It was necessary to await the return of the soldiers for the roll-call at four in the afternoon before being able to make them take arms.

Chateaubriand has said: "The day of the 27th began badly. The King invested the Duke of Ragusa with the command of Paris. That was to lean upon ill-fortune. No choice could have been more unfortunate. Neither the people nor the army had ever forgiven the Marshal the defection of Essonnes. A treason was called a *ragusade*. The man who was accused of ruining the Empire was to ruin the Restoration. At the very moment when he was installing himself at headquarters in the Place du Carrousel, numerous groups of workmen, clerks, and students were coming from all parts of Paris toward the centre, and arriving at the Palais-Royal, where they read and discussed with great vivacity the articles in the *Temps* and *National*, which had appeared in spite of the prescriptions of the Ordinances. As soon as this hostile crowd learned that the Duke of Ragusa had command of the troops, they uttered cries of indignation. Fanaticized by Béranger's songs and by memories of the imperial epic, Napoleon's former soldiers were enraged to the utmost. For them, the Duke of Ragusa was a traitor, and to fight him was to fight the enemy of France."

It was a day of disturbances; and while waiting until the garrison should have taken arms, the gen-

darmerie had difficulty in repressing the gatherings.
At five in the evening the troops were in position;
the first regiment of the guard, on the boulevard des
Capucines, with two pieces of cannon and fifty lancers; the third, on the Carrousel, with four pieces of
cannon and one hundred and fifty lancers; the Swiss,
on Place Louis XV., with six pieces of cannon; the
fifteenth of the line, on the Pont-Neuf; the fifth, in
Place Vendôme; the fiftieth, at the boulevards Pois-
sonnière and Saint-Denis; the fifty-third and the cuirassiers, in the Place de la Bastille. All these troops
were in communication with each other by means of
patrols in all directions. At first they encountered
no serious resistance. But let their leader, Marshal
Marmont tell the story: "Toward seven in the evening, the gatherings began again in the rue Saint-
Honoré, coming through the cross-streets. Two
barricades were raised near the rues Duc-de-Bordeaux
and Échelle, and destroyed by my orders. The
troops having withdrawn, they were begun again.
It was necessary to go back to them. The building
materials that were there served as weapons against
the troops. Some of the soldiers were wounded by
stones, and they fired twice. These hostilities on
the part of the Parisians could not be serious; and
this sort of intrenchments, constructed so near the
places where there were considerable bodies of troops,
seemed to have no other object than that of provok-
ing the troops and judging of their dispositions.
The patrols may have had some encounters else-

where, and probably did, because a man was killed near rue Feydeau. However, nothing of great importance occurred that day."

At Saint-Cloud Charles X. still continued to regard matters with complete tranquillity. Prince de Polignac would have reproached himself for disturbing his king apropos of a crisis whose issue he did not think doubtful, and as no one but him corresponded with the sovereign, and the bulletins sent to Saint-Cloud related no news but such as was favorable to the royal cause, Charles X. felt himself sure of success. During the day he received in special audience the Bishop of Beauvais, and Marquis de Dampierre, peer of France; he also worked with the Minister of the Interior, and afterwards with Count de la Bouillerie, steward of his palace. Etiquette was kept up in the most regular fashion, and absolute calm prevailed at the palace of Saint-Cloud.

To resume: Tuesday, July 27, seems not to have been a bad day for the royal cause. There were many liberals who did not as yet dream of a revolution. They would have been willing enough to profit by one, but without running any personal risk. The most audacious in words were the least resolved on action. On the subject of this day of July 27, Chateaubriand has written: "When the prefect of police sent to seize the presses of the *National*, M. Carrel resisted, but M. Thiers and M. Mignet, believing that the game was lost, disappeared for two days. M. Thiers went to hide himself in the valley of

Montmorency, at the house of one Madame de Cour-
champ, a relation of the two MM. Becquet, one
of whom was employed on the *National* and the
other on the *Journal des Débats*. The party of
usurpation did not yet show itself ; its chief, in hid-
ing outside of Paris, did not know whether he would
go to Saint-Cloud or to the Palais-Royal."

Some thirty liberal deputies had assembled at the
house of M. Casimir Périer ; but the majority of
them did not even seek to hide their fright. Their
host was perhaps the least courageous of them all.
In him the banker took precedence of the revolutionist. Moved to the utmost, he thus apostrophized his
colleagues : "Do you propose to render me responsible for the terrible events that seem to be preparing?
That would be insupportable ; I cannot endure it.
You are ruining yourselves. In departing from
legality you cause us to abandon a superb position."
The men in blouses were not of this opinion. As
happens almost always in times of revolution, the
laboring classes were to pull the chestnuts out of the
fire and the middle classes were to eat them.

Meanwhile, night had come. The royalists thought
the insurrection was discouraged. "At nine o'clock,"
says Marshal Marmont, "the groups broke up of
themselves, everybody returned to their lodgings,
and at half-past ten the streets were all clear. Tranquillity was perfectly restored, nothing foreboded any
disorderly plans for the night, and the troops received
orders to return to their barracks."

Charles X. received this news with satisfaction before going to bed. Yet in the midst of his serenity, he had a sort of vague presentiment that the situation was not altogether so good as those about him seemed to think. Seeing that General de Bordesoulle presented himself in place of the Duke of Ragusa to receive the watchword: "Ah!" said he, "you come instead of the Marshal. I have sent him to Paris. I authorized him to sleep at Saint-Cloud, but he has done well to remain where he was."

XI

JULY TWENTY-EIGHTH

VERY early on Wednesday morning, July 28, crowds were forming again, and the excitement was extreme. The gunsmiths and retail dealers in powder and shot willingly delivered their arms and ammunition to the insurgents. The cry was no longer, as on the previous evening, "Down with the Ministers! Down with the Charter!" but "Long live liberty! Down with the Bourbons!" At seven o'clock the cords of the street lamps were cut, the white flags at the mayoralties were dragged through the gutters, the royal escutcheons were broken, and barricades erected. Marshal Marmont sent everywhere orders for the troops to leave their barracks as soon as they had eaten their soup, and take their positions. Then he sent to Saint-Cloud a letter thus worded: "Wednesday, nine o'clock in the morning. I have already had the honor of rendering an account to Your Majesty of the dispersion of the groups that were disturbing the tranquillity of Paris yesterday. This morning they are forming anew, in greater numbers and more threatening. This is no longer a riot; it is a revolution. It is urgently necessary

106

that Your Majesty shall adopt means of pacification. The honor of the crown may yet be saved. To-morrow it may be too late. I am taking measures to put down the revolt. The troops will be ready at noon, but I await impatiently the orders of Your Majesty." Received at the moment when Charles X. was going to the Mass said in the chapel of the palace of Saint-Cloud, this letter was placed on a tabouret in the Gallery of Apollo and not opened by the King until after his return from the chapel.

The calmness of the old monarch remained imperturbable. His courtiers made it a point of honor not even to seem uneasy. The *Moniteur* had just appeared as usual. The number for Wednesday, July 28, the last of the Restoration, contained no mention whatever of the troubles in Paris, and people who read no paper but this would have imagined that the capital was enjoying the most complete tranquillity. The official sheet, after enumerating the special audiences given by the sovereign on the day before, added: "S. A. R. Monseigneur the Duke of Bordeaux went on Saturday last to Vincennes. After having visited the different parts of the arsenal of artillery established there, His Royal Highness repaired to the park and was present at the manœuvres of two field batteries. This was the first time that His Royal Highness had heard the firing of cannon so close by, and it was remarked that the young prince experienced no emotion but pleasure in assisting at a novel sight for him." Then followed a

piece of verse addressed to Vice-Admiral Baron Duperré by a sailor's apprentice at Brest, which ended
thus : —

> " Quand de pareils hauts faits sa tête est couronnée,
> Un mot doit le sauver d'éloges superflus.
> Pour lui du cinq juillet l'immortelle journée
> N'est qu'un laurier de plus." [1]

The number ended by the announcement of the
plays for the evening. The Opera was to give
Guillaume Tell.

At ten in the morning the populous quarters of
Paris were already in open revolt; but at other
points quiet still prevailed. The night had been
peaceful at the Champs-Élysées and in the faubourg
Saint-Honoré. The Duke de Broglie has related in
his *Souvenirs* that on going toward ten o'clock to
M. Guizot's house, in the rue Ville-l'Évêque, he
remarked no symptom of agitation. He found M.
Guizot in his cabinet, making a fair copy of the protest he had been deputed to draw up the day before.
Close by, in the salon, were several liberals, among
others M. de Rémusat and M. Cousin, who were in a
lively discussion. Presently M. Armand Carrel, the
editor of the *National*, came in. " All is over for this
time," he remarked sadly. " The Government is
master of the field: but patience ; it hasn't got to the

---

[1] When with like lofty deeds his head is crowned,
A word should spare him all superfluous praise.
For him of July fifth the immortal day
Is but one laurel more.

end yet." The discussion went on for some time over the chances of the present and the future, when suddenly the domestics entered, crying out that there was a riot. "We rushed into the street," adds the Duke de Broglie. "On entering the Place de la Ville-l'Évêque, at the end of the boulevard, we perceived in the corner opposite the church of the Madeleine, a squad of men in blouses, armed with guns, who looked as if they were aiming at us. Then, seeing that we were unarmed, they laughed and motioned us to pass on. Almost at the same instant we heard the tocsin sounding at full peal, first at the Hôtel-de-Ville and afterwards at the cathedral."

What is going on?

Numerous groups have gone from the Place de l'Hôtel-de-Ville to the open space in front of Notre Dame. The towers of the cathedral have been invaded. The great bell, weighing twenty-six thousand pounds, is set ringing, and the tocsin is sounded. All eyes are turned toward the summit of the towers. A flag is hoisted there. What flag is it? People are in doubt; they interrogate each other. Presently shouts of joy and triumph ring out. Old soldiers of the Empire take off their hats and bow. They remember Béranger's song: —

> " Ce drapeau payait à la France
> Tout le sang qu'il nous a coûté.
> Sur le sein de la Liberté,
> Nos fils jouaient avec sa lance.
> Quil prouve encore aux oppresseurs

Combien la gloire est roturière !
Quand secoûrai-je la poussière
Qui ternit ses nobles couleurs?"[1]

Very well! behold the dust is shaken off. The
flag hoisted on the towers of Notre Dame is the flag
of Austerlitz. The sight of it makes the liberals
tremble with joy and the legitimists with sorrow.
The tocsin that is sounding is the funeral bell of the
Restoration.

Almost simultaneously the ministers send Marshal
Marmont the royal order, declaring Paris in a state
of siege, and come to install themselves in the palace
of the Tuileries. As if overwhelmed by the weight of
his fatal name, the Marshal has just conceived a
plan which it would need thirty thousand soldiers to
carry out. He takes as his line of operation an arc
of the circle described by the boulevards from the
Madeleine as far as the Place de la Bastille, whose
chord is the rue Saint-Honoré as far as the market of
the Innocents, and the quays on the right bank from
Place du Châtelet to the Hôtel-de-Ville and rue Saint-
Antoine. Rue Richelieu and rue Saint-Denis cut this
arc perpendicularly from base to summit. Four
columns are charged with traversing these different
lines. They get in motion at noon. Their chiefs are
instructed to disperse all assemblies they find on their

---

[1] This flag repaid France — All the blood it has cost us. — On the
breast of Liberty, — Our sons played with its staff. — May it again
prove to oppressors — How plebeian is glory ! — When shall I shake
off the dust — That tarnishes its noble colors ?

line of march, to destroy all barricades that impede
their passage, and not to use their weapons unless
they are attacked. Marshal Marmont had added:
" Understand thoroughly, you are not to fire unless
they discharge a fusillade at you, not a few scattering
shots, but fifty fired all together at the troops."

Hardly had the four columns moved forward when
a horrible fusillade is poured in on them from the
windows of nearly all the houses. The troops return
it. A terrible combat ensues in every direction. A
heat like that of Senegal augments the anguish of
the soldiers. The thermometer marks thirty-five
degrees centigrade. Marmont's unfortunate army is
plunged into a bloody furnace.

Meanwhile Charles X. remains in tranquillity at
Saint-Cloud. The old King seems determined to
believe nothing but the reports of Prince de Polignac.
He will not allow any one to give him other information. The Duchess de Gontaut several times entreats
him vainly to go upstairs into the salon, where by
the aid of an excellent telescope he can see the second
floors of the entire rue de Rivoli, where from every
house and every window men and women are throwing missiles, pianos, commodes, furniture of every
sort they can lay hands on, so as to crush the troops
agglomerated in the street below. The tocsin and
the cannon can be heard in the palace of Saint-Cloud.
The courage of the Duchess of Berry rises. It is a
torment to her to do nothing. " What a misfortune
to be a woman!" she exclaims. She begs the King

to allow her to go to Paris and show herself on
horseback to the army and the people. The only
response of Charles X. is to order her in a severe
tone to keep quiet.

The situation becomes more serious hourly. The
Duke de Ragusa begins to think that affairs can only
be terminated by a negotiation. At three in the
afternoon he begins writing to the King, when announcement is made to him at his headquarters
on the Place du Carrousel, of the arrival of MM.
Laffitte, Casimir Périer, Mauguin, and Generals
Lobau and Gérard, who come to ask him to stop the
firing. Laffitte, who is the first to speak, has already
been an unlucky man for the Marshal. It was he
who had counselled the defection of Essonnes at Paris,
on the evening of March 30, 1814.

"Marshal," says he, "we come in the midst of the
anguish caused us by the state of things, to ask you
to arrest the effusion of blood."

"And we address ourselves," adds General Gérard,
"to a man with a French heart."

The Duke of Ragusa responds: "Gentlemen, I
make the same request of you. Grave disturbances
were evident this morning, and they presented all
the signs of a rebellion. I commanded the dispersion
of the assemblies and the restoration of good order.
On their way to the points indicated to them the
troops have been assailed by a murderous fusillade.
They returned this fire, and they were forced to return it. Let the Parisians suspend their hostilities,

and ours will cease on the instant. Those who were first to begin should be the first to leave off. That is just and right; men cannot let themselves be killed without defending themselves."

The Marshal's interlocutors then say it would be necessary to announce the withdrawal of the Ordinances, and that in that case they will use their influence to restore peace.

The Duke de Ragusa replies: "Having no political powers, I make no engagement on that head. But I propose, if you will cause the citizens' firing to cease, to go to Saint-Cloud at your head, so as to give more weight to your demands."

M. Laffitte and M. Mauguin wish to explain their griefs against the step taken by the Government. The Marshal interrupts them: "Gentlemen," says he, "do not enter upon an aimless and superfluous discussion. That would be to lose our time, for you would blame things that I am far from approving; but there is a military question here. At this moment it takes precedence of all others in my eyes, and I cannot abandon it." Generals Gérard and Lobau cannot refrain from giving their adhesion to this language.

"You see, gentlemen," resumes the Marshal, "what power I could have to support your wishes were quiet restored. For the rest, it is fatality that has laid this cruel command upon me. It was the greatest affliction that could overwhelm my life. But I can make no compromise with my duties, were proscription and death to be the cost of their fulfilment. Help me to conciliate everybody by causing the cessation, on the part of the inhabitants, of those hostilities which preceded and occasioned those of the troops."

Then the interlocutors of the Duke de Ragusa beg him to send to Charles X. at once the expression of their demands. He consents to do so. He afterwards proposes that they should see Prince de Polignac, who is in the adjoining room with the other ministers, but the President of the Council refuses to receive them.

The interview terminated, the Marshal adds the following lines to the letter he had begun: "Just as I was about to close my letter, MM. Casimir Périer, Laffitte, Mauguin, General Gérard and General Lobau presented themselves. They said they came to ask me to stop the firing. I replied that I would offer the same prayer to them; but they required as a condition of their co-operation a promise that the Ordinances should be repealed. I replied that, having no political power, I could take no engagement in that respect. After a somewhat long conversation, they asked me to report their application to Your Majesty. I think it urgent that Your Majesty should profit without delay by the overtures which have been made."

The Marshal intrusts his letter to Colonel Komiérowski, his first aide-de-camp, with an order to go quickly, present the letter himself to the King, and to give him verbal explanations on the situation of

Paris. The Colonel starts with an escort of twenty-five lancers, and reaches Saint-Cloud in four hours.

Introduced into the cabinet of the King by the Duke de Duras, first gentleman of the chamber, Colonel Komiérowski presents the letter of the Duke de Ragusa to Charles X., and gives a verbal account of the state of things to the sovereign. He explains to him that it is not merely the populace of Paris but the entire population which has risen, and that he had been able to judge of that for himself in crossing Passy, where musket shots had been fired at him by the citizens. Several times while the Colonel is insisting on details tending to demonstrate the gravity of the situation, the King interrupts him and says, "Abridge it." Far from disturbing him, the news he receives reassures him. He tells himself that if five liberal deputies have come to demand a cessation of hostilities from the Duke de Ragusa, it is because the insurrection believes itself vanquished. He orders the Colonel to retire and await his orders.

These orders not arriving, Colonel Komiérowski begs the Duke de Duras to go and ask the King for them. The Duke replies that etiquette forbids him to enter without being summoned. At last, the Colonel is recalled to the sovereign's cabinet. No written message is given him, but he is simply charged to tell the Marshal to remain firm, to reunite his forces at the Carrousel and Place Louis XV., and to operate with masses. Charles X. twice repeats this last word. The Duchess of Berry and the Dauphin,

who are then in the King's cabinet, maintain silence.
A few moments after the departure of Colonel Komić-
rowski, a man very devoted to the monarchy, General
Vincent, who has just come from Paris, arrives at
Saint-Cloud and says that the royal cause is incurring
the greatest perils if the Ordinances are not immediately withdrawn. Charles X. contents himself with
saying: " My dear fellow, you are a good general, but
you don't understand about such things as these."
    Meanwhile night falls. The four columns of troops,
commanded by Generals Quinsonnas, Talon, Saint-
Chamans, and Saint-Hilaire, have only been able to
effect their movements amid the greatest dangers,
while crossing the barricades and receiving the fire
and the missiles of every sort flung from the windows. By dint of courage and coolness they had
reached the goal assigned them by Marshal Marmont.
They had succeeded in recovering the Hôtel-de-Ville
from the insurgents, and in occupying the Place de
Grève, the Place de la Bastille, and the other points
fixed on. But as they had no longer food nor ammunition, they received at nightfall the order to retrace
their steps, to abandon the positions acquired with
such difficulty, and to encamp in the courts of the
Louvre, the garden of the Tuileries, the Place Vendôme, Place Louis XV., and the boulevard de la
Madeleine. During their retrograde march, which
was painful and dangerous, their officers had told
them that once back, they would find at the Tuileries
Charles X. and the Dauphin, who were waiting for

them, and that then they would want for nothing. The white flag was never hoisted on the dome of the Horloge Pavilion except when the King was at the Tuileries. On approaching, the troops saw that the flag was not floating, and they said with a surprise full of bitterness : " The King and the Dauphin abandon us. They give up defending themselves then ! "

Harassed by fatigue, devoured by a burning thirst, enfeebled by an insupportable heat, and having eaten nothing since morning, the unfortunate soldiers suffered both physically and morally. They regretted the blood shed in a fratricidal strife. Many of them who, after serving under the Empire, had entered the royal guard, murmured at being obliged to fight their former brethren in arms who recalled the tricolor. The Marshal could not even distribute bread to the troops. Two or three battalions only received a fourth part of a ration; the rest were obliged to wait until next day, and content themselves with a distribution of wine taken from the cellars of the Tuileries.

In the evening, the Duke de Ragusa received the following letter and order from Charles X.: —

" My Dear Marshal: I learn with great pleasure the good and honorable conduct of the troops under your orders. Thank them on my part, and grant them six weeks' pay. Reassemble your troops and wait for my orders to-morrow.

" *Order for the Marshal Duke de Ragusa, commander-in-chief of the first military division :* —

" 1. Reassemble all the forces between the Place
des Victoires, the Place Vendôme, and the Tuileries;

" 2. Provide for the security of the Ministries of
Foreign Affairs, Finances, and the Marine ;

" 3. Provide for the safe journey of the ministers
from Paris to Saint-Cloud, to-morrow, the 29th, between ten and eleven o'clock ;

" 4. In this position, await the orders which I may
have to give during to-morrow ;

" 5. Repulse assailants if they present themselves,
but make no new attacks against those in revolt.

" CHARLES.

"Done at Saint-Cloud, July 28, 1830."

The four columns which throughout the whole day
had loyally but with grief sustained so many losses,
shed so much blood, and retired only because they
had neither bread to eat nor cartridges to fire, found
themselves, after such useless heroism, in the positions they had occupied in the morning. As Duke
Victor de Broglie has remarked, no one could say
they had been vanquished; but they had been, so
to say, swimming in an ocean of riot whose waves
opened before them and closed up again behind them.
In the evening, all the troops being concentrated,
they had in their possession the Louvre, the Tuileries, the Palais-Royal, the Bank, and the Champs-
Élysées. The rest of Paris was given over to the
insurrection, which covered the quays, streets, and

boulevards with barricades. "In my long military career," Marshal Marmont has written, "and in the midst of events of all sorts in which I have been an actor, I have never experienced anything comparable to the torments and anxieties of that day. My head-quarters were established in the Place du Carrousel. At every moment I received a multitude of alarming reports. By means of calmness and painstaking I had succeeded in providing for everything, and the day came to an end as well as possible; that is to say, without grave accidents; but, for a reasonable man, all illusion was at an end, and, unless the reflec-tions of night, and the losses experienced, should com-pletely change the temper of the Parisians, there was no longer any possible hope save in a very speedy compromise."

And yet the royal cause did not seem desperate in the night of Wednesday and Thursday, July 28–29, 1830. Prince de Polignac, Minister of War *par interim*, came, at Marshal Marmont's request, to give some orders whose effects might be useful to Charles X. He had enjoined the pupils of the School of Saint-Cyr to repair to Saint-Cloud with their pieces of artillery. The two camps of Lunéville and Saint-Omer were raised, and the troops composing them were to go by forced marches to Paris. Other re-enforcements were expected there. The strategetic position occupied by the Marshal seemed not difficult to defend. He had the Seine on his right, the bou-levard on his left, the Louvre and the Place des

Victoires in front of him, and he thus covered the
Tuileries, the Champs-Élysées, and the road to Saint-
Cloud. He had told Prince de Polignac, and the
latter had written it to the King, that this position
was impregnable, and that he could hold it for three
weeks.

The combat having ceased at night, for lack of
ammunition, Charles X. felt reassured, and perhaps
fancied that the insurrection was vanquished, because
the sound of cannonading and firing was no longer
heard at Saint-Cloud. The old King was already
talking of the happiness he would have in granting
clemency to the insurgents. The calmness of a
beautiful, starry night contrasted with human agitations and passions. The Duchess de Gontaut says
in her Memoirs: "Importance was attached in the
royal apartment to not appearing disturbed. None
of the hours nor customs were interrupted: the little
promenade after dinner on the terrace, where the
children played, and where the poor governess,
though insupportable as they affectionately told her,
still received melancholy confidences; the whist
party which nothing disturbed, established just opposite the balcony. To see the four whist-players,
calm, entirely absorbed in their game, — dare I say
the word? — that scandalized me. I was wrong, for
the King confessed to me later on that he only
wished to seem tranquil, because he had promised to
be so."

Charles X., a man of the court if ever there was

one, was accustomed to conform scrupulously to etiquette. He did not say: "Come, I want to play; let some one get a table ready." He found it ready, and the first gentleman of the chamber said to him: "Sire, it is the hour for cards; your party is arranged." The Duke de Duras came to say that as usual, and the King sat down mechanically to the card-table, where he seated himself every evening at the same hour. It was for him a question of dignity to remain impassible and to change nothing in his habitudes.

XII

CHARLES X. did not reproach himself on account of his resolutions on Thursday morning, July 29, 1830. His eyes were not unsealed. He counted on the military re-enforcements which were, as he thought, to crowd into Paris; and he remained convinced that meanwhile the Duke de Ragusa's position was as impregnable as the Marshal had described it. Around him men's minds were growing gloomy, and the courtiers were well recovered from the optimism of the previous day; but he, always confiding in the protection of God, still imagined that his cause would triumph. He rose very early, and received the General Duke de Mortemart, captain-colonel of the Hundred Swiss, long before the usual hour for audiences. In spite of his high birth and his position in the King's military household, the Duke was considered very hostile to the ideas of the Extreme Right. A son of the late Duke de Mortemart and a Demoiselle de Cossé-Brissac, he had emigrated in 1791 with his family, and did not return to France until 1801. Entering Napoleon's army, he had won the cross at the battle of Friedland, distinguished himself at

122

Ratisbonne, Essling, Wagram, in Russia, at Leipsic,
and Hanau, and during the campaign of 1814 had
been charged by the Emperor to carry to Marie
Louise the flags taken from the Allies at Champau-
bert, Nangis, and Montereau.

King Louis XVIII. had made the Duke de Mortemart a peer of France and captain-colonel of the
Hundred Swiss. His liberal opinions did not prevent Charles X. from making him a lieutenant-
general and ambassador to Russia. The Duke came
back from Russia, and went to take baths in the
south of France. He had witnessed what took place
in Paris, July 28; and reaching Saint-Cloud in the
evening, he wished to give an account of it to the
sovereign at once. He could not be received until
the next day, July 29.

Charles X. received the Duke de Mortemart very
well; but when the latter assured him without cir-
cumlocution that it was no longer possible to sustain
Prince de Polignac and the Ordinances: "Mortemart," said the sovereign, "you are an honest and
loyal servitor; I know your worth; but you are still
young. Born in the midst of the Revolution, you
have assumed its prejudices and false notions without
observing it. My old experience is above all these
illusions. . . . I know where the concessions they
are asking would lead me, and I don't want to mount
a cart, like my brother. I prefer to mount a horse."
— "I think, Sire," replied the Duke de Mortemart,
"that the time is not far distant when you will be

obliged to mount one." — "We shall see, we shall
see," resumed the King, and then dismissed the
Duke.

Not long after, the ministers, coming from Paris,
arrived at Saint-Cloud to hold a council. Marquis
de Sémonville, Grand Referendary of the Chamber of
Peers, and Count d'Argout, peer of France, arrived
almost at the same moment, and entreated the sovereign to recall the Ordinances. Apprised of the
gravity of the situation, Charles X. began at last to
emerge from his quietude.

The hour of the Ministerial Council was not
changed, however. It took place at noon, after Mass.
The King was grave and sad, but not depressed.
He had just been praying with fervor, and his submission to the decrees of Providence rendered him
resigned in advance to all trials. As to the Dauphin, who from the first had ardently desired to
quell the insurrection himself, and had only been
detained at Saint-Cloud by the steadfast determination of the King, he was indignant at the thought
that a riot could be compromised with. According
to him, the danger of the situation was certainly
exaggerated; but even were it as great as it was
claimed to be, still they must hope and struggle to
the end. Baron d'Haussez declared that he considered that Paris was lost to the King, but that
Paris was not France; his opinion was that time
should be gained by a suspension of hostilities, and
under cover of this respite, a speedy move should be

made on the Loire, sending word to the troops of
Saint-Omer and Lunéville, who were going to Paris,
to turn toward the city the King should choose for his
residence. " M. d'Haussez," exclaimed the Dauphin,
" I dislike timid counsels. The better part, the most
dignified, is to let ourselves be killed." There was
but one minister who rejected all notion of a compromise: M. de Guernon-Ranville. He wanted fighting to go on at Paris and beyond Paris, and to uphold
the ministry and the Ordinances. " This," said he,
" is not the hour to deliberate and to compromise; it
is the hour to defend ourselves. By yielding we
should lose honor and gain nothing." The Dauphin alone was on the side of this advice. The King
no longer thought of fighting.

At court, meanwhile, everybody was blaming Marshal Marmont and attributing to him all the misfortunes of the last few days; the Dauphin demanded
his dismissal. The unfortunate Marshal had no
defender left except Charles X., who would not
inflict the stigma of a dismissal, but who ended by
taking a middle course. He appointed the Dauphin
commander-in-chief of the army, and by that very
fact placed the Marshal under his orders. In consequence, the son of Charles X. wrote the following
letter to the Duke of Ragusa during the council of
ministers : —

" My Cousin: The King having given me the
command-in-chief of all his troops, I order you

to retire at once with all the troops upon Saint-
Cloud. You will serve there under my orders. I
charge you at the same time to take all necessary
measures for transporting thither from Paris all bills
and papers in the Royal Treasury, according to the
decision just taken by the Minister of Finances. You
will be so good as to apprise the troops immediately
that they have passed under my command.

" LOUIS ANTOINE.

"From my headquarters at Saint-Cloud, July 29, 1830."

A courier was despatched with this missive.

The council of ministers was still in progress when
an officer well known for his devotion to the monarchy, General du Coëtlosquet, who came from Paris,
urgently requested to be received by the King. At
first no one was willing to introduce him, because he
was not in court dress ; but he insisted so vigorously
that he finally reached the sovereign. Harassed
with fatigue, scorched by the sun, his clothes in disorder, he wished to speak, but was unable ; his voice
was broken by emotion. " I still see him," writes
M. d'Haussez in his Memoirs, "I see him leaning
against the bookshelves, no cravat on, powdered with
dust, and hardly able to hold himself up. He came
to announce that all was being lost at Paris."

What had happened, then, since morning?

At sunrise Marshal Marmont did not yet think the
situation desperate. His troops, concentrated and
masters of the Tuileries, the Louvre, the Carrousel,

and the great routes which end there, occupied a
quadrilateral of which one side was formed by the
Seine, another by the rue and the faubourg Saint-
Honoré, and which extended from the Louvre as far
as the Bois de Boulogne. At dawn, the Marshal
placed two Swiss battalions in the court of the
Louvre. It was the head of the line, and he considered this post an impregnable fortress. The third
Swiss battalion, the third regiment of the guard, and
the sixth were on the Carrousel with six pieces of
cannon. The first and second regiments of the guard
occupied the Place Louis XV. and the boulevard de la
Madeleine with two pieces of artillery. The fifteenth
and fiftieth of the line were placed in the garden of
the Tuileries, and two pieces of cannon were opposite the rue Castiglione. The fifth and the fifty-third
of the line were in the Place Vendôme. The Marshal
established posts in the houses at the entry of the
streets abutting on the Carrousel, and at the Place
which separates the Louvre from the Tuileries. In
the rue de Rohan he placed a battery which commanded the rue Richelieu and prevented all offensive
movements from that side. He put a detachment in
the houses on the rue de Rohan, facing the rue de
Rivoli, to prevent the inhabitants of these houses
from firing at the troops massed in the latter street.
He did the same for the houses in the Place du
Carrousel, opposite the palace of the Tuileries.

It was a very good strategetic position. But, to
profit by it, the Duke of Ragusa would have needed

an inflexible character, and it was that he lacked. In
street combats still more than on battle-fields, a general must know what he wants. The combat of the
thirteenth Vendémiaire had been fought on very
nearly the same site as that of July 29, 1830. But
Marmont was not Bonaparte. Bonaparte made nothing heard but the voice of cannons; Marmont par-
leyed. In Marmont's place, Bonaparte would have
arrested without scruple the five deputies who had
come to negotiate with him at headquarters. Marmont did not content himself with practising; he was
preaching politics. By hesitating, through humanity
or self-interest, to employ his artillery; by forbidding
his troops to fire except to defend themselves against
an attack; by convoking the mayors and their deputies to send them around among the environs of the
Tuileries and talk to the people, he paralyzed the
military action.

The thing most desired by the Duke of Ragusa
was the fall of the Ministry, even while defending it
by arms. "I expected every moment," he says,
"news and powers. If at eleven o'clock even, I
had been authorized to promise the withdrawal of the
Ordinances, the dynasty would have been saved. In
circumstances so critical it was of the greatest importance to treat while we still occupied Paris, while
the palace of the Tuileries, the real seat of the capital, was still in our possession; hence I had decided
to risk everything rather than retire voluntarily."

Now see the circumstances in consequence of which

the Marshal thought himself obliged to beat a retreat some minutes later. One of the liberal deputies, M. Casimir Périer, came before the fifth and fifty-third of the line, who occupied the Place Vendôme, and induced their defection. Then the Marshal made the fifteenth and fiftieth of the line, who might have been led away by this example, depart from their cantonment in the Tuileries garden, and sent them to the Champs-Élysées. A large number of people gathering in the rue de Richelieu, the captain of artillery commanding the cannon placed in the rue de Rohan sent to the Marshal asking an authorization to fire upon them. The Duke of Ragusa himself approached the cannon, and, although the persons in this gathering fired on the troops, he forbade the latter to fire lest they should hit the women. Desiring, nevertheless, to put a stop to hostilities at this point, he ordered the chief of battalion, de La Rue, his aide-de-camp, to go and parley once more, and to announce to the insurgents that negotiations were in progress, but that if they came any nearer they would be fired on. This officer managed to stop the firing.

It was an hour past noon, and the Marshal, who was still in the rue de Rohan, thought that calm was restored, when he heard a lively fusillade. The Swiss battalion that he had ordered to quit the Louvre and occupy the Place du Carrousel, had left a company behind them, stationed at the left angle of the Louvre, beside the rue du Coq, where the buildings then in process of construction facilitated the approach of the in-

surgents. The adjutant-major of this battalion, having
come in search of this company, retired it immediately
without giving notice to Colonel de Salis, who might
have replaced it. Seeing the post vacated, the insurgents rushed upon it and succeeded in making their
way into the apartments of the Louvre. Then ensued
a real panic among the troops. Thinking themselves
blockaded, they fled in disorder from beside the arch
of triumph in the Carrousel. The Duke of Ragusa
rejoined them.

"I get on horseback," says he in his Memoirs.
"Men and horses are killed beside me, and I arrive
in the courtyard of the palace. There I rally sixty
Swiss. With this feeble troop I oppose those pressing on us. . . . The Parisians penetrate the very
courtyard of the Tuileries, and one of them falls,
pierced by a ball, at the very moment when he was
about to fire on me at a distance of ten paces. I had
a charge made on them by four officers who accompanied me, and they were driven out. I had the
gate locked under fire. My sixty Swiss remained
masters of the field of battle."

The troops pass through the vestibule of the Pavilion of the Horloge, and continue their retreat with
the Marshal by the garden of the Tuileries and Place
Louis XV.

Meanwhile, the insurgents on the left bank, finding the wicket near the Pavilion of Flora open, rush
into the court of the Tuileries, just abandoned by the
troops, pass through the ground-floor apartments,

arrive beneath the central dome, go up stairs into the Hall of the Marshals and to the roof of the Pavilion of the Horloge, where they plant the tricolored flag.

At this moment the Duchess of Berry, leaning against a window-seat in the second story of the palace of Saint-Cloud, turns a glass in the direction of Paris, whose principal monuments define themselves clearly against a limpid sky. " Ah! my God," she cries, " I see the tricolored flag."

The Duke of Ragusa continues his retreat. " I occupy," says he, " the upper part of the faubourg du Roule, certain that in this position no one will present himself before us. In sight of the palace, having the artillery in an open place, we were still menacing. That was something for the negotiations. So long as we were in sight our words carried weight. If the court had then evacuated Saint-Cloud and gone to establish itself at Saint-Denis, free from care about its security, we might have been able, once rejoined by the artillery of Vincennes which was to arrive during the day,—we might, I say, have been able to go and take up a position on Montmartre, and from there destroy the city or at any rate menace it. Instead of that, they had decided differently at Saint-Cloud, and at this very moment I received news that the King had given the command of his army to the Dauphin. The latter ordered me to evacuate Paris and bring the troops to Saint-Cloud." The sufferings of the troops had been extreme. They had been under arms for thirty hours, and had had to sustain the most obstinate and bloody combats.

The council of ministers went on. After the tidings brought him by General du Coëtlosquet, Charles X. decided to yield; M. de Guernon-Ranville was the only minister who continued to speak of resistance. "If the legitimate throne must fall once more," cried he, "let it at least fall with honor. Shame alone has no future." The Dauphin approved this language, but the King gave way more and more. "Gentlemen," said he, "they impose on me the obligation of dismissing ministers who possess all my affection, in order to take others given me by my enemies. Here I am in the situation of my unhappy brother in 1792. Since it must be so, I am going to summon the Duke de Mortemart. I pity him for having attracted the confidence of my enemies. If he has been in fault, here is a very cruel punishment. Every one has his griefs; one of those which I feel most keenly is this cruel separation." The voice of Charles X. was altered by tears.

The sorrow of the old King was again augmented by the arrival of Marshal Marmont. "Sire," said the Marshal, "this is a lost battle! A ball aimed at me killed one of my officers at my side. I regret that it did not go through my head; I would prefer death to the sad spectacle I have just witnessed."

One consolation for Charles X. in this day of mourning was the arrival at Saint-Cloud of the pupils of Saint-Cyr, who, unlike those of the Polytechnic School, remained faithful to him. Accompanied by the Duchess of Berry, the Duke of Bordeaux and Mademoiselle, he passed through the ranks of their battalion. "Watch over this precious child," he said to them. "One day, I hope, he will be your King and know how to appreciate your devotion." Mademoiselle, who was but eleven, came forward, holding the hand of the Duke of Bordeaux, her junior by a year. "Ah! gentlemen," said she to the young men, "I beg you to defend my brother well!" All the students responded with a shout of "Long live the King!"

The question now was to induce the Duke de Mortemart to take the Ministry. The Duke's first reply had been this: "I beg you to say to the King that I will defend His Majesty at the head of my company to the last drop of my blood. But I will not meddle with any political affair, and with this one less than any other." The King, having summoned him, said: "You were right; the position is more difficult than I thought this morning; it is believed that a ministry of which you should be the head might arrange everything. I have appointed you." The Duke replied: "I do not think myself capable, Sire, of accomplishing your views. I entreat Your Majesty to choose some one else." Charles X. insisted; then drawing a paper from his pocket: "There," said he, "is your nomination. From this moment you are Minister of Foreign Affairs and

President of the Council." M. de Mortemart refused
to take the paper. The King was absolutely bent on
putting it in his hand. The Duke constantly drew
back. Charles X., seeing him literally at the wall,
with his arms close to his body, thrust the paper
inside his general-officer's belt. The Duke drew it
out to give back to him. "Sir," said the King at
this, "you refuse then to save my crown and the
heads of my ministers?" M. de Mortemart could
not resist words like these. He accepted, only saying: "May Your Majesty never forget what I have
had the honor of saying to him. If I succeed in re-
establishing the royal authority at Paris, it cannot be
otherwise than at the cost of the most painful concessions extorted by necessity. No doubt I shall be
held responsible for the consequences they may produce. If I fail in my negotiation, I shall be not less
to be pitied, and but too happy if no one claims that
I have betrayed." — "And that is how," the Duke
will say later on, "I found myself invested with that
dignity of prime minister which is usually so much
desired."

M. de Mortemart should have started immediately
for Paris, where the royal cause was not yet absolutely lost. But Charles X. detained him at Saint-
Cloud, perhaps with the ulterior thought that during
the night some unlooked-for event might change the
face of things. He contented himself with sending
MM. d'Argout, de Sémonville, and de Vitrolles to
the capital, charging them to announce the with-

drawal of the Ordinances and the nomination of a liberal Ministry presided over by the Duke de Morte- mart, with General Gérard as Minister of War, but without giving them a writing to certify the authen- ticity of the news. To their great astonishment these three negotiators found at Paris a provisional Government installed at the Hôtel-de-Ville, under the presidency of General Lafayette.

At Saint-Cloud people were still under illusions. They said to themselves that the troops surrounding the King would be joined by forty pieces of artillery from Vincennes, a Swiss regiment which was coming from Orleans, and all the troops of the camp of Saint- Omer. They thought the appointment of a liberal Ministry would have a quieting effect, and that in any case the throne would be saved. The cannon were no longer roaring; they thought everything was over; Paris, from a distance, seemed tranquil, and they liked to persuade themselves that next day the Duke de Mortemart could install himself peacefully in the Ministry of Foreign Affairs. " The court," has said M. Louis de Viel-Castel, "had resumed, or, better, preserved, its ordinary aspect. In the evening the King was still seen forming his whist party, in which M. de Polignac and M. de Mortemart took part suc- cessively. The Dauphin had his game of chess as usual. M. de Polignac seemed calm and serene ; but M. de Mortemart was uneasy and disturbed. He would have liked to start for Paris with MM. de Sémonville and d'Argout; but the King opposed

this, wishing to await the return of Count Alexandre
de Girardin, whom he had despatched to investigate
the situation, and still counting on some turn of
fortune, or, at the very least, thinking that, as M. de
Sémonville had induced him to hope, when things
were less advanced, the great State bodies would
come the next day to implore his clemency, which
would save the royal dignity and allow him to limit
his concessions." The King retired at the usual
hour, without having signed the ordinances which
the Duke de Mortemart had been vainly waiting for
during several hours. The lights were extinguished;
the palace of Saint-Cloud was at peace.

XIII

CHARLES X. was far from believing when he went to bed on Thursday evening, July 29, that his throne was lost. If he had not yet despatched the Duke de Mortemart to Paris, it was because he could not accustom himself to the idea of a liberal Ministry. Almost all sovereigns who make concessions desire to take back with one hand what they give with the other; the new President of the Council, confronted with the King's repugnances, dared not formulate a programme; on both sides there was equivocation. Can one reproach Charles X. with his delays and hesitations? At that moment the Duke of Orleans and the liberal deputies hesitated as much as he did. Both were waiting for fortune to declare itself before taking up a definite position.

Meanwhile, MM. d'Argout and de Vitrolles arrived at Saint-Cloud at half-past one in the morning. The most profound silence reigned in the palace, all of whose doors were closed. The Duke de Mortemart, ill and very uneasy, had finally thrown himself on a sofa for a little repose. Surprised to find him

137

still at Saint-Cloud, MM. d'Argout and de Vitrolles
waked him up and urged him to start for Paris
without losing a moment. "I would have been
there long ago," he said to them, "but what would
you have me do? I have neither the ordinance
which withdraws the Acts of the 25th, nor those
which name General Gérard and M. Casimir Périer
as ministers. I have no powers; in fact, I have nothing." Then his interlocutors entreated him to force
open the King's door. At such an hour the thing
was difficult. Nevertheless, the Duke de Mortemart
succeeded in entering the bed-chamber of Charles X.
The sovereign awoke. He seemed more disposed to
recall his concessions of the previous day than to
make new ones. The Duke conjured him to receive
MM. d'Argout and de Vitrolles, who, coming from
Paris, could make him understand the gravity of
the situation and the necessity of making a decision.
The King would not see M. d'Argout, but he
received M. de Vitrolles, who ended by convincing
him. The ordinances were drawn up. One recalled
those of July 25; the other convoked the Chambers
for August 3d; a third named the Duke de Mortemart, President of the Council and Minister of Foreign Affairs; General Gérard, Minister of War; and
M. Casimir Périer, Minister of Finances: a final one
re-established the National Guard. But no one dared
mention the tricolored flag to the King, nor M. de
Lafayette, and the name of the commander-in-chief
was left in blank. The new President of the Council

had another struggle to obtain the royal signature. The restoration of the National Guard above all inspired the sovereign with profound repugnance. Quite worn out, he, nevertheless, concluded to sign. The Duke de Mortemart called for a horse. It was refused him, an order of the Dauphin forbidding any horse to be taken from the royal stables. Then he borrowed a private carriage, in which he started for Paris at six on Friday morning, July 30. Obstacles of every sort hindered him on the road. Obliged to alight from the carriage, he walked part of the way, and only succeeded in entering Paris through a breach opened near Vaugirard in the *octroi* wall, which was being repaired. On his road he had hurt his heel. "I sincerely pity a man of courage and honor like M. de Mortemart," Chateaubriand has said, "when I think that the legitimate monarchy was possibly overthrown because the minister charged with the royal powers was unable to meet two deputies in Paris, and because fatigued with walking three leagues he had rubbed the skin off his heel."

And yet the liberals were still very uncertain as to the resolutions they ought to take. One of them, M. Mauguin, has written: "Charles X. still had considerable forces at his disposal. . . . We feared an attack. People deceive themselves and judge after the event, when they think that Charles X. was at the end of his resources on July 29; the weakness of his character and the incapacity of his advisers counted for much in the changes of his for-

tune." The greatest divisions existed in the liberal
camp. Some desired the Republic, some the Empire,
some royalty under the Duke of Orleans. There
were also many who consented to uphold Charles X.
with a liberal ministry. On July 30, at six in the
morning, at the very moment when M. Mortemart
left Saint-Cloud for Paris, M. Laffitte was saying in
his house to M. Alexandre de La Borde: " Things
are arranged; the Duke de Mortemart is President
of the Council, Gérard and Périer are ministers;
I could have desired something different, but what
would you have? everything seems decided."

M. Thiers had not shown himself during the three
days of combat. He reappeared on the scene July
30. During the night he had drawn up a placard
thus worded, which was posted at eight o'clock in
the morning: —

" Charles X. can never enter Paris again; he has
shed the blood of the people;

" The Republic would expose us to frightful divisions; it would embroil us with Europe;

" The Duke of Orleans is a prince devoted to the
cause of the Revolution;

" The Duke of Orleans has never fought against
us;

" The Duke of Orleans was at Jemmapes;

" The Duke of Orleans has worn the national
colors, the Duke of Orleans only can wear them
still;

" The Duke of Orleans has declared himself; he

accepts the Charter as we have always desired and intended it;

"He will hold his crown from the French people."

At half-past twelve, a certain number of liberal deputies assembled at the Palais-Bourbon in the place where the deliberations of the Chamber ordinarily took place. M. Laffitte, who came in a sedan chair, presided. "Twelve or fifteen hours before," M. de Vaulabelle has said, "they would have accepted the Duke of Bordeaux and the regency of his mother; in the morning, the royalty of this young prince, with the Duke of Orleans for regent, would have been received with acclamations." At noon people were dreaming of a change of dynasty. However, the deputies consented to wait for the Duke de Mortemart; but the Duke did not come. Fulfilling his mission loyally but against his wishes, overwhelmed by fatigue, burnt up with fever, limping so much from his fall in the morning that he needed the assistance of two persons to stand upright, he did not make his appearance at the Palais-Bourbon. He was seen at the Luxembourg, where a certain number of peers had assembled, but he could do nothing useful there. He contented himself with sending Count de Sassy to the Palais-Bourbon, and then to the Hôtel-de-Ville, with the new ordinances. This step produced no result; in spite of the ardent opposition of the republicans of the Hôtel-de-Ville, the chances of the Orleanist cause were augmenting hourly.

What was the man doing at this moment who was about to become King? He kept himself hidden from Tuesday, July 27, at Raincy, in the midst of a wood, at the lodge of one of his foresters. None knew the place of his retreat except his family. To all who inquired for him, his servants invariably made the same response: "Monseigneur is absent, and we do not know where he is." In the morning of July 30, M. Thiers repaired to Neuilly. He did not find the prince, but he had a long conversation with the Duchess of Orleans and Madame Adelaide. He withdrew with the conviction that the Duke would end by accepting the crown, and, returning to Paris the same day, he aided more than any one in deciding the liberal deputies, assembled at the Palais-Bourbon, to beg the Duke of Orleans to come to Paris for the purpose of exercising the functions of lieutenant-general of the realm and of hoisting the tricolored flag there.

After the departure of M. Thiers, the Duchess of Orleans had sent her chevalier of honor, Count Anatole de Montesquiou, to Raincy, to urge the Duke to come out of his retreat. The prince hesitated long. Several times he gave the order to set out, and several times he retracted it. Chateaubriand has said: "At last, persuaded by the chevalier of honor of the Duchess of Orleans, Louis Philippe got into a carriage. M. de Montesquiou set out before him; at first he went very fast; but, looking behind him, he saw the carriage of His Royal Highness stop and turn back toward Raincy. M. de Montesquiou returned in haste, and implored his future Majesty, who was speeding to hide himself in the desert, like those illustrious Christians of olden times who fled from the weighty dignity of the Episcopate; the faithful servant obtained a last and unfortunate victory. In the evening of the 30th, the departure of twelve members of the Chamber of Deputies, who were to offer the lieutenant-generalship of the realm to the prince, sent a message to him at Neuilly; Louis Philippe received this message at the park gate, read it by torchlight, and took the road to Paris without delay, accompanied by MM. de Berthois, Haymès, and Oudart. He wore a tricolored cockade in his buttonhole; he was going to carry off an old crown from the garret."

We have just seen what went on at Paris and at Neuilly on Friday, July 30. Let us now examine the aspect of the palace of Saint-Cloud during the same day.

Charles X., confident of the success of the Duke de Mortemart's mission, still flattered himself that the only result of the crisis would be a change in the Ministry, but the courtiers began to think it was about to end in a revolution. False and contradictory tidings were in circulation; sometimes they thought all was saved, and again that all was lost. The ambitious asked themselves from what quarter the wind was going to blow, and thought of nothing but their private interests. Every one had an in-

stinctive persuasion that this court, so majestic even
yesterday, was about to go to pieces. Those who
had flattered Charles X. the most were to be the first
to deny him. Little by little the rising tide of recan-
tations and apostasies was to overspread all. But on
this 30th of July, — the last day the old monarch
passed at Saint-Cloud, — the royal cause did not
seem absolutely desperate. Many courtiers thought
that Charles X. might possibly abdicate, but that in
any case the interests of his grandson would not be
put in jeopardy: these were already addressing the
protestations of a selfish devotion to the Duchess of
Berry.

In the morning the Duke of Ragusa visited the
troops of the guard to give them confidence, and to
provide their rations as far as possible; but one thing
annoyed him much: their pay was already in arrears,
and a gratuity ordered by the King had only been
paid in part. There were several desertions during
the day; confusion and disorder began to appear on
all sides. The royal guard was dissatisfied with
the Duke of Ragusa. It contained many former
officers and soldiers of the Empire, who had never
forgiven him for the defection of Essonnes, and who
found his conduct during the last three days equivocal. Chateaubriand has said: "The wounds and
tatters of the exhausted troops caused nothing but
wonder in the titled, gilded, and cloyed domestics
who ate at the table of the King. No one dreamed
of cutting the telegraph wires; couriers, travellers,

mail coaches, diligences, went freely over the roads, carrying the tricolored flag, which incited the villages to insurrection by passing through them. The enticing away of the soldiers by means of money and women began. The proclamations of the Paris Commune were hawked hither and thither. The King and the court were still unwilling to persuade themselves they were in danger. In order to prove that they contemned the doings of certain mutinous *bourgeois*, they let everything go as it would: the finger of God is visible in all that."

The royal family was already divided. The Duke of Angoulême and the Duchess of Berry did not approve the King's policy. During the day, the Dauphin, conversing with the Duke of Ragusa, blamed Charles X. for having promised to withdraw the Ordinances and create a new Ministry. "But what means has he?" asked the Marshal. "No matter," replied the prince, "it would be better to perish than to retreat." — "But to perish is the last thing of all; that comes when nothing else can be done, and there are resources if one chooses to employ them." — "The electors have insulted the King by returning the deputies who had voted the Address." — "Perhaps that was neither polite nor pleasant for the King; but when people are busy in defending their rights they don't think about politeness; and the country was defending itself in this instance with the weapons given it by the Charter." The prince thus ended the interview: "Well, the King is mas-

ter, but I am far from approving what he has done."
And thereupon he dismissed the Marshal.

Prince de Polignac and the rest of the former ministers, so surrounded and so flattered the day before, were already abandoned. They were held responsible for existing evils and for all those that were yet to come. Dissatisfied with others and with themselves, they wandered like ghosts through the salons and gardens.

As for the Duchess of Berry, she was constantly lamenting the inactivity to which the King had reduced her since the beginning of the week. All through the three days' combat she had never ceased inwardly repeating : " How ! so many brave men are facing death to defend the cause of my son, and I am not among them to thank them, to encourage them, and to share their dangers ! " Looking from the roofs of Saint-Cloud at Paris, the huge city lying on the horizon, she was like a valiant soldier, who should witness a battle from afar but would be prevented, in spite of his ardor, from hastening at the summons of the cannon. The detonations of the artillery, the noise of the fusillading, far from intimidating the courageous princess, only excited her; the instincts of an Amazon wrought up her intrepid soul. All the respect she bore toward the old King was needed to prevent her from setting out in spite of him, or breaking into recriminations. Who knows ? If the courageous mother, leading her son by the hand, had followed the Duke de Mortemart and come to an-

nounce to the Parisians that the Ordinances were
revoked, and that a liberal Ministry was coming into
power, the legitimate monarchy might possibly have
been saved. But Charles X., who remained absolute
master in his family, had formally forbidden both the
Duchess of Berry and the Dauphin to leave the palace of Saint-Cloud. He told himself that if he, an
old pilot accustomed to so many storms, could not
resist the actual tempest, a very young and inexpe-
rienced woman would certainly not have strength to
do so. He feared, moreover, lest the princess, once
at Paris, might serve as a hostage to the Revolution.
Such anxieties are comprehensible. Was not the
King the brother-in-law of Marie Antoinette, the
brother of Madame Elisabeth? But the memory of
the women sacrificed by the Revolution did not
intimidate the Duchess of Berry. The greater the
danger was, the more the worthy daughter of Henri
IV. desired to brave it. When the armed contest
was over, the princess felt an increasing regret that
she had not taken part in it; the sight of arms and
uniforms revived her martial ardor. The troops knew
she was courageous and did not include her in the
criticism they passed on the King, that he should
have been at the Tuileries during the struggle, instead of remaining at Saint-Cloud. If Charles X.
had already lost much of his prestige, the Duchess
of Berry retained all her own.

The sky was as luminous as the situation of the
monarchy was sombre. A dazzling sun, shedding

floods of light over lamentable scenes, seemed to be insulting the afflictions of the race of Louis XIV. by the splendor of its beams. A southern nature, the Duchess of Berry, far from being weakened by the temperature of these hot July days, drew from them an increase of energy and exaltation.

At this movement, when so many defections were preparing, and when treason began to insinuate itself in the palace of Saint-Cloud, the children of the amiable prince still had the gift of charming and softening by their grace and innocence. The soldiers, after so many hours of privation and fatigue, of dangers and sufferings, forgot all their ills whenever the two children showed interest in them. The wounded were in the court. They lacked bread. The son and daughter of the Duchess of Berry, who were about sitting down at table, wanted to nourish them with their own dinner. " I approved this good sentiment," says the Duchess de Gontaut, "and I even assisted them. Never shall I forget the animated, intelligent expression, and the heart-felt enthusiasm of Monseigneur when, seizing an immense leg of mutton, he went down with all speed. Mademoiselle followed him, laden also with whatever she could reach. Arriving near the soldiers, these admirable little princes cried: ' Take it friends ; it is our dinner. Take everything, even the dishes.' I let them do as they pleased, and they were covered with benedictions."

On reascending the stairs of the palace, the gov-

erness met Prince de Polignac, calm as ever, who said
to her: "Give me some dinner."—"There is no more
dinner here," she answered. "The princes have distributed everything to the poor fellows who are dying
with hunger in the courtyard." M. de Polignac
tranquilly replied: "Very well! let us go and dine
with M. de Cossé." Turning toward the apartment
of the latter, he found in the corridors the domestics
of the princes, who were lamenting because all their
demands were responded to by: "Everything is exhausted; there is no more money; there are no more
provisions."

The day wore on thus between alternating hopes
and discouragements. The messengers sent to Saint-
Cloud by the Duke de Mortemart could not reach
there, having been intercepted by armed insurgents.
Hence Charles X. knew nothing of what was going
on at Paris; he might have been a hundred leagues
from there.

Towards evening the Duke of Ragusa saw the
King and tried to induce him to leave without delay
with all the troops, so as to get away from the fatal
atmosphere of Paris, and to go without stopping to
the Loire; to Blois, for example. Charles X. spoke
of Tours, adding: "In any case, we must await the
results of de Mortemart's journey." The Marshal
replied that the silence of the Duke since morning
left small hopes for the issue of his proceedings; by
going away promptly, he thought the fidelity of the
troops could be preserved. If the King officially

recalled the Ordinances, if he at once convoked the
Chambers in some city in the centre of France, if
he summoned the diplomatic corps about him, His
Majesty, by the dignity and firmness of his attitude,
would smite with illegality all that should be done at
Paris. The conversation went no further, and the
Marshal withdrew.

Shortly afterwards, at six in the evening, he had
an interview with General Tromelin, who had come
afoot from Paris. On his way the general had met
deserters, and he announced an imminent attack on
Saint-Cloud by the insurgents. The Marshal, alarmed
by these tidings, decided, in order to repair the silence
the Dauphin had observed toward the soldiers, to issue
the following order to the guard, to whom alone his
command extended : —

"Soldiers, you come in these days of combats to
give proofs of courage and devotion. The King is
contented with you. Recompenses have been awarded
you. The Ordinances are withdrawn. M. the Duke
de Mortemart, named Prime Minister, is about to
assure a pacification. This is the moment to close
up your ranks about the throne which you have so
valiantly defended, and to remain close to your flags.
The Marshal, major-general of the guard :
                              "DUKE OF RAGUSA."

The Marshal did not take time to submit this
order of the day to the Dauphin, in order that it
might be read in the bivouacs before the evening

muster. But he went to Charles X. towards nine
o'clock, wishing to ask his orders for the next day,
and to report to him what he had done. The King
then said to the Marshal : —

" You were wrong; you should never talk politics
to the troops."

" That is true when all is in order; but when all is
going to pieces, we must try to preserve it. Politics
are in the soldiers' minds necessarily. They are not
automatons; it is necessary to address their intelligence, their honor, and their interests."

" Did you say so to my son ? "

" No, Sire; time pressed; I only addressed the
guard, and I waited to acquaint Monseigneur with
it when I came for orders to Your Majesty."

" You have been wrong. Hurry to him now and
tell him."

The Marshal left Charles X. and went to the apartment of the Dauphin. This prince had been exasperated ever since the week began. Furious that he
also had been detained at Saint-Cloud instead of
going to Paris to fight, he would have preferred
death a thousand times to the humiliations to which
royalty had been subjected. The liberal ideas, the
delays, the hesitations of the Duke of Ragusa, had
revolted him. He had come to the point of sharing
the rancor of Napoleon's old soldiers, those who called
a treason a *ragusade*. He had long sought to dissimulate his fury. He could do so no longer. It broke
out.

The Marshal himself shall recount this lamentable
scene : —

"M. the Dauphin had entered the King's room as
I was leaving it, but by another door. I did not
meet him, therefore, but I did not wait for him long.
Barely two minutes had elapsed when he arrived
with a distraught air. Passing in front of me, he
said to me with a furious look : 'Enter!'

"Hardly was I in his salon when he caught me
by the throat, crying: "Traitor! miserable traitor!
You take the notion to issue an order of the day
without my permission!'

"At this sudden attack, I seized him by the
shoulders and pushed him away from me, he re-
doubling his cries and beginning anew his insults.

"'Give me up your sword!'

"'It may be taken from me, but I will never give
it up!'

"He threw himself upon me and drew it; he
seemed to wish to strike me with it, and shouted:
'Hither, body-guards! Seize this traitor and take
him away!'

"To describe the sensations I experienced at this
horrible moment is a thing impossible. A sentiment
of horror, indignation, contempt, overmastered me.
But I dwell on it, because I shall be no longer
living when these Memoirs shall appear. The recital
of the facts shall be, for posterity, my only ven-
geance. I was surrounded by six body-guards and
thus conducted to my lodging. The six body-guards

remained in my chamber, where I was detained a prisoner."

In ordinary times, Marshal Marmont would have been a model of devotion, discipline, honor. At the troublous epochs in which he lived, in those moments of supreme crises when the greatest evil is uncertainty as to what right and duty may be, he was beneath the part he had to play by trying to be skilful when he should have limited himself to being heroic. A sort of fatality pursued him; it was his destiny to ruin by turns the cause of the tricolor and that of the white flag. He was not less fatal to Charles X. than to Napoleon, and yet he loved both sovereigns sincerely. He was a man of heart, a soldier of great bravery and high intelligence. One comprehends what he must have suffered when the Dauphin addressed him the same reproaches as the Emperor. Was he then condemned by a cruel fate to endure identical accusations under two régimes so opposite, and was the name of traitor to pursue him everywhere like an indelible stigma?

"I sought for the cause of such folly," he adds in speaking of the conduct of the Dauphin. "An exaggerated susceptibility, over-excited by the misfortunes of the moment, and the natural feebleness of his powers are the motives on which it was necessary to rest in order to banish the suspicion of an odious calculation by means of which he would have designated me to public opinion as the veritable

cause of the catastrophe. Nevertheless, this idea
came into my mind, and I firmly believed my end
was near; but I may say with pride that I was not
disturbed by it, so overwhelmed were my faculties
by the other sentiments animating me."

At the end of half an hour, the Duke de Luxembourg, captain of the guards on duty, arrived, in
company with all the superior officers of the body-
guards, bringing back the Marshal's sword and
announcing that he had been sent for by the King.
The Marshal repaired at once to Charles X., who
said : —

"You did wrong to publish an order of the day
without submitting it to my son; but I admit that
he has been too quick. Go to his apartment. Admit your error, and he will recognize his own."

"Too quick, Sire! Is this the way one treats a
man of honor? See M. the Dauphin! Never! A
wall of brass is between him and me henceforward.
This is the price then of so many sacrifices, the recompense of such devotion! Sire, my sentiments for you
are not equivocal, but your son horrifies me!"

"Come, my dear Marshal, calm yourself; do not
add to our afflictions that of separating yourself
from us."

Charles X. pronounced these last words in a most
affecting tone; then drawing the Marshal toward him
by both hands, and putting his arms around him, he
led him to the threshold of his cabinet, the door of
which had been left open, doubtless with the inten-

tion of making all the officers on duty witnesses of
the reparation offered. Then the King charged the
Duke de Guiche to conduct the Duke of Ragusa to
the Dauphin. Let us go back to the Marshal's
story.

"Once alone with the Duke de Guiche, my fury
seized me anew, and I said with an energy I could
never estimate: 'Heaven grant that France may
never fall into the hands of a man like that!' After
a quarter of an hour's debating, and in the sad circumstances surrounding us, I saw well enough the
necessity of concluding to obey. I went to the
Dauphin's room. I said to him haughtily and in the
most formal manner: —

"'Monseigneur, it is by the express order of the
King that I approach you and admit that I was
wrong in publishing an order of the day without
your consent.'

"He waited a moment, and replied: —

"'Since you admit you were wrong, I admit that
I have been a little too quick.'

"I made no answer, and he added: 'Moreover, I
have been punished, for I wounded myself with your
sword.' And he showed me the cut he had given
himself in the hand. I answered sharply: —

"'It had not been destined to shed your blood, but
to defend it.'

"'Come,' said he, 'don't think any more about it,
and let us embrace each other.'

"He embraced me with difficulty, for assuredly I

did not bend my back in order to be nearer his
height. He took my hand, which I left limp. I
made a profound bow without looking at him and
went back to my lodging."

This painful and melancholy incident marked the
last evening that Charles X. and his court passed at
Saint-Cloud. No message from the Duke de Mortemart reached the palace, and the King, more and
more uneasy, was in complete uncertainty as to what
might have occurred during the day at Paris. He
ended by commissioning General Count Arthur de
La Bourdonnaye, gentleman of the chamber and
deputy of the Right Centre, to go in search of the
Duke, in order to bring back positive news, and
while awaiting the time of M. de La Bourdonnaye's
return, he went to bed.

XIV

CHARLES X. was asleep for the last time at Saint-Cloud, and his slumber was not to be a long one. Hardly had the old King begun to repose after so much emotion and anxiety, when a rumor spread that the insurgents assembled between Auteuil and Boulogne would take advantage of the darkness to surprise the palace. The news was false, but courtiers always pass from an excess of confidence to excessive discouragement, and the more alarming the rumors were, the more likeness they thought they bore to truth. Some one frightened the Duchess of Berry by persuading her that her children were in danger. The Princess was as averse to being surprised by night and imprisoned without a struggle, as she was willing to combat the Revolution face to face in open day. Hence she implored the Dauphin to get the King away from Saint-Cloud. The Dauphin refused at first to disturb his father's slumber, but the Princess finally induced him to do so. The King was awakened. "What is the matter?" exclaimed Charles X. He was answered: "Sire, Monsieur the Dauphin sends to beg you to start for

157

Versailles." Weakened and discouraged, the sovereign made no objections. He arose and made ready to depart. He charged Marshal Marmont to take command of the four companies of body-guards who were to be his escort, and had carriages brought into the palace courtyard for himself, his daughter-in-law, and his grandchildren.

An eye-witness, M. Théodore Anne, a body-guard of the Noailles company, thus describes the scene: "We had been lying beside our horses, with the bridles on our arms, since eight o'clock in the evening, when at two in the morning, July 31, the quartermasters came to order us to bridle, go out, and mount our horses quietly, as the King was about to leave Saint-Cloud. We had been expecting this order for a long while, and it did not surprise us; we executed it at once and were drawn up in line of battle by the number of our companies behind the palace, facing the Orangery, our right resting on the Ville-d'Avray road, our left at the park entrance beside the palace. The court carriages made their appearance at half-past three in the morning; the King was in the last one. At the left-hand door of it rode Marshal Marmont. The greatest silence prevailed during the entire journey. Every one was a prey to his reflections. The King, so lately surrounded by courtiers at high salaries, and now reduced to the escort of a few soldiers loyal to their oaths and to their duty; the young Prince who but the day before had been saluted with the title of heir to the beautiful

crown of France; the young Princess, an angel of
grace and beauty, and near them their mother, an
angelic, adored being, whose stay in France had been
marked only by the benefits she had spread around
her: all this evil fortune which befell an august and
deceived family, betrayed, but innocent of the evil
that had been done, — all this, I say, contracted the
heart and left no room for any but the saddest
thoughts."

On passing through Ville-d'Avray, they noticed
that the inhabitants, in order to placate the Revolution, had already effaced from their signs all words
which might cause them to be suspected of royalist
sentiments. A wine merchant, *À la chasse royale*,
had crossed out the word *royale*. Another, whose
sign was *Au garde à pied*, had likewise dissimulated.

The King mounted a horse while on the road. The
Duchess de Gontaut, who was in the same carriage
as Mademoiselle, has written: " I saw a hand resting
on the door beside me. Day had begun to break, and
as I bent forward, I met the eyes of the King, sad but
not dejected. He said nothing, but silently continued
to escort the carriages of his grandchildren, all that
was precious which was left to him on earth. I had
not sighed on leaving Saint-Cloud, the court and its
grandeurs, but I wept on beholding the sad and
resigned lineaments of the King."

They marched slowly and in silence. The Marquis
de Vérac, governor of Versailles, presented himself
before Charles X. at the embankment of Picardy, and

told him that the Place d'Armes was crowded with
National Guards who had already put on the tricolored cockade and were making hostile speeches.
The King thereupon decided to turn towards the
Grand Trianon. On arriving there, at six in the
morning, the party alighted at the great marble salon,
where by the light of the rising sun they recognized
each other. Madame the Duchess of Berry was in
a riding-habit, with small pistols at her belt. The
King asked what they were for. " To defend my
children," responded she, " in case any one comes
near them." His Majesty gave her a friendly pat on
the shoulder, and smiled.

Charles X. was affected on seeing once more, and
in such doleful circumstances, the poetic spots which
recalled the sweetest memories of his childhood and
youth. The Grand Trianon comprises a ground story
only, but its proportions are elegant and harmonious,
and all the prestige of Louis XIV. still lingers there.
As he passed through the avenue leading to this
delightful palace, Charles X. glanced at the Little
Trianon, situated a few paces distant on the right; it
evoked the remembrance of his unfortunate sister-in-
law, who had been as it were the goddess of that
little shrine.

Here the fugitive sovereign would have liked to
meditate and collect his thoughts, but the cruel exigencies of fate left him no leisure to do so. He reas-
sembled his former ministers at the Grand Trianon
for a final council. There was question of summon-

ing the great bodies of State to Tours, convoking the
Chambers for August 15, and adopting military
measures for intercepting communications between
Paris and the departments. Ordinances, proclamations, and circulars were prepared. The ministers
perhaps imagined that they were about to renew
their struggle against the Revolution.

The arrival of the Dauphin dispelled the last illusions. This prince, instead of following Charles X.
when the King quitted Saint-Cloud, had determined
to remain with the troops some time longer, perhaps
in hope of some favorable turn of fortune. "It was
an impolitic and unmilitary measure," Marshal Marmont has said. "To provoke a sort of action at a
moment when even the least appearance of combat
should have been avoided, was to give a pretext to
disorganization and disorder, and, in a fashion, to
desire to produce them.

"The twenty-six hours that had elapsed since the
evacuation of Paris," continues the Marshal, "had
given time for men's minds to ferment, influence
to be exerted, and the force of example to seduce.
What he should have done, was to retire slowly,
providing for all the needs of the troops, and, once
far enough away to escape the influence of Paris,
to busy himself in trying to change their minds and
invigorate their moral tone; but the thought of this
necessity did not occur to the Dauphin. . . . Instead
of that he wanted to retire fighting, which is always
a *pis-aller*, even in war, and it was his unhappy fate
to be beaten by the inhabitants of Sèvres alone."

The entrance of the bridge, at the side of this
village, was occupied by a battalion of lancers of the
guard, commanded by the Duke d'Esclignac. The
insurgents, stationed at the other end of the bridge,
attempted to force the passage. The Dauphin, advancing towards them, urged them not to begin
the struggle. They responded by a sharp fusilade.
The Duke d'Esclignac was grievously wounded. The
troops weakened. There were some desertions. All
the Prince could do was to concentrate his little
army and go to rejoin Charles X. Shortly before
noon he left Saint-Cloud, followed by a dozen pieces
of artillery and about twelve thousand men.

All along the route, in every village between
Saint-Cloud to Trianon, the Dauphin encountered
manifestly hostile dispositions on the part of the inhabitants. The incident at the bridge of Sèvres had
impressed him deeply; he was no longer sure of his
troops. The town of Versailles was in commotion.

The Prince arrived at the Grand Trianon between
one and two o'clock. His first word was to advise
his father to go on toward Rambouillet. Charles X.
followed this advice. The former ministers were
given to understand that they must retire forthwith,
and were furnished with blank passports and small
sums of money. They desired, however, to go in
the carriages belonging to their master's suite; but
just as they were preparing to enter, one of their
number, M. Capelle, who had just seen the King,

apprised them that the sovereign regretted his inability to take them, lest their presence might interfere with some arrangement with the leaders of the Parisian movement. "I thank them for their services," Charles X. had added; "they should now consider their own safety."

The Duchess of Berry set off first with her children by the usual road to Rambouillet. The King, taking another route on horseback, was to rejoin her after having reached open ground and crossed the line of woods which might serve as ambuscades for insurgent skirmishers. The Princess had left Trianon some time before; but the old King, as if foreboding that he would never again see this pleasure-palace, could not make up his mind to depart. He cast a melancholy glance toward the beautiful shades which had sheltered his infancy and that of his two brothers, — shades which had been witnesses of the games chanted by Victor Hugo: —

"Beaux enfants qu'on berce et qu'on flatte,
Tout surpris, vous si purs, si doux,
Que des vieux en robe écarlate
Viennent vous parler à genoux!
Quand les sévères Malesherbes
Ont relevé leurs fronts superbes,
Vous courez jouer dans les herbes,
Sans savoir que tout doit finir,
Et que votre race qui sombre
Porte à ses deux bouts couverts d'ombre,
Ravaillac dans le passé sombre,
Robespierre dans l'avenir! . . ."

" Que l'aîné, peu credule à la vie, à la gloire,
Au peuple ivre d'amour, sache, d'une nuit noire,
D'avance emplir son cœur de courage pourvu.
Qu'il rêve un ciel de pluies, un tombereau qui roule,
Et là-bas, tout au fond, au-dessus de la foule,
Quelque étrange échafaud dans la brume entrevu.

" Frères par la naissance et par le malheur frères,
Les deux autres fuiront, battus des vents contraires ;
Le règne de Louis, roi de quelques bannis,
Commence dans l'exil, celui de Charles y tombe.
À l'un Reims doit manquer, à l'autre Saint-Denis." [1]

----

[1] Fair children, whom men flatter and delude,
You so pure, so gentle, who are surprised
When old men in scarlet robes
Come to speak with you kneeling !
When the severe Malesherbes
Have raised their haughty foreheads,
You run away to play in the shrubbery,
Not knowing that all must end,
And that your foundering race
Bears at its two shadow-covered ends,
Ravaillac in the gloomy past,
Robespierre in the future.

Let the eldest, little credulous of life, of glory,
Of a people intoxicated with love, learn some dark night
How to fill his heart beforehand with provided courage.
Let him dream of a rainy sky, of a rattling cart,
And yonder, in the background, above the crowd,
Of some strange scaffold seen amid the mist.

Brothers by birth, by sorrow also brothers,
The other two will fly, beaten by adverse winds ;
The reign of Louis, king of a few exiles,
Begins in exile, that of Charles ends there.
The one will have no crowning, the other no tomb.
To the one Rheims will be lacking, to the other Saint-Denis.

The brother of Louis XVI., the brother-in-law of
Marie Antoinette, did not say adieu to the Trianons
without a painful contraction of the heart. The
officials of his household were impatient to see him
depart. One of them said to him, "The King for-
gets that he must go." "Ah, yes," replied Charles
X. The old monarch crossed the apartments with
slow and measured steps. Reaching the steps, he
cast a sad glance about him, mounted his horse, and
went away without a single word.

When you visit the Grand Trianon, reader, remember the thirty-first day of July, 1830. Pause in the
marble-pillared vestibule which is to this palace what
the Gallery of the Mirrors is to the palace of Versailles. There the remaining courtiers of the King
who was going into exile assembled for the last time.
Souvenirs of different régimes, from that of Louis
XIV. to our own days, blend in this majestic vestibule. At present you may see there a fine group
in marble offered to the Empress Eugénie by the
Milanese ladies the day after the battle of Magenta;
it represents the City of Milan under the form of a
woman whose chains lie broken at her feet, and who
is embracing another woman, the Sovereign of France.
There the council of war was held which tried Marshal Bazaine. In our opinion, other surroundings
should have been chosen for the debates of this painful trial, the sight of which M. Thiers had wished to
spare the vanquished country.

How many sorrows are linked to this joyous dwell-

ing! It was at the Grand Trianon that Napoleon I.
sought a refuge for his melancholy on the day when
his divorce from the Empress Josephine was pronounced, that divorce which brought misfortune to
the Emperor and the Empire. It was the Grand
Trianon which was the first halting-place in the
flight of King Charles X., and, as if by a sort of
retaliatory punishment, it was in the same palace
that Louis Philippe rested for a moment, February
24, 1848, as he was flying from Paris forever.

A visit to celebrated palaces is the best lesson in
history and philosophy. Beyond the Grand Trianon,
on the right of the esplanade that precedes the palace,
all along the short avenue which leads to the Little
Trianon, is the carriage-house wherein are assembled
all the gala-carriages that recall the greatest splendors of Royalty and the Empire. Of all these magnificent vehicles, the mere sight of which awakens the
souvenir of brilliant processions, triumphal entries,
resplendent pomps and ceremonies, among these
gilded and escutcheoned carriages, fairy-like in aspect,
with windows that resemble mirrors, the finest, the
most majestic, that which surpasses all the rest by
its richness and its proportions, is undeniably the
one used at the coronation of Charles X. This
marvellous carriage served also on the occasion of
the baptism of the Prince Imperial during the reign
of Napoleon III. The only alteration made was to
replace the royal arms by those of the Empire. The
latter still figure on it. But where have the lilies
gone? What has become of the eagles?

XV

THE ARRIVAL AT RAMBOUILLET

CHARLES X. rode away from the Grand Trianon on Saturday, July 31, 1830, at half-past two in the afternoon, keeping sometimes in advance of his body-guards and sometimes in their midst. He was surrounded by the Marshal Duke of Ragusa and several officers. In passing Saint-Cyr they saw, drawn up in battle array, their colonel at their head, the remnant of the mounted and foot gendarmerie who had survived the bloody combats of the capital. Colonel de Foucault and the gendarmes cried: "Long live the King!" The cortège continued its march. On the road Charles X. rejoined the Duchess of Berry. A halt was made shortly before reaching Rambouillet. The company of Noailles, which had followed the carriages of the princes, was ordered to go on ahead when the march was resumed. "When we came up to that of Madame," M. Théodore Anne has said, "Her Royal Highness, who wore a man's costume, and was with her children, stood on the carriage step to see us file past; she saluted us affectionately and seemed to be thanking us for the support we were lending, at this sad moment, to her and her children, for whom she displayed such a touching solicitude. This worthy princess, against whom no complaint could arise, and who did all the good which her slender revenues permitted her to accomplish, will bear away with her all my regrets."

When Charles X. had come to Rambouillet on July 26, to hunt there in his favorite forest and seek to forget his political preoccupations, — that, one remembers, was the day when the Ordinances appeared, — he hardly suspected that he would return there under very different circumstances before the week was over. He was no longer a powerful king, coming to divert himself amidst a few courtiers. He was a fugitive recoiling before an insurrection, and feeling his crown tottering on his head.

It was night. The sovereign had not been expected. His reception bore traces of passing events. No acclamations, no trumpets, no torches. The moon alone illumined the old tower where Francis I. had died. At ten in the evening, the royal carriage silently entered the courtyard of the chateau where Napoleon, flying from Malmaison, had also come to spend the first night of his eternal exile. The King descended sadly from the carriage. He stopped on the first landing to give his arm to the Duchess of Berry. On reaching the principal salon, — that room with three large windows in the form of arcades which is called the Salle du Bal, — he found the town authorities assembled. It was only a few minutes since they had been apprised of his coming,

and they had had no time to make any preparations.
" Well, Monsieur Delorme," he said to the mayor,
"are your inhabitants still well disposed? " — "Yes,
Sire." " Ah! why is it not so everywhere? " He
addressed a few words to other persons, and then,
turning again to the mayor: " You say then that
your inhabitants are well disposed? " — "Sire, I answer for them as for myself." The Duke of Bordeaux and his sister, who were to be put to bed on
the first story, were brought to the King. He wept
as he embraced them; then, drawing out his watch:
"Only ten o'clock," said he; " I thought it was
later." And he retired to his chamber.

"Get us some bread!" the Duke of Ragusa at
once exclaimed, addressing the authorities. " Bread
for these gentlemen who have taken nothing all day.
Bread for the troops of the escort, who have eaten
nothing in twenty-four hours! "

The destitution was such that even the royal
family suffered from it. Listen to the Duchess de
Gontaut: " The probability of the King's arrival not
having been foreseen, the chateau was closed up
completely; there were no provisions and no succor
to be hoped for. I had a small apartment opened,
where I established tired Mademoiselle; I put her to
bed; but she was hungry. I sent to the town.
' There is nothing to be had,' was the reply brought
back to me. The troops that had arrived before us
had exhausted everything. My poor little princess
told me she could not sleep because she was so

hungry. I went to the kitchen, to the pantry, everywhere; not even an egg, which would have seemed a great resource to me; I could have cried with chagrin. I went back up-stairs to her, hoping to find her asleep; she was waiting for me. Hunting all over the chamber, I found at last a piece of stale bread forgotten on a commode, a long while before, probably, for it was very hard; she seized it, made efforts to break it, succeeded at last in dividing it into two pieces, and giving me half, she said to me in a touching voice, the expression of which I shall never forget: 'Let no one ever say I did not share my last bit of bread with you; eat it, here it is.'"

Moved by this souvenir, the Duchess de Gontaut adds: "Dear, adorable Princess! after having devoured the wretched scrap of bread she had kept for herself, she went peacefully to sleep in my arms. I passed a sorrowful night beside her. I regretted the past; I feared the future; but my courage returned with the daylight and never abandoned me."

Charles X. had a great predilection for Rambouillet. He remembered having spent very agreeable hours there in his youth, when the chateau belonged to the virtuous Duke de Penthièvre, and afterwards to Louis XVI., who acquired it in 1778. He could evoke the radiant images of the Princess de Lamballe and Queen Marie Antoinette. He could still see in the gardens the shell-work pavilion which the Duke de Penthièvre had had constructed for his daughter-in-law, the Princess de Lamballe, and the dairy which the Queen had established here as well as at the Little Trianon. No hunting-parties had pleased Charles X. more than those at Rambouillet. It was not without emotion that he found himself once more in this residence where he was to pass such painful moments.

Bizarre caprice of fate by which pleasure-houses become for the Bourbons as well as for the Bonapartes the stations of Calvary and the halting-places of affliction! The two rival dynasties have a common itinerary of humiliations and exiles, and the palaces that have beheld their joys end by sheltering nothing but their sorrows.

At the chateau of Rambouillet, the Duchess of Berry was to find herself in the same position as the Empress Marie Louise. The wife of the Emperor had sojourned there from April 13 to April 23, 1814, with her son, dispossessed as the Duke of Bordeaux was going to be. There she had her painful and discouraging interview with her father. There the young eaglet, as the poet calls him, had become the prisoner of Austria; from there he started for Vienna, where the Duke of Bordeaux was to go likewise. The analogy between Napoleon II., the phantom of an Emperor, and Henri V., the phantom of a King, is striking.

Does not one remark a great likeness between Napoleon's journey to Rochefort and that of Charles X. to Cherbourg? The Emperor starts from a pleasure-house, Malmaison; the King also starts from a

pleasure-house, the Trianon. Both stop on the way
at Rambouillet; both arrive there at the same hour,
ten in the evening; both are in the same state of
mind, have the same ulterior notions of resistance,
the same perplexities, the same anguish. Both, in
fine, soon acknowledge themselves vanquished by an
inexorable fatality.

Was the departure from Malmaison, June 29, 1815,
less mournful than that from the Grand Trianon,
July 31, 1830? Read the story of General Beker,
quoted by the Marquise de Blocqueville in her
beautiful work on her father, Marshal Davout, Prince
d'Eckmühl, and you will be yet more impressed by
the similarity of the two situations: —

"The journey was accomplished in the greatest
silence as far as the chateau of Rambouillet, where
there had been originally no thought of stopping, but
where, either through fatigue or in hopes of a change
of fortune, the Emperor determined to halt at about
ten in the evening. There was a melancholy supper
at which not a word was exchanged; Grand-Marshal
Count Betrand had recommended that no questions
should be asked, a great reserve maintained, and no
explanations of accomplished facts suggested. But all
were too deeply penetrated with a sense of decorum
to be willing to disturb by any reflections the respect
due to such a supreme misfortune.

"After supper the Emperor retired to his bed-
chamber, where he remained alone with General
Betrand. It was not known that he intended to

pass the night at Rambouillet, and all were astonished when the Marshal came to announce that His
Majesty had gone to bed very much fatigued, and
would not continue his journey until the next morning. Thereupon Generals Savary, Beker, and Rovigo
installed themselves in the salon until it should please
the Emperor to transmit them his orders.

"The night slipped by in this expectation; they
were always thinking that some less disastrous news
might come to revive hopes and afford opportunities
for a less rigorous fate. Receiving no favorable
reports, Napoleon resolved to depart, and at eleven
in the morning, June 30, 1815, they set off again in
the same order as on the night before."

When the Emperor was at Rambouillet, although
he had lost thousands of deserters, there still remained to him an organized force of seventy thousand men inured to war, and asking nothing better
than to fight against the enemy that had rashly
advanced upon Saint-Germain and Versailles. To
Charles X. also the nucleus of an army still remained,
and with it he might have put to flight the disorderly rabble of Parisians who marched against Rambouillet on August 3. But, like the Emperor, the
King felt that fortune had condemned him. Can he
be reproached with his hesitancy when one reflects
that a man of iron, an inflexible monarch, a giant of
battles like Napoleon, hesitated also? When the
wind of misfortune blows on sovereigns, the strongest
becomes weak, the most resolute undecided.

Napoleon's perplexities at the time of his abdications at Fontainebleau and the Élysée were not less
keen than those of Charles X. when he abdicated at
Rambouillet; and the King turning toward Cherbourg, where he was to embark on an American
vessel, reminds us more than once of the Emperor
arriving at Rochefort, and going on board an English
vessel.

Those who are interested in the history of
Charles X. will do well to visit the chateau of Rambouillet. Exteriorly it is unchanged. Its proportions
are not grandiose, but its façades present a picturesque aspect; that on the side of the courtyard, with
its two feudal towers, one large and one small, which
flank it to right and left; and that looking on the
garden, with its small spiral iron stairway and its
revolving balcony, whence there is a view of the
sheet of water and the magnificent foliage. The
interior, on the other hand, is the picture of solitude
and decay. The rooms, although intact, no longer
contain a single piece of furniture. During the
Franco-German War, Rambouillet was occupied by
the Prussians. The chateau, which they converted
into a hospital, was cleaned from top to bottom
after their departure. In 1871 the State rented it
for a dozen years to the Duke de la Trémouille.
The Duke's maître d'hôtel occupied a very small
chamber, with only one window, in the great tower,
in which Francis I. had yielded his last breath.
Nothing could be more humble than this room, sup-

ported in the middle by a great beam, whose narrow
alcove contained the bed whereon died so wretch-
edly the most artistic of all sovereigns, the monarch
of the Field of the Cloth of Gold, the king knighted
by Bayard, the victor of Marignan, the father of
letters, the resplendent host of the palaces of Fontainebleau and Chambord. The lease of 1871 was
not renewed in 1883. The Duke de la Trémouille
naturally removed the furniture he had placed in the
chateau, and it was not replaced.

To-day the chateau of Rambouillet is inhabited by
nobody but three or four keepers, who show it to
infrequent visitors. The outhouses are occupied by
a school for soldiers' children. The fine establishment for breeding merino sheep, which belongs to
the State, is in the gardens, where tourists may still
see the shell pavilion and Marie Antoinette's dairy.
The President of the Republic comes sometimes to
shoot in the archery-grounds, and the other hunting
is let to private persons.

In spite of the dilapidation of the interior, a visit
to the chateau of Rambouillet is very interesting.
One is shown, at the extremity of the Salle du Bal,
the place where the table stood where the brother of
Louis XVI. and of Louis XVIII. signed the abdication which he thought would be merely that of
himself and his son, but which was that of the entire
elder branch. One contemplates also the chamber
where Napoleon passed the cruel night of June 29–30,
1815, and that wherein Charles X. spent two nights

not less painful, that between July 31 and August 1,
and that of August 2–3, 1830. When one has the
historic passion, he is always keenly impressed by
the sight of localities where great historical events
have been accomplished. To reconstruct the past,
one must behold with his bodily eyes as well as with
those of the imagination, and the best way to evoke
and resuscitate the actors who have figured in human
annals, is to contemplate the places where they had
to play the parts assigned them by the decrees of
Providence.

We left Charles X. at Rambouillet in the evening
of July 31, 1830. We shall find there the next
morning a new personage in the dolorous drama
whose vicissitudes are about to be unfolded. It is
Madame the Duchess of Angoulême. The orphan of
the Temple has seen the death struggle of the royalty
of Louis XVI. She will be present also at the death-
struggle of the royalty of Charles X.

XVI

THE DUCHESS OF ANGOULÊME

THE only member of his family whom Charles X.
had made acquainted with his plans was his
son. The Duchess of Angoulême had been no better
informed than the Duchess of Berry. She was quietly
taking the baths at Vichy while the sovereign had
been preparing. Perhaps if she had been near the
King her uncle and father-in-law, the daughter of
Louis XVI. and Marie Antoinette would have dis-
covered the secret of his resolutions and might have
dissuaded him from fulfilling them. But Charles X.,
who divined that the Princess did not share his ideas,
was not very sorry to have her at a distance. He
told himself that all would be over when she returned,
and that she would find the royal cause consolidated
once for all by the triumph of the Ordinances.

The Dauphiness had left the King July 7, and her
journey from Saint-Cloud to Vichy had been nothing
but a series of ovations. At Moulin, on the 9th, she
had reviewed the first regiment of dragoons; all the
houses had been decorated. The next morning she
had gone to Souvigny, to visit the priory church containing the tombs of the former Dukes of Bourbon,

and was conducted processionally, under a canopy, to her prie-Dieu. After Mass she went down into the vaults. "A visible imprint of emotion showed itself on her countenance," said the *Moniteur*. "All hearts were softened by the sight of the august daughter of our kings, thus lost in meditation." The pious Princess continued her excursion, which was a sort of pilgrimage amidst the souvenirs of her ancestors, and at Bourbon-l'Archambault, the first residence of the Sires de Bourbon, they showed her the ruins of the Sainte-Chapelle, once celebrated for the riches of its reliquary and the splendors of its stained glass windows.

On her way back to Moulins, the Dauphiness met a courier just arrived from Lyons, who gave her the despatches announcing the surrender of Algiers. She had the news immediately communicated to the inhabitants of Bourbon-l'Archambault. At Souvigny, through which she passed anew, large crowds thronged the roads and stopped her carriage under a triumphal arch of foliage erected in her honor. Her joy was at its height. "Come nearer," said she to the crowd. "Algiers has surrendered! Our wrecks are saved!"

The next day, July 10, the Princess finally reached Vichy at half-past five in the evening. Her first act on entering the city was to send a note to the mayor, Baron Lucas, announcing the taking of Algiers. "Transmit this good news to everybody," exclaimed the daughter of Louis XVI.; "I want every one to

share my joy." She said afterwards to the hospital
sisters : "My sisters, I do not doubt that you have
offered fervent prayers for the success of our armies."
—"And also for the King and Madame the Dauphiness," responded the sisters. The Princess afterwards took a long walk. Admiring the banks of
the Allier and the Sychon, and the magnificent land-
scape bordering the valleys, she stopped frequently
to chat with the village women whom she met. At
the decline of day the gardens of Vichy were illuminated. The next morning the Princess received
the authorities and the officers of the first dragoons.

However much inclined by the memory of past
woes to see all things under a gloomy aspect and
to distrust fortune, the daughter of Louis XVI.
could never have imagined during her pleasant stay
at Vichy that the moment was so near when the
Odyssey of her exiles was to commence anew. In
the *Moniteur* of Tuesday, July 27, might be read
the announcement, " S. A. R. Madame the Dauphiness is expected at Saint-Cloud next Friday or Saturday." And yet the unfortunate Princess was never
to see that city again.

Count de Puymaigre, who was then prefect of
Mâcon, has written in his curious *Souvenirs :* "We
had just celebrated the victory of Algiers when I
was officially informed that Madame the Dauphiness,
leaving the baths of Vichy, would be at Autun July
26, and at Mâcon the 27th. I was pleased with this
news. In my devotion to this august Princess there

is what I would call a profound attachment if she
who inspires it were not the daughter of Louis XVI.
and the granddaughter of Maria Theresa. Everything was soon ready to receive her. Encouraged
by her former goodness to me, I paid little attention
to the order she had given me, as well as all the
other prefects, not to come to meet her, and I hastened to do so at Autun."

On Tuesday, July 27, the Princess left this city,
where she had slept at the episcopal palace. A
courier dressed in green preceded her. Six post-
horses drew her carriage, in which she had seated
three persons with her: Madame de Sainte-Maure,
Marquis de Conflans, and Count de Puymaigre.
This immense berlin, whose panels were blazoned
with fleurs-de-lis, could hardly squeeze through the
narrow and winding streets of Autun, thronged
as they were with people uttering shouts of joy.
White flags hung from the windows. Everything
wore a festive appearance. And yet the Dauphiness
seemed depressed, as if preoccupied by the foreboding of some fatal event.

Hardly had they left Autun when the Duchess of
Angoulême opened a very large green bag which she
always travelled with, and drew from it a quantity
of journals. After rapidly glancing through them
she said: "There is nothing new," and seemed more
at her ease. She stopped for some minutes at Chalon-
sur-Saône, and left there at noon.

It was extremely warm. Thick clouds of dust

penetrated all parts of the berlin. The Dauphiness maintained an anxious and profound silence. Reaching the table-land of the mountain dominating the town of Tournus, she alighted from the carriage and contemplated the magnificent panorama unrolling on the immense horizon. Then she spoke in terms that betrayed emotion of the taking of Algiers, that feat of arms so glorious for France and so envied by England. "And yet," she added with an accent of bitterness, "Frenchmen have been found who could form desires against the success of a French army!"

The same day — Tuesday, July 27, 1830 — the Princess entered Mâcon at four o'clock in the afternoon, where, still received with all the honors due to her rank, she alighted at the prefecture.

It was there she learned of the Ordinances of the 25th. The news had been brought by telegraph to the prefect of Lyons, M. de Brosses, who came to give her an account of it. "She seemed greatly troubled," says Count de Puymaigre; "her altered features, her abrupt movements, the brevity of her remarks, all proclaimed that this woman, so strong and so acclimated to ill-fortune, could hardly dissimulate her too just alarms. Nevertheless, she resumed all her dignity to conform with the exigencies of her lofty position, and to receive what are called presentations, — those scenes of padding in princely life which so often exhale a contraband devotion, a cowardly and grasping servility, hypocritical oaths, and which must have been such a burden to her especially at that time." All the array of pomp was still displayed around the daughter of kings. A triumphal arch with the Bourbon arms commemorated the conquest of Algiers. A numerous guard, bivouacking in the court and gardens of the prefecture, gave them the aspect of a brilliant headquarters. In the evening fireworks were set off.

The next day, Wednesday, July 28, at five o'clock in the morning, the Princess was on the terrace overlooking the beautiful banks of the Saône, a terrace adjoining the chamber where she had slept. She had the prefect and M. de Puymaigre summoned, and spoke to them about the Ordinances, the text of which she did not yet know. "She disapproved the Ordinances," the latter has written, "and yet, without consulting the immense interest she had in this frightful game of heads and tails in which the monarchy was staked in the streets of Paris, she wished to abide by her duties as wife of the king's first subject. These words, tinged with the bitterest regrets, 'It is perhaps a great misfortune that I was not at Paris,' revealed her mind to me. She promenaded, or rather marched, heedlessly in the garden, as if succumbing under the weight of her preoccupations; then, as if mastered by the inflexible necessity of completing a journey which seemed arrested by a will higher than her own: 'I foresee painful things at Dijon. I will tell them that I count for nothing in the State, and that I know only how to obey the King. For the rest I fear nothing for myself, but only for the King and for France. I rely on your devotion.'" Such were the last words addressed by the Dauphiness to Count de Puymaigre and the prefect of Lyons.

The following day, July 29, at Dijon, the Princess, who was still officially received, was present at a theatrical representation. As she entered the playhouse she heard cries of "Long live the Charter! Long live the Two hundred and twenty-one! Down with the Ministers! Down with the Ordinances!" She withdrew after the first piece. But the crowd followed her to the prefecture, uttering the same cries. Force had to be employed to shelter the daughter of Louis XVI. from the insults of a hostile populace.

The Princess continued her route. Before arriving at Tonnerre, where she was to spend Friday, July 30, she stopped at the chateau d'Ancy-le-Franc, the home of Marquis de Louvais. M. de Partouneaux, sub-prefect of Tonnerre, wrote the same day: "What a reception we were preparing for Madame the Dauphiness! I had succeeded in rousing everybody up. For two days I had had my hands full of workmen, and the sub-prefecture is no longer recognizable; everything has been freshened up, and decorated luxuriously and with elegance; I had arranged twenty-eight chambers, and our streets and public places were to be adorned with trees, garlands, and triumphal arches. The people of the whole town and the environs were to be present at our festivities. The disastrous news from Paris, related by travellers, has spread consternation into all hearts."

M. de Partouneaux repaired to the chateau d'Ancy-le-Franc. The Dauphiness said to him: "They are not willing that I should sleep at Tonnerre." — "I answer for the inhabitants of that town," replied the sub-prefect; "but we shall have no demonstrations of joy; all hearts are overwhelmed with grief." — "Demonstrations of joy!" returned the Princess. "Ah! I cannot desire them. My heart is lacerated. French blood is being shed! Why was I not near the King!" And at these words plenteous tears flowed from her eyes. She complained afterwards of the absence of tidings. Not knowing where her family were, she was in mortal anxiety.

The sub-prefect returned to Tonnerre, where he made ready for the silent entrance of the Dauphiness. The population behaved respectfully, and when she passed through the town she heard no shouting nor a single hostile word. After having visited the asylum and the church of Notre Dame, she arrived at the sub-prefecture, where she learned the news from Paris, the establishment of a provisional government, with Lafayette as commander-in-chief of the National Guard. Troyes, Sens, Auxerre, Joigny, were none of them tranquil. People were aware, from the official notices, that the Dauphiness was to leave Tonnerre July 31, at five o'clock in the morning. Who knew whether insurgents might not carry off a hostage so precious on the route?

After a reception at the sub-prefecture, where more than one was seen weeping, the Princess asked for M. Partouneaux and apprised him of her intention to depart secretly in the evening. At the time when she was supposed to be asleep, she descended by a private staircase and succeeded in leaving the town without being recognized.

"The next day," M. Partouneaux has written, "I looked again at the vestiges of that reception which, a few days earlier, I had thought would be so brilliant. In the vestibule the two medallions still remained, where, amidst a bouquet of lilies, might be read the date of the journey of Louis XIV. to Tonnerre, and that of Madame the Dauphiness: 22 June, 1674 — 30 July, 1830. A magnificent crown and festoons of foliage ornamented the steps of the hotel; the front of the mantelpiece in my salon represented the conquered city of Algiers. The white flag floated over all its towers and forts, carried by the army of Charles X., who sees his own flag proscribed to-day, and who, like the Dey of Algiers, whom he had just driven from his dominions by armed force, is seeking refuge in a foreign land."

After leaving Tonnerre, the Dauphiness met on the road the eldest son of the Duke of Orleans, the Duke of Chartres, who was then nineteen years old and already colonel of a cavalry regiment. The Duke de Broglie has thus described the meeting: "Between Joigny and Sens, the carriage of the Princess crossed that of M. the Duke of Chartres, returning from the barrier of Montrouge, where he had been arrested by the insurgents and set at liberty by order of M. de Lafayette. He knew that the Dauphiness was expected. Having recognized the officer sitting on the box, he had him stop, and alighting, he related to the Princess all that had occurred, warning her of the impossibility of her arriving at Saint-Cloud by passing under the walls of Paris, and placing himself at her service for all that lay in his power. The Dauphiness loved the Duke of Chartres. She thanked him with effusion.

" And you," she asked, " where are you going? "

" To Joigny, where my regiment is."

" That is well," said the Dauphiness ; " keep it for us."

The Princess arrived at the palace of Fontainebleau at five in the afternoon of July 31, and rested there for several hours. There was a striking contrast between the sorrows and the magnificence of this palace of her ancestors, where she recalled the triumphal entrance of the Duchess of Berry in 1816. At nine in the evening she left it in a carriage belonging to the governor of the palace, Count Melchior de Polignac, who passed her off as one of his relatives. The chamber-maids were sent away at the same time in the Princess's own carriage with an escort of gendarmes, by a different route, and at the post-house they were convinced that it was the Dauphiness who was travelling in this conveyance.

Having learned at Croix-de-Berny that Charles X.

had abandoned Saint-Cloud, the Princess went round
Paris, did not change horses at Versailles, where
the people displayed hostile dispositions, and finally
reached the chateau of Rambouillet in the morning
of August 1. "As soon as she was perceived," says
the Duchess de Gontaut, "the troops recognized her
and rushed toward the hand she held out to them.
She was beloved by them, for she had always testified
a frank and constant solicitude for the royal guard.
She was welcomed and saluted by loyal shouts that
were heard at the chateau. Everybody ran; I holding Mademoiselle by the hand. She sprang towards
her aunt. The King received the daughter of Louis
XVI. in his arms. 'Never leave us again,' he exclaimed; 'that will be the greatest of consolations.'
Profoundly affected, I kissed her hand. I found
Madame the Dauphiness sad, but not dejected. Her
soul, habituated to misfortune, knew how to endure
it with that dignified resignation of which her features always bore the impress."

The arrival of the pious Princess was a ray of joy
in the midst of so much gloom. Charles X., who
beheld the Revolution of 1830 through the souvenirs
of 1793, had been very uneasy about the fate of his
niece. On finding her safe and sound, he thanked
God with an overflowing heart.

XVII

THE FIRST OF AUGUST

ON Sunday morning, August 1, Charles X. at Rambouillet did not yet despair, and he felt himself in safety amidst the body-guards encamped in the park. One of them has said, "The night was tranquil; yet we were not without anxiety concerning the intentions of the inhabitants, some of whom were prowling round us, and we took turns in watching near the horses, which could be untied and stolen while we were asleep."

The Dauphin had passed the night at Trappes, with the regiments of the royal guard, who were without provisions. Their temper did not cease to be alarming. Desertions grew more numerous, and the colonels were afraid to remain exposed with a few officers and flags to the insults and attacks of the peasants. One of them even proposed to send an envoy to Paris to make an agreement with the provisional government, by virtue of which the regiments should return to their garrisons. The sentiment of military honor prevented the French colonels from accepting this proposition. The disorder constantly increased, the soldiers deserted in bands, the discouraged leaders no longer trying to prevent them. "I remained an entire stranger to what was going on," says Marshal Marmont, Duke of Ragusa, in his Memoirs. "A simple spectator of the most melancholy scene, I was anxiously awaiting the end of this horrible drama. The wife of one of my friends wrote me from Paris, to warn me of the exasperation against me, and asking me to betake myself to a distance. She sent a trusty man to guide me; she offered me money, and every aid and guarantee of personal safety which I could require. I refused her offers, while thoroughly appreciating the sentiments that dictated them. Honor obliged me to remain, whatever might be the consequences."

Meanwhile, the Dauphin had left Trappes at daybreak with the regiments of the royal guard. In the morning he also found himself at Rambouillet, having brought with him the infantry and light cavalry. He left the 2d Swiss regiment from Orleans at the village of Perey, and the division of heavy cavalry at Cognières. The infantry took up position in front of the chateau of Rambouillet. The forty-two pieces of artillery of this little army were packed in the hamlet of Rue-Verte, behind Perey. The defence of the chateau was confided to the bodyguards, the mounted grenadiers of the guard, the picked gendarmerie, and a Swiss regiment. Spite of the difficulty of paying and feeding the troops, there was still an imposing military equipment, and the greater part of the regiments remained faithful.

As the sojourn at Rambouillet seemed likely to be prolonged, the officers and soldiers began to think of organizing themselves. Cabins were erected, trellises torn down, and trees felled to make fires; the branches served for roofing. Everybody named his house according to his own fancy. One dwelt at the *Quinconce des Tuileries;* another established himself at the *Rotonde du Palais-Royal;* the sign of a third was the *Barreaux-Verts;* a fourth baptized his dwelling the *Petite-Provence.* The park resembled a camp.

A false alarm was given by several musket shots. It was nothing but some hunters. The King had just ordered the shooting to be opened, and had authorized the officers to kill pheasants. They massacred them. A stag which had escaped crossed through the camp; he was chased, killed, roasted, and eaten. The soldiers, deprived of the resources of the chase, revenged themselves by bathing in the ponds in the park, almost under the eyes of the princesses. While the park was in such disorder, the interior of the chateau was still subjected to the laws of strict etiquette. The Duchess of Angoulême, however, for lack of vestments, could not lay aside her travelling-dress, and complained of needing underlinen. The Duchess of Berry, who also had brought no robes with her, continued to wear the male dress in which she had left Saint-Cloud. But all the courtiers of Charles X., both soldiers and civilians, still wore the uniforms of their grades and functions, and the King was surrounded by the same respect and homage as in the happiest days of his reign.

What occurred in Paris on the 1st of August? One could read in the *Moniteur* of that morning: "Summary of July 31, addressed to General Dubourg. The victory is ours! The tricolored flag is being run up on every side. Charles X. went away last evening. The Duke of Angoulême left Saint-Cloud at thirty-five minutes past eleven this morning, by way of Ville d'Avray, in a carriage with six horses, followed by eight or nine pieces of artillery and their caissons. The traitorous Duke of Ragusa galloped, courtier-wise, ahead of his carriage; the latter gave orders that the chateau should be locked up after his departure. He was accompanied by the 1st infantry regiment of the guard, the choice dragoons, and the feeble remnant of lancers of the guard. The remaining soldiers asking nothing better than to be ranged under the national colors; their horses are with the peasants, we shall go and take possession of them, and bring back our misguided brothers with cries of: Long live the Charter! Long live the grand nation!"

If this was the language of the official sheet, one can fancy what Charles X. had to expect from the new government. And yet the old King still entertained illusions. Throughout his entire reign he had maintained that the Duke of Orleans would always be faithful to him, and even after the events of July, he was not willing to retract his words. On

the 31st, Viscount de Conny having come to him to
say: "How does it happen, Sire, that in the terrible
circumstances in which the monarchy is placed, M.
the Duke of Orleans has not hastened to Your Majesty?" Charles X. had replied: "I think he is at
Saint-Leu; but my cousin will not accede to the
propositions which will be made to him. The souvenir of his father is present to his mind. The Duke
of Orleans is attached to us." August 1, at Rambouillet, General de Girardin, who came from Paris,
did not dispel the King's illusions. According to
what the Duke of Ragusa notes in his Memoirs, the
general announced that the Duke of Orleans, to
whom the crown had been offered, declared he did
not want it, saying and repeating that he would
never be a usurper.

On that day, however, the lieutenant-general of
the kingdom took measures most disquieting for the
elder branch. He appointed M. Dupont (de l'Eure),
General Gérard, Baron Louis, and M. Guizot commissioners of the departments of justice, war, finances,
and the interior. He substituted the tricolored cockade and flag for the white cockade and flag. He
convoked the two Chambers for two days thence,
August 3. It was the date fixed by Charles X. on
two different occasions, but it was not he but the
Duke of Orleans who was going to open the session.
At this news the unfortunate sovereign, hoping
against hope, essayed to give a legal character to
what was occurring, by himself investing the Duke

of Orleans with the powers of lieutenant-general of
the kingdom. "In such a disorder," said he, "I shall
try to make an appeal to my cousin; I have never
done him anything but good; he cannot fail to re-
spond to my confidence."

Then Charles X. dictated the following act : —

"The King, wishing to put an end to the troubles
existing in Paris and a part of France, counting,
moreover, on the sincere attachment of his cousin,
the Duke of Orleans, appoints him lieutenant-general of the kingdom.

"The King, having thought it fitting to withdraw
his Ordinances of July 25, approves the reassembling
of the Chambers on August 3d, and desires to hope
that they will re-establish tranquillity in France.

"The King will await here the return of the person charged to carry this declaration to Paris.

"If any attempt shall be made on the life of the
King and his family, or on their liberty, he will
defend himself unto death.

"CHARLES.

"Done at Rambouillet, August 1."

The King, who had a good heart, easily fancied
that others were as good as himself, and he was
simple enough to believe that his declaration would
result in a general pacification at Paris.

The Dauphin, who had chief command of the little
army of Rambouillet, announced to the troops, by
an order of the day, that campaign rations were

allowed them. In the evening another order of the
day was read to them, expressed as follows: " The
King informs the army in an official manner that he
has entered into arrangements with the provisional
government, and everything points to the belief that
this arrangement is about to be concluded. His
Majesty brings this news to the knowledge of the
army in order to calm the agitation displayed by several regiments. The army will feel that it should
remain calm and imperturbable, and await events
with tranquillity.

" (Signed) LOUIS-ANTOINE."

In the evening, after his dinner, Charles X.,
accompanied by the Duke and Duchess of Angoulême, the Duchess of Berry, the Duke of Bordeaux
and Mademoiselle, passed in front of the army drawn
up in line of battle. "He was received," M. Théodore
Anne has said, "with signs of attachment but without acclamations. How could we have shouted?
Everybody was weeping; the princes themselves wept
as we did. There is something so touching in the
ill-fortune of a crowned head, something so painful
in the destiny of this unhappy and innocent family,
thrice condemned to exile, that this grief ought to
seem very natural."

The message announcing to the Duke of Orleans
that Charles X. had appointed him lieutenant-general
of the kingdom was brought to the Palais-Royal in the
night of August 1–2. When he received it, Louis-

Philippe had not yet gone to bed. He was noting down on paper, in company with M. Dupin, the heads of his discourse for the opening of the Chambers, which was to take place August 3. Seeing the Prince troubled, M. Dupin said to him that, having accepted the first commission from the Chamber of Deputies, he could not accept that of the King, and he drew up a letter by which the Duke of Orleans simply acknowledged the reception of the message, at the same time noting that he was lieutenant-general of the kingdom by the choice of the Chamber. Louis-Philippe read this reply several times over; he afterwards copied it with his own hand, and ordered his aide-de-camp, M. Berthois, to keep himself in readiness to carry it to Rambouillet; then, before sealing it, he said to M. Dupin: "I will go and acquaint my sister with it." The Prince did, in fact, go out, and when he returned at the end of a few minutes, he gave the despatch to his aide-de-camp. M. Dupin has written on this subject in his Memoirs: "It has been claimed (Berryer even has affirmed it to me) that the letter I prepared is not that which M. Berthois was commissioned to deliver to Charles X.; that this letter was the ostensible letter which the aide-de-camp was to present at the barrier if he was arrested on his mission; but that he was the secret bearer of another letter hidden in his cravat, and that this second letter, expressed in different terms, was the only one delivered to Charles X. Is this true? I do not know. Louis-Philippe was not

obliged to declare his whole mind to me. I relate
nothing but what I heard and saw. The letter which
I concurred in drawing up is the only one that I
have known." However it may be, the general
opinion is that the response received by Charles X.
contained words of affection and devotion which
determined the credulous monarch to the resolution
which he took on August 2.

XVIII

THE ABDICATION

WE are now at Monday, August 2. Before relating what is about to take place at the chateau of Rambouillet, let us consider the Palais-Royal at Paris. It is ten o'clock in the morning, and M. Odilon Barrot is invited to see the Duke of Orleans on pressing business. He finds the lieu-tenant-general of the kingdom alone in his cabinet. The Prince says to him: "I have just received a letter from Charles X., who, on the point of quitting France, asks me for a convoy. I have thought of you for this mission. It is proper that the Chamber, the army, and the population of Paris should be represented in it. Marshal Mortier, Duke of Treviso, will represent the army; Baron Schonen and Colonel Jacqueminot, both deputies, will represent the Chamber; will you consent to represent the Parisian National Guard?"

M. Barrot bows.

"Time presses," adds Louis-Philippe. "Go and make your preparations for travelling, and in two hours a carriage will be ready to transport you to Rambouillet. The Duke de Coigny, who has per-

sonal relations with Charles X., will introduce you
to him. Here is the reply I have addressed to the
King and which you will deliver. . . . Be so good
as to call again at the Palais-Royal before starting,
as I shall have some private instructions to give you."

M. Barrot hardly takes time enough to go to his
own house, and then returns to the Palais-Royal.
This time the Duchess of Orleans is in her husband's
cabinet. The Duke exclaims against his fatal destiny which condemns him to be the instrument of
the deposition and exile of a family which has overwhelmed him with benefits, and for which he has
such profound affection. The Duchess, a prey to
extreme agitation, throws herself upon her husband's
neck, seeks to console him, and, turning to M. Barrot, says to him: " Do you see him? He is the most
honest man in the kingdom." " Monsieur Odilon
Barrot," says Louis-Philippe, " I have chosen you
because I know your heart and because I have
already had opportunities of appreciating the generosity of your sentiments."

Meanwhile the situation was becoming more ag-
gravated at Rambouillet for Charles X. The troops
that remained to him — already insufficient to protect his person — were constantly diminishing. On
Monday morning, August 2, three regiments of
heavy cavalry of the guard went over to the new
government and started from Cognières for Paris
with their colonels and unfurled standards. The
Swiss colonels demanded a written safeguard and a

map of the route from the new power, so as to retire
with their troops into Burgundy. As to the five
infantry regiments of the guard which were at Rambouillet (the sixth was in Normandy), they were
decimated by desertions. There still remained four
regiments of the guard, one of artillery, and three of
light cavalry. But it was becoming very difficult to
feed and provide for them. The 2d Swiss regiment had just retired from Perey, and the chateau of
Rambouillet was completely exposed, and at the
mercy of the first alarm and the first panic that
should lay hold on men's minds.

The word "abdication" began to circulate amongst
the last courtiers of Charles X. The Duke of
Ragusa recommended this measure with much
warmth in the grand salon of Rambouillet. The
King was informed of it. He had the marshal summoned to his cabinet, where he expressed himself in
much these terms: "With the movement already
given and what is now occurring, Sire, to tell you
that you could still continue to reign would be to
deceive you. Every day our situation will become
more unpleasant, and, I venture to say, more miserable. There is still grandeur in rising voluntarily,
and by one's self, above a great misfortune. Your
Majesty should not allow his falling crown to be
snatched away; he should know how to despoil himself of it by setting it on the head of his grandson.
This action might rally many to his side; it would
consecrate the principle of legitimacy and deprive

Europe of the right to meddle in our painful affairs;
it would conserve our institutions, — our only remaining elements of government and of opinion, —
and may preserve us from anarchy. This resolution
is a great act of prudence, since it cuts short immense difficulties, whose consequences no human
prevision can foresee."

Charles X. listened calmly and with coolness.
After thanking the marshal for his candor, he said:
"I have already thought of this step, but there are
many inconveniences about it; in the first place, my
son must consent to it, for his rights are the same as
mine; and again, it would be necessary to confide
my grandson, poor child, to the care of M. the Duke
of Orleans."

The Duke of Ragusa replied: "On the first head,
I cannot suppose that M. the Dauphin would separate
himself from his father in a resolve deemed necessary
for the welfare of his people. As to the second, it is
an executive measure, and certainly nothing must be
neglected to assure the life and safety of the young
Prince."

Charles X. and his interlocutor viewed the question under all its aspects. Then the King dismissed
the marshal, after thanking him anew, and took some
time for reflection. The King had a generous and
Christian soul; the thought of putting a stop to
bloodshed, of ending civil discords, the idea of a personal immolation, of a sacrifice made to France, encouraged him to abdicate. He cherished, moreover,

the illusion that although his people had misunder-
stood the intentions of an old monarch, the innocence
of a child could arouse no hatred. According to the
Duchess de Gontaut, he had been touched by the
last letter of the Duke of Orleans, which was full of
testimonies of attachment and fidelity, and he believed
that Henri V. could not be less well treated by Louis-
Philippe than Louis XV. by the regent. This last
consideration decided him, and convinced of having
conciliated everybody by fulfilling a supreme duty,
he drew up and signed the following act of abdication : —

"RAMBOUILLET, THIS 2D AUGUST, 1830.

"MY COUSIN: I am too profoundly pained by the
woes which afflict or may threaten my people, not to
have sought a means of averting them. I have
therefore taken the resolution to abdicate the crown
in favor of my grandson, the Duke of Bordeaux.

"The Dauphin, who shares my sentiments, likewise
renounces his rights in favor of his nephew.

"You will then, in your capacity as lieutenant-
general of the kingdom, cause to be proclaimed the
approaching accession of Henri V. to the crown.
You will, moreover, take all the measures in which
you are concerned for regulating the forms of government during the minority of the new King. Here
I limit myself to acquainting you with these dispositions ; it is a means of escaping many evils yet.

"You will communicate my intentions to the diplomatic bodies, and you will acquaint me as soon as

possible with the proclamation by which my grandson
shall be recognized King under the title of Henri V.

"I am commissioning Lieutenant-General Viscount
de Foissac-Latour to deliver you this letter. He has
orders to come to an understanding with you concerning the steps to be taken in favor of the persons who have accompanied me, as well as suitable
arrangements for what concerns me and the remainder of my family.

" We will regulate afterwards the other measures
which shall result from the change of reigns.

" I renew to you, my cousin, the assurance of the
sentiments with which I am your affectionate cousin,

" CHARLES."

The King had just finished this letter when the
Duchess brought the Duke of Bordeaux and Mademoiselle to him. He held out his arms to his grandson, pressed him to his heart for a moment, and then,
putting him down, he took the letter and said: " Here
is my abdication. The wording of it does not exactly
please me."

Listen to Madame de Gontaut. " We were reading this act when Madame the Dauphiness entered.
The King presented it to her; she read it, was respectful, and, touching her own abnegation, sublime.
Then the Dauphin came in. After glancing over
the paper, which he knew already, he took the pen
and signed it. Never could an abdication, made in
an instant, be more frank, spontaneous, and affect-

ing; the same devotion, the same respect, the same
object: the welfare and peace of France.

"Mademoiselle was close by; seeing tears flow,
she said in an undertone: 'Some misfortune is going
to happen to us, brother, for they all weep when
they look at us. Come, let us pray to the good
God.' And she drew him gently out on the balcony.
They kneeled down. . . .

"The abdication being signed, the King said to
me: 'Take away the children; their sadness troubles
me. Go and try to divert them; but I shall have to
speak with you; I will give you notice.' The Dauphin, the Dauphiness, Madame the Duchess of Berry,
who came in then, remained with the King, and also
Baron de Damas."

Not long after, Marshal Marmont having gone
down into the courtyard of the chateau to give some
orders, perceived the Dauphin at a window. The
Prince beckoned him to come up. "Monsieur the
Marshal," said he, "you know the resolutions taken
by the King, and in which I have associated myself;
I am, therefore, destined 'never again to play any
political part in this country. I ask you now, as a
man and a Christian, to forget what has passed between us." The Dauphin then held out his hand to
the marshal, and he, affected by so great a misfortune, pressed it with a painful emotion.

Now let us return to the Duke of Bordeaux, or,
better, to Henri V. The sadness of childhood is
generally of brief duration. That of the little Prince

yielded to the efforts made by his sister to amuse him. She helped him make himself a team out of some chairs, and a high seat on which he sat, whip in hand, when his governor, Baron de Damas, came in, bowed, and said: "Sire!" Silence ensued. "Sire, I am commissioned to apprise you that the King, your august grandfather, being unable to create the welfare of France in spite of his heartfelt desire, has just abdicated. It is you who are going to be king, under the name of Henri V."

The child got down from his seat and, coming face to face with his governor, said to him: "Grandfather, who is so good, cannot create the welfare of France, and so they want to make me king! What stupidity!" And he added, shrugging his shoulders: "But, Monsieur the Baron, what you are telling me is impossible!" Then, picking up the whip and reins again, he said: "Come along, sister, let us play!" Baron de Damas left the room.

To this recital the Duchess de Gontaut adds: "Presently the King sent for me. He was alone, and seemed to me calm; he asked me how Bordeaux had received the news of his royalty. I told him, and he could not help smiling. His Majesty said to me: 'It is only a few days ago since Louise wrote to the Duchess of Orleans inviting her to make a visit to Dieppe, and the answer she received was charming. Remind her of that when you announce to her that we are going to entrust her with all that we have dearest in the world. I have just apprised her of it; but I know she loves you, and a letter from you would be received in a friendly spirit. I do not dictate it to you; you will know how to say what we experience, and, my God! what you experience yourself at this cruel separation.' To obey was my duty; but how should I, a simple woman, do it? To recommend my king to his aunt? Impossible, unfitting! I meditated for an instant, and, God assisting, I did it, but in the name of Mademoiselle, in a manner to touch the heart of her good and pious aunt."

The Duke and Duchess of Angoulême approved, or seemed to approve, the resolutions of Charles X. But it was otherwise with the Duchess of Berry. The courageous and tender mother rejected the idea that any one could snatch her child from her. It was her intimate, immovable conviction that it was her duty and her right to keep him with her, and that there could be no regency but her own. If Henri V. were proclaimed, it was she who, in virtue of the ancient laws of the French monarchy, should govern in the name of her minor son. She thought herself, and not without reason, in possession of rights similar to those of Blanche of Castile, Maria de' Medici, and Anne of Austria. Less a foreigner than these princesses, since she belonged to the Bourbon family by birth as well as by marriage, she considered her exclusion from the regency as an affront she knew she had not deserved, and against which she protested with all the energy of her character. Could

any one say she was not popular? Had she not known
how to conciliate the sympathies of all classes of
society? Could she not recall the enthusiastic, almost
idolatrous protestations of devotion addressed to her
at the time of her marriage, her widowhood, and,
above all, at the birth of her son? Did not her ears
still ring with the blare of trumpets, the frenzied
acclamations which had greeted her but recently, when
she passed through the different provinces of the
realm? She had taken in earnest — and could one
blame her for it? — the protestations everywhere re-
iterated in a manner so respectful and so formal. Had
it not been often enough repeated to her that were she
in the slightest peril, she would need only to make a
sign in order to see every good Frenchman become
her defender? Could she doubt that the French
nation was a race of knights who would blush
to abandon a woman? Moreover, what accusation
could be formulated against her? Never had she
meddled in politics, and could her son, a child of
nine years, be held responsible for the faults or errors
of Charles X.? She determined, therefore, to plead
in person the cause of Henri V., and to present the
little King in person to the Chambers, the people, and
the army. An officer of her household went to the
house of the sub-prefect of Rambouillet, bearing an
order to procure post-horses. While they were being
harnessed to the berlin, she begged, she entreated,
Charles X. to let her take her son to Paris. The
King replied that he would never consent that the

royal child should incur such dangerous risks, or be exposed to the fury of parties. " Well then," said the Princess, "I will not take Henri." Then she added in a resolute tone: " I will go alone; I will go alone." But the entreaties of the Dauphiness, who recalled the fate of Marie Antoinette, Madame Elisabeth, and Louis XVII., were so eager, and the orders of Charles X. were so positive, that, in spite of all her efforts and her supplications, she was forced to remain where she was.

Charles X. had just abdicated as king, but, as head of the family, he was always obeyed. The berlin, with six post-horses, remained in the court-yard of the chateau several hours, and it was not until seven in the evening that the Duchess of Berry came to countermand her order for departure. The mother of Henri V. was weeping.

M. Alfred Nettement has said: "There was the intelligence of a political situation in these tears. In the existing crisis everything lay in being on the spot. Once at Paris, the Duchess of Berry could influence the people, neutralize the Duke of Orleans, and embarrass the Chamber. Fortune is like men; she puts the absent in the wrong."

The Dauphin had retained command of the troops until six in the evening, when he delivered it up to Marshal Marmont. The act of abdication having been printed, the marshal read it to each regiment. Speaking to the officers of every grade and to the soldiers congregated around him, he tried to make

them feel how important it was for both the safety
and the dignity of Charles X. that he should remain
surrounded by the greatest possible number of men.
He said it was a duty of honor and conscience for
the troops not to abandon him; the resolution of the
monarch was magnanimous, and they must let him
find its reward in redoubled attention and respect.
The marshal repeated the same remarks five or six
times while proclaiming Henri V. in every direction.

The dinner hour for the royal family had been
delayed. For the first time Charles X. appeared in
a frock coat, having left off his uniform. After dinner, the old King, taking his grandson by the hand,
went to the bivouac of the body-guards. When they
perceived him they wished to present arms; he forbade them; and, advancing toward the assembled
troops, he apprised them of his abdication in favor of
the Duke of Bordeaux, whom he presented as king,
asking for him the same fidelity and devotion which
had always up to that very day been testified by the
bodyguards and the royal guard. Enthusiastic shouts
resounded. Every sword, every sabre, was brandished
in air. The Dauphin united with his father in
recommending the royal child to the troops. The
Dauphiness addressed the soldiers in encouraging,
dignified, and affectionate terms. But it was the
Duchess of Berry above all who electrified them by
her courage; she spoke to them of glory and of hope.
The watchword was given that evening by General
Baron de Damas, in the name of Henri V.

General de Foissac-Latour, who was to deliver the
act of abdication to Louis-Philippe, had quitted Rambouillet at half-past three in the afternoon. He was
met on the road by the commissioners whom that
Prince had sent to Charles X., the Duke de Coigny,
M. Odilon Barrot, Colonel Jacqueminot, and Baron
de Schonen. M. Barrot says in his Memoirs : "Marshal Mortier had refused to go with us. The reason
he gave was that, being a knight of the orders [1]
(*chevalier des ordres*), he could not dispense himself
from appearing in the King's presence vested in his
blue ribbon, such being the rule. This brave old
soldier could allege no better motive for his refusal
than to fall back upon a question of etiquette that
was at least puerile ; in spite of the gravity and the
danger of the situation, we could not avoid smiling
when he offered us this strange excuse. Marshal
Maison, designated to replace Marshal Mortier, having accepted, rejoined us at Rambouillet, where we
arrived between nine and ten in the evening."

The five commissioners alighted at the tavern, and
caused Marshal Marmont to be apprised of their
arrival by praying him to put himself in communication with them. The marshal had just re-entered
the chateau and given an account to Charles X. of
his round among the camps. He went to find the
commissioners. All of them wore the tricolored
cockade, excepting the Duke de Coigny, who had

---

[1] *Un chevalier des ordres du roi* signified a Knight of Saint
Michael and of the Holy Ghost.

kept his white one. They explained their mission in
few words, and asked to be presented to the King.
M. Odilon Barrot adds in his Memoirs: —

" The marshal, having gone to receive the King's
orders, came back in a few moments to say that the
King had returned to his apartments, and that it was
etiquette (always etiquette) that no one could be introduced at such a moment. We implored him to go
back to the King, accompanied this time by the Duke
de Coigny, to whom we delivered the letter from the
Duke of Orleans of which we were the bearers. Marshal Marmont returned very soon, saying that the
King had not read without surprise the letter addressed him by his cousin ; that he had not demanded
a convoy, and needed none ; that he was surrounded
by a faithful army, and that he would await in this
situation the result of the communications he had
ordered to be made to the Chambers. The Duke of
Ragusa added that, nevertheless, the King would not
take it ill that we should remain at Rambouillet until
the misunderstanding was cleared up."

The commissioners replied to the marshal that they
had come to Rambouillet in the capacity of convoys,
to fulfil a mission of peace and protection; that,
since they were not accepted by Charles X. in this
capacity, they could not remain a moment longer.
As the horses had not yet been taken from their carriages, they started immediately for Paris.

Almost at the same moment, General de Foissac-
Latour had succeeded, not without difficulty, in

reaching Louis-Philippe, at the Palais-Royal, with the abdication of the King and the Dauphin. He was told at first that the Prince was at Neuilly and suffering. He waited, skulking in the back of a cab on the Place du Palais-Royal, fearing every instant to be attacked by an uneasy and tumultuous crowd. An aide-de-camp of the Duke of Orleans came at last to deliver him from this painful situation, and led him, by way of the rue Valois, up to the top of the palace, whose stairs and vestibules were encumbered by men of the people, and individuals of every class in society, some lying on the flags and steps, others leaving the apartments, others going thither, every one coming and going freely. Through a half-opened door the general distinctly saw the Duke of Orleans, lying on a folding-bed, and seeming prostrated with fatigue. Still conducted by the aide-de-camp, he got as far as the great gallery. The Duchess of Orleans was there all alone. She came to meet him. He delivered to the Princess the letters he had been charged with. On reading that addressed to her by the sister of Henri V., tears came to the eyes of the Duchess of Orleans. She confined herself to this remark: "Tell the royal family that my husband is an honest man, and repeat it to the Duchess de Gon-taut." It was eleven o'clock in the evening. Thus ended the second day of August, 1830.

XIX

AUGUST THIRD AT PARIS

LET us now examine what occurred at Paris and
at Rambouillet on Tuesday, August 3. The
commissioners, coming from the latter town, reached
the Palais-Royal at four o'clock in the morning and
had the Duke of Orleans awakened: he hardly gave
himself time to dress; his feet were bare in his
slippers. M. Odilon Barrot said to him: "Monseigneur, Charles X., replying to the message we bore
him on your part, has caused us to be informed that
he had not asked for convoys, and that, moreover,
surrounded by a faithful army, he had no need of
any. It seemed evident to us that he is trying to
gain time; this situation is perilous, and an end ought
to be put to it; and if a blow is to be struck, it belongs to you, and to you alone, to take the initiative."

M. Barrot adds in his Memoirs: "I emphasized these
last words; we had no time, in fact, to demand an
explanation of that strange blunder which sent us
out of Paris as *convoys*, a blunder which had put us
in a very false and even very dangerous position;
for if Charles X. had been resolved to play his last
card and to expose his remaining forces in a supreme

212

effort, he could have done nothing better than have us shot as spies and rebels, according to the rumor that got about, and then to order an immediate march on Paris."

In reality, the commissioners had been most anxious. The voice and manner of M. Barrot doubtless smacked of what he felt; for Louis-Philippe, instead of expatiating at length, as was customary with him, replied, after looking at him: "You are right; a movement must be made on Rambouillet. Give notice to General Lafayette, and have the call to arms beaten in all quarters of Paris; every legion of the National Guard will furnish a contingent of six hundred men, and you, gentlemen, will lead this column to Rambouillet."

The *Moniteur* of August 6 has established the fact that the march of the Parisians was ordered by Louis-Philippe. We read there, in fact: "Charles X. had formed a camp at Rambouillet, where several corps of the royal guard were gathered around him. An armed force not dependent on the established government could not be allowed to exist at the doors of the capital, where its very presence so close to Paris kept the population in a dangerous state of irritation. There was room to fear at every moment that the popular masses might rise and march thither. The lieutenant-general of the kingdom recognized the necessity of anticipating the movement which the prolonged sojourn of Charles X. at Rambouillet could not fail to produce, in order to place leaders at the head of it who, by making it regular, could prevent the excesses that might be feared. He ordered General Lafayette to march six thousand men in the direction of Rambouillet, hoping that this demonstration would be sufficient to decide Charles X. to take the only step which so many circumstances combined to make him adopt; that of going away, and dissolving the assemblage by which he was surrounded."

The Parisians were much excited in the morning of August 3. At first a rumor was spread that the commissioners, on presenting themselves at the outposts of the royal army, had been butchered there. As soon as their return and the negative results of their journey were known, the crowd became still more agitated. Groups were forming on all sides, where people said: "Charles X. will not quit Rambouillet. He and his former ministers pretend to govern France. He is marching on Paris with his army to compel us, at the cannon's mouth, to recognize his grandson. He is waiting for the Chouans to recommence the war." Paris was at the morrow of the Revolution. The fighting impulse was still in full force. The streets were still blocked with barricades. When the call to arms was beaten in the twelve legions of the National Guard, it thrilled the people. Men of the people followed the drums. A pupil of the Polytechnic School, standing up in a cabriolet, beat the general alarm amidst the applause of the crowd. All of a sudden, with that electric rapidity that is pro-

duced in times of revolution, there arose a shout of:
"To Rambouillet! to Rambouillet!" from one end
of Paris to the other, and in the outskirts likewise.
The Champs-Élysées was the meeting-place whence
they were to start. Nothing could be stranger than
this improvised army. One might have thought it a
masquerade. Urchins, grown men, old men, national
guards, the common people; uniforms, vests, blouses,
peaked caps, hats, grenadiers' bearskin caps, cuirassiers' helmets, lancers' Polish caps; muskets, fowl-
ing-pieces, carbines, horse-pistols, daggers, swords,
sabres, lances taken from the troops during the three
days of July, bayonets stuck on the end of canes, —
such was the aspect of an indescribably disorderly
crowd and confusion.

"To this army, which knew neither obedience nor
discipline," Duke Victor de Broglie has said in his
Souvenirs, "General Pajol, a man of great energy,
was assigned as commander, with General Jacqueminot as chief of staff; pupils of the Polytechnic School
were placed at the head of companies formed by
chance. As no military man could be under any
illusion concerning the fate of this multitude if it
were met on open ground by the regiments of the
royal guard, General Pajol had instructions, in case
of attack, to plunge into the woods and there disperse
his followers."

The Duke de Broglie adds: "These instructions
were drawn up in council. I held the pen; the
minute of it, in my handwriting, exists entire in

the papers delivered to King Louis-Philippe after
the Revolution of 1848. When I was charged at
this epoch, by M. Dufaure, Minister of the Interior
under General Cavaignac's administration, to preside
over a commission which was itself charged to effect
a separation between the papers of the King found in
his cabinet and delivered like them to pillage at the
sack of the Tuileries, the minute in question fell
under my notice. I could not deny either its language or its existence. I was on the point of reserv-
ing it with the intention of sending it to the King
myself, and asking his permission to keep it; but, all
things considered, I thought it more delicate to leave
it in the packet, intending, however, to entreat that
good prince to give it back to me himself. I never
saw him again until a few days before his death, at a
moment he scarcely had full command of himself."

On being furnished with his instructions, General
Pajol gave the signal of departure from the Champs-
Élysées. The sovereign people did not intend to
travel the fifteen leagues afoot. They requisitioned
every vehicle they could find, — omnibuses, cabs, vans,
cabriolets, diligences, trucks, private carriages. All
of these were · crowded as full as possible. There
were bunches, so to say, of human beings in the in-
teriors, on the boxes, and on the roofs. Even the
foot-passengers hoped to find other means of locomo-
tion, for they had decided to seize all vehicles they
should encounter on the way. They laughed, they
sang, they howled, they bandied quips and jests.

M. Odilon Barrot says : " A stranger who should
have seen such a strange procession passing by without knowing the cause that impelled it, would not
have known how to characterize it ; he would much
sooner have taken it for one of those grotesque processions by which some of our northern provinces
are accustomed to celebrate a local anniversary, than
for an army going to decide the fate of the monarchy."

The expeditionary column had been gone for some
time in the direction of Rambouillet, when a salvo of
artillery from the cannon of the Invalides announced
that the Duke of Orleans was arriving at the Palais-
Bourbon, where the opening of the session of the
Chambers was to take place. It wanted a quarter of
one o'clock. About one hundred and fifty deputies
and a small number of peers, not in uniform, had
assembled. The throne, on which Louis-Philippe did
not yet expect to sit that day, was on a platform and
covered with draperies sown with lilies. The flag
floating above the royal crown was tricolored. The
Duke of Orleans was received at the door of the
palace by the grand deputations which came to meet
him. He was greeted with acclamations on entering
the hall. He took his place on a stool placed at the
right side of the throne, and his second son, the Duke
of Nemours, on another at the left. The Duke of
Chartres was absent. The Duchess of Orleans, Madame Adelaide, and the young princes and princesses
occupied a tribune. " Gentlemen, be seated," said

the Duke; then he delivered a discourse in which occurred the following passages: —

"In the absence of all public power, the desires of my fellow-citizens have turned toward me; they have deemed me worthy to co-operate with them for the safety of the country; they have invited me to exercise the functions of lieutenant-general of the realm. Their cause has seemed to me just, the peril immense, the necessity imperious, my duty sacred. I have hastened to the midst of this valiant people, followed by my family, and wearing the colors which, for the second time, have marked among us the triumph of liberty. . . .

"Respect for all rights, care for all interests, good faith in the government, are the best means to disarm parties and lead back men's minds to that confidence in institutions, that stability, which are the only assured pledges of the welfare of peoples and the strength of states. Gentlemen peers and deputies, as soon as the Chambers shall be constituted, I will make known to them the act of abdication of S. R. King Charles X. By the same act S. A. R. Louis-Antoine of France, Dauphin, likewise renounces his rights. This act was placed in my hands at eleven o'clock last night, August 2. I have this morning ordered it to be deposited in the archives of the Chamber of Peers, and I will cause its insertion in the official part of the *Moniteur.*"

Thus, Louis-Philippe, who spoke in his discourse of respect for all rights, said not one word concerning those of the Duke of Bordeaux, now become Henri V. He omitted to announce that it was in favor of the young Prince that the abdications of Charles X. and the Dauphin had been made, and he did not even pronounce the name of the royal child who, according to the charter, was the legitimate sovereign of France.

XX

ON Tuesday morning, August 3, Charles X. still indulged the illusion that his grandson would that day be proclaimed King of France and Navarre by the Chambers. The Duke de Luxembourg, captain of the guards on duty, put this sentence in his order of the day to the four companies: "Bodyguards of Charles X. or of Henri V., your position does not change." The courtiers imagined up to the last moment that they were going to retain their posts and their high salaries under the new reign. " The efficacy of the abdications was so little doubted at Rambouillet," says Chateaubriand, " that they were preparing the young Prince for his journey; his ægis, the tricolored cockade, was already fashioned by the hands of the most ardent partisans of the Ordinances. Supposing that the Duchess of Berry, setting off suddenly with her son, had presented herself at the Chamber at the moment when the Duke of Orleans was there making his opening speech, there were two chances left — perilous chances! But, at the least, a catastrophe occurring, the child escaping to heaven, would not have dragged out wretched

220

days in a foreign land. My counsels, my wishes, my cries, were useless; I asked in vain for Marie Caroline." Marie Caroline did not appear; but, as we have said already, it was not the fault of the courageous mother.

Charles X. awaited tidings from Paris with dignity and patience. Marshal Marmont has admired his touching attitude, his calm and pious resignation, his noble countenance, sad and benevolent. He is less just to the Duke of Angoulême, whom he did not forgive the scene at Saint-Cloud. "The Dauphin," he says, "by his gaiety and indifference presented a revolting incongruity. Did he not go so far as to say to Gerardin: 'What am I going to do with my dogs?' — 'Monseigneur, you have other interests which outrank that one.' 'Well, I will occupy myself with nothing but my dogs.' — 'Just as you please, Monseigneur; but for my part, I will not talk about dogs.'

"Moreover," adds the vindictive marshal, "the Dauphin is an unaccountable man, peremptory, despotic, susceptible, and full of self-love when he had any power. He has said and repeated since the catastrophe, and, I believe, with sincerity, that he regretted nothing at all but his dogs and horses."

Toward noon an event occurred which was of a sort to give the little court of Rambouillet hopes that the fidelity of the troops could be depended on. An ardent revolutionist, Colonel Poques, had been commissioned by the government of the Hôtel de Ville to go to Rambouillet and demand the crown diamonds. Surrounded by a certain number of disbanded soldiers, he placed himself in front of the outposts of the royal army and delivered a haughty summons. He was ordered to retire. Instead of obeying he stayed where he was and set up the tricolored flag in the grand avenue of the chateau. A discharge was fired. The colonel was wounded in the leg. The Duchess de Gontaut relates that he was carried to an out-house of the chateau, where attentions were lavished on him, the King sending his own surgeon. "Colonel Poques," she adds, "had a mother whom he worshipped; she lived in Pau, where my family was at the time. He wrote her an affecting letter which he asked General Trogoff to give to me, begging me to see that it reached his mother. I promised, and I did it. I was blamed for this *sentimentality*. But only by persons without mothers. The King had permitted me."

During the day, there arrived at Rambouillet one of the most faithful servitors of the monarchy, one of the most distinguished diplomats of the Restoration, the Duke de Montmorency-Laval.

Anne Pierre Adrien de Montmorency, Duke de Laval, cousin of Duke Mathieu de Montmorency, had been ambassador in Spain from 1814, in Rome from 1821, and in Vienna in 1828. In 1829 he had refused the portfolio of Foreign Affairs. From September in that year he had been ambassador to London. He had treated the affairs of Greece and of Algeria with equal intelligence, patriotism, and firmness. On July 25, 1830, the very day the Ordinances were signed, he said to Lord Aberdeen: "I do not know what may be hoped from the generosity of France, but what I do know is that nothing can be gained by threats." The Duke de Laval came to Paris on leave of absence. He hardly expected to find a revolution there. (We have read the account of his visit to Rambouillet, August 3, 1830, in his papers, the sight of which we owe to the kindness of his grandson, Count de Couronnel, who received them from his father, Marquis de Mailly-Couronnel.)

The ambassador of Charles X. was struck by the tranquillity manifested by the old King. As if forgetting the gravity of events possessing a more immediate interest, he conversed long and eagerly with his ambassador on the diplomatic questions which had occupied the attention of Europe a few days before. It was even necessary for the duke to recall the sovereign's mind two or three times to the imminence of the danger which had been increased within three days by the inaction of Rambouillet. "It was then," is said in the ambassador's papers, "that the Duke de Laval broached to Charles X. an idea whose boldness struck to his heart and which he demanded to put into execution. It was the Duke of Bordeaux himself for whom he asked the King, that he might take him to Paris and to the Chambers, which would be disarmed by the courage of the guardian and the innocence of the child. No hatred or popular prejudice was excited by the name or character of M. de Montmorency. Herein he had a great advantage over Baron de Damas. The Duke de Laval went to the Duchess of Berry to renew his proposition. But in the dejection and consternation everywhere prevailing at the chateau of Rambouillet, the audacity of such a plan could not be adopted on the instant. It would have required new entreaties, more ample developments of a plan foolhardy in appearance, but which was the only one that might yet save the situation. The rapidity with which events proceeded in the evening annihilated the hopes of those who wished Madame to play the part of Maria Theresa, and the counsellors of Cherbourg carried the day."

The King and the royal family dined at four o'clock. What was left of the court dined in an adjoining room. There may have been forty at table. The Duke of Ragusa was there, looking anxious and dejected, the Duke de Luxembourg, the Duke de Lévis, the Duke de Guiche, Madame de Castéja, etc. The dinner was sad, gloomy, and shorter than usual, as circumstances required.

Meanwhile, the spirit of the picked troops that yet surrounded the King continued good, and, in fine, the day had not passed too badly. True, there was some complaint of a lack of food and money which occasioned several desertions, but the chief complaint was on account of an inaction which it was hoped might end that very evening, for the rumor of the movement of the Parisians on Rambouillet had already spread among the ranks, and those of the officers and soldiers who remained sincerely devoted to the elder branch of the Bourbons were waiting with impatient ardor for what they considered the moment of retaliation.

The Parisians, marching in disorder but rapidly enough, were not far now from Rambouillet. The commissioners, when their carriage had passed the head of the column already arrived at Sèvres, thought it prudent to summon General Pajol, who had command, nominally at least, of this strange army. They expressly recommended him to place a rather strong advance guard at Trappes, a little village lying just on the hither side of Rambouillet, and to give orders to the officers who should command this post to permit no person whatever to pass beyond it, adding that the success of their mission might depend on the strict execution of these instructions.

The Parisians had left the Champs-Élysées at midday. At eight in the evening, the head of the column had reached Coignières, three leagues from Rambouillet. There General Pajol established his headquarters. The artillery, composed of six pieces of ordnance, was placed on the left side of the road. The volunteers, worn out with fatigue, and suffering from heat, thirst, and hunger, bivouacked on the right, in the fields of wheat and clover, and, very much concerned about their means of subsistence, distributed themselves about the neighborhood, seeking to obtain provisions by money or otherwise. The car-

riages were so disposed around the camp as to form
an enclosure. According to M. Odilon Barrot, a few
squadrons of artillery would have sufficed to get the
better of this disorderly multitude.

On arriving at Trappes, the three commissioners,
M. Barrot, Báron de Schonen, and Marshal·Marquis
Maison, halted and sent an emissary to Marshal Marmont, Duke of Ragusa, to announce to him that they
were again at the disposal of the King, and to ask him
for a safe-conduct. This safe-conduct reached them an
hour later, and their carriage, surrounded by a squadron of body-guards, entered Rambouillet by the park
gate. It was dark. The bivouacs of the troops of
the royal army were lighted up. The guides of the
commissioners took pains to make them pass in front
of the regiments of infantry and cavalry massed
along the road and in the park, and especially in
front of the forty pieces of cannon in battery near the
chateau.

"Nothing could be more striking and mournfully
solemn," M. Barrot has said, "than the aspect of the
chateau of Rambouillet at this critical instant. At
the moment when we entered the grand salon it
was thronged with functionaries of every grade, who
separated, on seeing us, into two ranks, between
which we advanced. How describe the different
sentiments depicted on all faces — terrible despair on
some, ill-concealed joy on others? But the domi-
nant one was the keen anxiety caused in all by our
presence. Was it peace or war that we were bring-

ing? Were they to lie under the necessity of letting
themselves be slain in a last and supreme struggle
for the reigning dynasty, or would a compromise
permit each one, after having preserved his honor, to
consider his own interests and turn toward the rising
sun? All this was written on the countenances at
which I could give a rapid glance in passing. To
questions addressed me by one and another as to
whether they must fear or hope, I confined myself
to replying: 'Hope!' And this word, circulating
quickly in the throng, had already changed its physiognomy, when the door of the cabinet of the King
was opened and closed again behind us."

Charles X. was alone, standing near a table. He
had a severe aspect. "Well!" said he, "what do
they want of me?" — "Sire," responded M. Barrot,
"we are followed by an armed column of the people
of Paris. We have outstripped it, and we have hastened to approach you in order to spare France a
horrible conflict in which your most faithful adherents, those who should be dearest to you, would ·
infallibly perish; a conflict henceforth without object,
since you and your son have abdicated." "I have
abdicated, it is true," said Charles X., "but in favor
of my grandson, and we are all resolved here to
defend his rights to the last drop of our blood." The
King pronounced this last phrase in a forcible tone,
and with an energy which seemed to express an irre-
vocable resolution.

M. Barrot replied: "It does not belong to me to

pre-judge the rights of which you speak, nor the hopes which attach to them; but take care lest the name of your grandson become the signal of the approaching catastrophe. Whatever fate God may reserve for him, let it not be soiled with the blood that will be shed, even in the interests of that future."

Charles X. felt himself affected: "Very well!" said he, "what must be done?"

Forgetting the laws of etiquette, his interlocutor took him by the hand and, pressing it, said: "You have already begun the sacrifice, Sire; it must be consummated, and consummated at once, for there is not a minute to lose."

Charles X. afterwards dismissed the three commissioners, and then, as they were retiring, he expressed a wish to speak privately with Marshal Maison. "When they were alone," adds M. Barrot, "according to what the marshal told us about the interview, Charles X. must have said to him: 'You are a soldier, Marshal, and consequently incapable of deceiving me. How many of them are there?'—'Sire,' must have replied the marshal with that apparent simplicity which does not exclude a certain finesse, 'I have not counted them; but, approximately, there must be from sixty to eighty thousand men.'"

In reality, there were not more than fifteen thousand, and Marshal Maison perfectly well knew it. Is not that a singular euphemism which lays this inexact declaration to the account of an *apparent simplicity which does not exclude a certain finesse?*

"That is sufficient," returned the King; "in a quarter of an hour I will let you know my decision." Consulted by Charles X., Marshal Marmont urged an immediate departure. From the beginning of the crisis, the author of the defection of Essonnes, discontented and discouraged, had acted half-heartedly and under the stroke of fatality. The commissioners had been struck by his language on their first visit to Rambouillet. He had said to them: "I was the pronounced adversary of the Ordinances, and yet I saw myself forced to execute them." He had added, as if to excuse the three days' combat: "The street should be free to the soldiers as well as to the citizens; and the mere fact that it was interdicted to them, made it necessary to order them to fire." Then he had avowed his intention of withdrawing from the proscribed family as soon as he should have accompanied them to their land of exile and thus fulfilled his duty. He had asked an official acknowledgment of this from the commissioners, and they had given it, making meanwhile sad reflections on the vicissitudes of this existence.

It is plain that with such an attitude of mind, Marshal Marmont must find many objections to a supreme combat. In contradiction to General Vincent, who entreated Charles X. to allow him to lead the troops against the Parisian bands, the marshal declared such an enterprise impracticable. On this subject he has written in his Memoirs "However little to be dreaded from the military point of view

were the tumultuous bands advancing against us,
yet, considering the actual temper of the troops; we
were not prepared to stop them or to fight them.
It would have been quite simple to march against
this disorganized mass with six thousand horse and
six pieces of cannon. It would have been quite easy
to put them to flight; but in all our cavalry, we had
no reliable troops except the body-guards, and their
destination could not be changed. They could not
quit the King's person. On the other hand, to be
able to act with cavalry, it would have been necessary
to go nearly three leagues, since the forest of Rambouillet extends to that distance in the direction of
Paris."

The marshal adds that the head of the column of
Parisians had already arrived at Perey, that is, at the
entrance of the forest; that they would have been
there in still greater numbers by morning; that the
least troop which should have fired in the woods
could have arrested the cavalry; that for this reason
he would have had to take a few foot-soldiers with
him, and that Charles X. had hardly any left. His
conclusion is that an offensive movement was not
practicable, and that, on the other hand, Rambouillet
affords no positions capable of being defended; that
it is a crater in which troops cannot even be regu-
larly drawn up, and that there was in consequence
but one thing left for the King to do: to withdraw.

The royalist party has not accepted Marshal Marmont's views and has keenly resented his attitude.

It has been claimed that on leaving the chateau, Marshal Maison said: "If I were in Marmont's place, with troops like his and forty-two pieces of cannon, it would be these rattle-pated Parisians who would run!" and that General Pajol afterwards owned to General Vincent that on the least attack "all those fellows would have scattered like frightened sparrows."

According to the figures given by M. de Chateaubriand there were still remaining at Rambouillet on August 3, thirty-five hundred foot-soldiers of the guard, and four regiments of light cavalry, forming twenty squadrons and presenting a total of two thousand effective men. The military household, body-guards, etc., cavalry and infantry, amounted to thirteen hundred men: in all, eight thousand eight hundred men, and seven mounted batteries composed of forty-two pieces of artillery.

"And before whom were they retreating?" says the author of the *Memoires d'Outre Tombe.* "Before an almost unarmed troop arriving in omnibuses, cabs, and little carriages. General Pajol gave himself up for lost when he was forced to assume command of this multitude which, after all, did not amount to more than fifteen thousand individuals even when increased by the arrivals from Rouen. Half of this troop were left on the roads. A few enthusiastic young men, valiant and generous, mingled with this mass, would have been sacrificed: the rest would probably have dispersed. Had the line and the artil-

lery opened fire in the fields of Rambouillet in open
ground, a victory, according to all appearances, would
have been gained. Between the people's victory at
Paris and the King's victory at Rambouillet negotiations could have been established."

However this may be, what is almost certain is that
if Marshal Maison had told the King the truth about
the numbers of the Parisian hordes, and their absolute disorganization, Charles X. would not have
quitted Rambouillet. But believing that he had a
real army of from sixty to eighty thousand men in
front of him, who, it was said, were going to make
their attack at night, he ordered a retreat toward
Maintenon, where he was about to ask hospitality
from the Duke de Noailles.

At ten o'clock in the evening the call to saddle
was sounded, and all the camp made ready to depart.
"Thus they surrendered to the perfidious representations of Marshal Maison," it is said in the papers of
the Duke de Laval, "and fled before an enemy more
to be despised than feared. What shame! what
despair for all the young officers, but an instant
before still full of the hope of avenging their reverses
and outrages by a brilliant victory, and now certain
of adding utter failure to a first defeat! The heart
of the King was moved by the fearful picture of a
civil war, of the horrors that were about to follow
and of those that had already gone before. In the
confusion of this precipitate retreat the Duke de
Laval sought to reach Charles X. and speak with

him again. But he only arrived in time to kiss His Majesty's hand at the moment when he was entering his carriage."

The Duchess de Gontaut has said: "I had to awake Mademoiselle. Poor little Princess! She was sleeping so well, so soundly, that she did not even comprehend the cruel word: *partir!* I had to repeat it. She so gentle, so submissive to manifest duty, said, sobbing: 'No! no! Not go away!' I made her a sort of little sofa composed of five or six pairs of sheets which I had hastily picked up in our apartment. In order to lead Mademoiselle to her carriage, we had to pass in the court over the chafing-dishes on which the royal silverware had been melted in order to pay for the soldiers' food."

Meanwhile the commissioners were very joyful. M. Odilon Barrot wrote the following letter to General Pajol: —

"General, you may arrest your movement; we have just decided the King to depart *by dint of frightening him.* [This phrase, *à force de lui faire peur,* is italicized in M. Barrot's Memoirs, where the letter occurs.] His forces were considerable and well placed. Marshal Maison estimates that there were not less than ten thousand altogether. Receive, general, my sentiments of esteem and cordiality."

M. Barrot also wrote the subjoined letter to Louis-Philippe, which contains almost a prophecy of the events of 1848: —

"Monsiegneur, it is with happiness that we an-

nounce to you the success of our mission. The King
decides to go with all his family. We have made him
understand that the interests of his grandson might
indeed determine him to offer resistance and shed
more blood, but that it was much better, whatever
might be the future of that cause, to keep it apart
from all violence and bloody conflict. This argument
seems to have decided him. Occupy yourself, therefore, in giving satisfaction to what may be reasonably
required by the republican principle, for I believe
that to be the only enemy you need to fear; the partisans of the fallen family will constitute themselves
its auxiliaries. You have, Prince, as aids in combat-
ing this enemy, that frankness, that honesty of heart,
and that simplicity of manners which should effect
your triumph. We will write you in fullest detail
all the incidents of our journey. God grant that it
may terminate happily. I am, with respect, Monseigneur, of Your Royal Highness the very humble
and very obedient servitor."

The commissioners, after having placed seals on
the van containing the crown diamonds, and surrounded it with a tricolored flag, confided it to the
safekeeping of the mayor of the town. Then they
had four mules that were in the stables harnessed to
their carriage, and undertook the convoy of royalty,
proceeding slowly through the beautiful forest of
Rambouillet, illumined here and there by infrequent
lights.

XXI

IN the month of December, 1674, Françoise d'Au-
bigné, widow of the poet Scarron, finding em-
ployment for her graceful gifts as governess to the
children of Madame de Montespan and Louis XIV.,
just granted her by the King, acquired, for the sum of
two hundred and forty thousand livres, the estate of
Maintenon, situated fourteen leagues from Paris, ten
from Versailles, and four from Chartres. In February, 1675, she wrote to her brother: " It is a large
castle at the extremity of a large town ; a situation
according to my taste, — fields all about it, and a
river which passes through the moats. It produces
an income of ten thousand livres, and will bring in
twelve thousand in two years." And to Madame
de Coulanges: "I have been two days at Maintenon, which seemed but a moment. It is a fine
enough house; a little too large for the retinue I
intend for it. It is a very beautiful property, with
woods in which Madame de Sévigné could dream
to Madame de Grignan quite at her ease. I wish I
were able to live there ; but the time has not yet
come."

On her return from this little journey, an unexpected word pronounced by the King produced a great effect at court. In addressing a remark to Madame Scarron, Louis XIV., always courtly towards her, styled her Madame de Maintenon, in presence of everybody. Thus she became a marquise. "It is quite true," she wrote to Madame de Coulanges, "that the King called me Madame de Maintenon, and that I had the imbecility to blush at it. My husband's friends are wrong in accusing me of having concerted this alteration with the King. They are not his friends who say so: they are my enemies or those who envy me; a little good fortune attracts many such."

The castle from which the celebrated companion of Louis XIV. derived her historic name was destined to give asylum to the last sovereign of the elder branch of the Bourbons. Duke Paul de Noailles, one of whose ancestors had been Madame de Maintenon's heir, reminded himself, in a truly noble and generous fashion, of the benefits by which royalty had honored his family.

At Rambouillet, at the moment when he had just learned that the Parisians were marching on Paris, and had decided to start at once, in the middle of the night, Charles X. had met the Duke de Noailles in the grand salon, and had said to him in the affectionate tone of intimacy: "My dear Duke, to avoid great misfortunes I have decided to go away. Receive us at Maintenon." The duke bowed, and had departed in great haste, and arrived there in advance of the King.

The court almanac for 1830 contained four engravings representing four castles: Chenonceaux, Maintenon, Lude, Montfort. Concerning that of Maintenon it had a little explanatory note. When, at the beginning of 1830, the brother of Louis XVI. and of Louis XVIII. glanced over this almanac, — the last one of his reign, — he hardly suspected that before the end of the year he would come, a dethroned and fugitive king, to ask a few hours' shelter in this castle, still full of the glorious souvenirs of the greatest of his ancestors, the Sun-King.

It was two o'clock in the morning when Charles X., accompanied by the royal family, arrived at Maintenon. The Duke de Noailles received him at the foot of the staircase with tokens of the most profound respect. The entire castle was illuminated as if for a festival. Near the duke was the duchess, a sister of General Duke de Mortemart, that elect lady, so noble in heart and mind, who died in 1887 at the age of eighty-seven. The duchess was pregnant at the time. She was to bring into the world the ensuing month her second son, Marquis Emmanuel de Noailles, who has represented France with distinction as minister plenipotentiary at Washington, and as ambassador to Rome and to Constantinople. The King remarking that the duchess seemed fatigued and suffering, insisted that she should go to rest. She was replaced in doing the honors of the castle by her niece, Mademoiselle de Beauvilliers de Saint Aignan, who was to marry, in 1832, the Prince de Chalais,

eldest son of the Duke de Périgord, and to die in
1834,—a woman as worthy as she was charming; of
whom her uncle, Duke Paul de Noailles, said: " Her
life on earth was like the apparition of an angel."

They all assembled at first in the salon which had
been the bedchamber of Louis XIV. The commissioners came there and joined the persons composing
the King's suite. The Duke de Noailles afterwards
conducted Charles X. to the chamber he was to
occupy on the first story. It was that of Madame de
Maintenon. A body-guard was put on duty in the
little balcony outside the window of this chamber.
Then the Duchess of Berry and her children were
led to the apartments intended for them on the
ground-floor.

During this time the commissioners, seated about
a round table in the salon, were already occupying
themselves in tracing the itinerary of the journey
Charles X. was about to undertake. They sent and
received despatches. Near them was the Duchess
de Gontaut, who was writing sad farewells to her
daughter, the Duchess de Rohan. She told them
so, begging them to forward her letter to Dieppe.
M. de Schonen promised to do so.

As the night advanced, the commissioners separated, and Madame de Gontaut returned to Mademoiselle at the very moment when the King and the
Duchess of Berry were entering the chamber where
the little Princess slept. " We come," said Charles
X., " to speak to you about the arrangements to be

made for the future, as we find ourselves under the necessity of restricting as far as possible the number of persons who shall accompany us. You will readily understand that we are forced to a separation which I know will be painful to you: that of Madame de Rivera. Announce it to her, adding my sincere regrets at finding ourselves obliged to make this sacrifice." (Mademoiselle Eugénie de Rivera was styled Madame, and had the title of countess in her quality as canoness. She was a young Spanish orphan without fortune, very sympathetic in character, who acted as under-governess to Mademoiselle.) "What!" said the Duchess de Gontaut with animation, "abandon her like this!" — "She will not be abandoned," replied the King. "We leave her momentarily in the most respectable asylum. She will await here, near the friend of her early youth, the moment when we bring her back to us."

The unfortunate sovereign said afterwards: "I am completely ignorant of the fate reserved for me." Thereupon the Duchess de Gontaut repeated to him the conversation between the commissioners who had traced in her presence the itinerary of the journey, settling every halting-place between Maintenon and Cherbourg, the port selected for the embarkation. This name: Cherbourg; this word: embarkation, which had so vividly impressed Madame de Gontaut, did not seem to excite any emotion in Charles X. The Duchess of Berry did not conceal her own. Then the old King turned back to his sleeping-cham-

ber, climbing painfully the steps of the staircase up
which Louis XIV. had bounded.

"This unexpected visit," adds the Duchess de
Gontaut, "this painful decision reached at the very
moment when I had just written my last farewell to
my daughter, filled me with a discouragement foreign
to my character; but I soon felt that it was a matter
of duty to endure without feebleness any future which
it might please God to impose. . . . It was a profound
grief to me to announce our separation to Madame
de Rivera. . . . Her devotion had not been weakened by any obstacle. She would have worked with
pleasure for her Princess; but to leave her at the
moment of her exile caused her a mortal sadness;
she said so to me even with harshness.

"Dear Eugénie," adds Madame de Gontaut, "we
were both ignorant that Providence had its own views.
Providence watched over you. This desertion which
I have wept over placed you high, and you have been
able to procure the pleasure and happiness of the
husband who was granted to you. This divine
Providence has given you daughters and a circle of
friends who love you, and of whom you are the animating spirit. Let us bless then the hand of God
who has sustained the orphan and protected virtue."

The King had just made his sacrifice. He decided
to leave for Cherbourg. On arriving at Maintenon,
Marshal Marmont had supposed that after suitable
repose the royal family and the troops would continue
their retreat to Chartres in order to gain the Loire

and make an attempt at government in the name of Henri V. The marshal had even sent an advance guard to Chartres commanded by General Talon, and in that city some officers to prepare provisions for them. But, on coming to receive the King's orders as to the continuation of the movement, he learned that Charles X., giving up the struggle, had abandoned the idea of repairing to the Loire, and was making ready to start for Cherbourg and take ship there.

During the night march of the troops from Rambouillet to Maintenon, a courier sent from Paris had brought to the two Swiss regiments of the royal guard a safe-conduct from the lieutenant-general of the realm, to bring them to Châlons and Mâcon. This safe-conduct fell into the hands of General Vincent, who sent it to the Duke of Ragusa. " I experienced a profound sentiment of indignation," says the marshal, "on seeing these two regiments, overwhelmed with benefits from the King, making haste to abandon him just at the moment when their presence seemed to be most useful and necessary. . . . I inquire: What advantage resulted to the Bourbons from having had, at the cost of money and a wounded public sentiment, troops that were good, no doubt, but which assuredly could not pretend to be superior to French troops? What was the use of these privileged troops which in certain cases were exempt from service? What good end did it serve if these troops did not at least devote themselves to the personal defence of the King?"

Charles X. having definitely given up the struggle, a part of the troops was sent back. The French infantry of the royal guard, whose total was now reduced to twelve hundred men, was directed to Chartres, where it should find provisions, and was from there to be sent into its garrisons, there to receive the orders of the new government, to which the heavy cavalry of the guard had rallied already; it was disseminated to several points. The lancers, hussars, and the artillery, which were near Chartres, were ordered to go thither, and afterwards return to their respective garrisons, like the infantry. There remained the chasseurs, dragoons, picked gendarmes, and the body-guards. The chasseurs were disorganized, since one of their squadrons had been led to Paris by one of their chiefs. The dragoons, the picked gendarmes, and the body-guards remained absolutely faithful.

Although exhausted by fatigue, the commissioners occupied themselves before going to rest with the disbanding of the troops that were not to follow Charles X. and settling the halting-places for the succeeding days.

The Duke de Luxembourg was present at this sort of council of war. The conversation turned on the events that had just occurred. "I am not quite sure," said the duke to the commissioners, "that you have not made us commit a gross piece of folly in persuading the King to withdraw." — "Why so?" said M. Barrot. "I suppose that with the forces you commanded you could have obtained a momentary advantage over the disorderly troop that was marching on Rambouillet, and that you could have succeeded in taking it back to Paris. On the very instant the tocsin would have sounded in all the country places; this population whose temper you have had an opportunity of judging would have risen *en masse*, you would have been attacked, and not one of you perhaps would have escaped." — "All the same," replied the Duke de Luxembourg; "confess that in wiping out this rabble we should have rendered a great service to your Louis-Philippe."

After relating this conversation, M. Odilon Barrot adds: "Just as I was about to stretch myself on a camp bed which had been arranged for me in the billiard room, the Duke de Noailles entered; he had not hesitated to give hospitality to his unfortunate King, but he was not easy concerning the consequences of this act of devotion. He was afráid of seeing the insurgent column from Paris arrive at any moment, and he feared especially for his pregnant wife the shocks that might be caused her by a contest, followed perhaps by grave excesses; I reassured him by telling him what orders we had given, and then went to sleep."

In the morning of August 4, the park of Maintenon was still full of troops encamped under the trees. At an early hour, Charles X. was present at Mass in the small chapel of the castle. The company of the ordinary foot-guards of the King, also called the Com-

pany of the Hundred Swiss — whose captain-colonel
was General Duke de Mortemart, brother of the
Duchess de Noailles — afterwards returned its standard to Charles X. The officers, and those of the
other corps that were about to depart, took leave of
the royal family. The King gave them his hand to
kiss and thanked them for their fidelity. Profound
as his grief was, he succeeded in mastering it. His
attitude remained grave and dignified. The eyes of
the Duchess of Angoulême were filled with tears.
She said: "Adieu, my friends; be happy!" It was
ten o'clock in the morning when some one came to
tell the King that they were awaiting his orders to
depart. He then took leave of the Duke and Duchess
de Noailles and thanked them in affecting terms for
their noble hospitality. The Duchess de Gontaut
says that the grace of his manners was still admired,
and that in this final moment he knew, as he had
always done, how to find words which console and
which are never forgotten.

The souvenir of the sojourn of Charles X. at the
castle of Maintenon has been religiously preserved
by the Noailles family. In the chamber used by the
King this inscription on a plaque of gilded wood has
been placed: "Here His Majesty King Charles X.
passed the night of August 3–4, 1830." Above this
plaque is a picture representing the last sovereign of
the elder branch of the Bourbons, vested in the mantle
and collar of the supreme head of the order of the
Holy Ghost. The little chapel where he heard Mass

on the morning of August 4 has remained just as
it was then with its beautiful sixteenth century
stained glass windows.

Duke Paul de Noailles, who gave hospitality to
Charles X., and who died in 1885, a member of the
French Academy, has written a masterly work on
Madame de Maintenon, and has labored with as much
zeal as intelligence at the restoration and preservation
of the castle whose name was taken by the companion of Louis XIV. It is very picturesque, this
manor, in which the architecture of the Middle Ages
combines so harmoniously with that of the Renais-
sance. How many things contribute to the beauty of
the edifice; the towers which date back to Philip
Augustus, the moats filled with ever limpid and pure
water, the elegant medley of stones and bricks, the
windows, the balconies, the arcades which date from
Cottereau, treasurer of finances to Charles VIII. and
Louis XI., the great gallery which reminds one of
that of the castle of Don Ruy Gomez de Silva, and in
which appear the portraits of the most celebrated
members of the Noailles family: admirals and marshals of France, cardinals and ambassadors! At
Maintenon the souvenir of Charles X. is not brighter
than that of Louis XIV. The present Duke de
Noailles, the remarkable author of *Cent ans de répu-
blique aux États-Unis*, was four years old when the
fugitive King came to pass several hours at the
castle, and he recalls the impression produced on him,
the morning of August 4, 1830, by the sight of the

troops camped under the trees of the park, which, with the forty-eight arches of its gigantic aqueduct, makes one think of Poussin's most beautiful landscapes. One likes to see historical castles belonging to worthy inheritors of their former possessors, and is pleased to salute an illustrious family which has a veneration for the past.

XXII

DREUX AND VERNEUIL

CHARLES X. and his cortège made their way without difficulty from Maintenon to the environs of Dreux, which had been designated as the first stopping-place. The carriages of the King and the royal family were followed by those of the commissioners, and the peasants along the route manifested no hostility. A quartermaster of the palace, Count de Geslin, had gone ahead to prepare lodgings at Dreux. He found the town closed and barricaded. He was arrested and taken to the Hôtel-de-Ville, and told that the whole population, in arms, would oppose the entry of Charles X. into the town. He was afterwards released, so that he might carry this news to the commissioners. He retraced his steps, and meeting them at the entrance of the town, he apprised them, in great alarm, of what had happened.

Listen to the account of M. Odilon Barrot: "Our carriage, outside of which our tricolored scarfs were floating, had taken lead of the escort, and when we were in sight of Dreux, Schonen and I alighted and went toward the post of National Guards. Recognized and received with acclamations, we were car-

ried, so to say, to the Hôtel-de-Ville in the midst of
an immense throng of people belonging to the town
and the surrounding country, and there each of us,
mounted on a table, harangued the crowd. 'The cause
of right and liberty has triumphed,' we said to them,
'there is no more conflict, and consequently no more
enemies. There is nothing left except to respect the
misfortune of a family fallen and making its way into
exile. The people of Paris, who have shed their
blood for the triumph of the common cause, have set
the example of this respect for misfortune. Will you
be less generous than they?'—'No! no! let them
enter!' Such was the response which rang from the
crowd throughout every corner of the Hôtel-de-Ville
as well as in the streets and public places."

The quartermaster who had accompanied the commissioners, instead of rejoicing at their intervention,
broke into lamentations. "Have I lived so long,"
he exclaimed, "to hear my master treated thus?"—
"You are mad, my dear fellow," replied M. Odilon
Barrot; "tell me what means must one employ to
enter a closed town when we cannot enter it by
force?"

On returning to meet the King, the commissioners
encountered the Dauphin, who was on horseback at
the head of the escort. They gave him an account
of what they had done and obtained. "That does
not concern me," returned the Prince; "go and tell
it to my father." The commissioners then approached
the carriage of Charles X. and announced to him

that the obstacle to his entry into Dreux was removed, but he must be prepared to find the whole
city decked with the national colors. "It is all the
same to me," replied the King, "provided I can enter,"
and he gave orders to go on.

That same day, August 4, toward four o'clock in
the afternoon, Charles X. entered Dreux, where, in
the chapel belonging to the castle belonging to the
Orleans family, are the tombs of the princes and princesses of his house. The promise made by the
inhabitants of the city was kept exactly. The populace, so excited but a few moments before, beheld
the long cortège of men and baggage pass by with
the utmost calmness. There was not an insult, not
a cry.

A squadron of body-guards bivouacked in front of
the dwelling of the King. The rest were dispersed
along the bank of the river or in the fields.

The dragoons of the guard, commanded by Lieu-
tenant-Colonel Cannuet, a very distinguished officer
of the former army, had followed the King without
the desertion of a single man. "On arriving at
Dreux," says Marshal Marmont, "the King sent
back this brave regiment, which had been a model of
good discipline and fidelity, and praised it in terms
which it had deserved. The escort was now composed solely of the body-guards, the *gendarmerie
d'élite*, and two pieces of cannon. The King drew
up his own itinerary; but he made the travel of each
day so short and so many halts, that his journey

would have been eternal. I was charged with com-
municating this itinerary to the commissioners. They
demanded certain changes which were the object of
subsequent arrangements."

The vague hopes entertained until then by certain
body-guards were now dispelled. One of them, M.
Théodore Anne has written: "It was at Dreux that
we knew we were going to Cherbourg, where the
King would embark. Some hope still remained, it
was said, for the Duke of Bordeaux, and short journeys for the sake of awaiting events were spoken of.
But the presence of the commissioners showed us
how illusory was such a hope."

M. Odilon Barrot relates, in his Memoirs, that at
Dreux the King was rejoined by one of his aides-de-
camp. He was questioned concerning all the circumstances of the previous day. He was asked how many
men there were in the column marching from Paris to
Rambouillet; if it was orderly and well armed. He
replied that there were about fifteen thousand men, a
great part of whom were not seriously armed, and
that the greatest disorder was noticeable in the whole
crowd, who marched pell-mell, without being formed
into battalions. "This officer," adds M. Barrrot,
"perhaps exaggerated in an opposite sense from the
exaggeration of the marshal; but one can judge of
the exasperation which this account created in the
minds of all these men who regretted not having
fought, and who loudly complained of the King's
having allowed himself to be deceived by Marshal

Maison. Such as had loudly congratulated themselves on the pacific denouement which had been substituted by the retreat from Rambouillet for a bloody
conflict which had its hazards, now exclaimed most
vigorously against the infamy and treason. But
reflection on the situation of this little troop of loyal
men, whom every step enlightened further, and who,
surrounded by hostile populations, could not even
pass through a town without the intervention of a
convoy, soon banished all anger."

It is M. Barrot, again, who thus relates an interview he had the same evening with the Duchess de
Gontaut: "Madame de Gontaut made this spirited
and sensible remark: 'If on the *thirtieth* of *July* I
had brought the young Prince to you at the Hôtel-de-
Ville and set him on General Lafayette's knees, what
would you have done?' — 'Faith, Madame, it is probable that in that case neither you nor we would be
here.'"

The night of August 4-5 was spent at Dreux. In
the morning there seemed cause for anxiety. "We
were awakened," says the Duchess de Gontaut, "by
the noise, so well known, alas! of a riot; I ran to the
window; I saw the hotel surrounded by peasants
armed with scythes; I had a moment of disquiet
which was soon dispelled when some one came to tell
me that there was nothing political involved in this
popular movement; that it was simply the harvesters
of the environs, who, desiring an increase of wages,
rose in arms to follow the example of Paris. This

agitation, which continued during part of the day, was disagreeable but not dangerous."

Verneuil was to be the next stopping-place. The commissioners started from Dreux at four o'clock in the morning of Thursday, August 5, preceding the royal family by an hour, in order to induce the population to be quiet, and prevent all offensive manifestations. The journey from Dreux to Verneuil, where they were to rest that night, was accomplished without hindrances. In every village along the road they found tricolored flags floating from the church steeples, and National Guards wearing the three colors. This spectacle was extremely disagreeable to the King. In other respects, the people showed themselves calm and silent, the result of their personal dispositions, their instincts, and also of the representations of the commissioners, who, preceding the cortège, had taken care to repeat them constantly.

When they arrived at Verneuil, where they passed the night of August 5–6, M. Odilon Barrot wrote to Louis-Philippe : " Everywhere along our route we have found an at least apparent unanimity for the new government. The National Guards were under arms and wore the national cockade. . . . The suite of the King now comprises only some five hundred bodyguards, a few picked gendarmes, two pieces of cannon, many valets, and much baggage. We have hinted at the dismissal of a good many of the attendants ; but the force of custom prevails. The King appears sat-

isfied with the cares with which we surround him; we
advance but slowly; the King says he is not able to
make long journeys, and it is neither our mission nor
our desire to constrain him to travel faster. . . . We
despatched a courier to Paris yesterday; to-day we are
sending one to Caen for money; the King is in absolute want of it; he speaks of his willingness to repay
the sums disbursed; this point does not concern us.
Madame the Duchess of Berry entreats S.A.R. the
Duchess of Orleans to protect her château of Rosny.
The Duchess of Angoulême appears completely
absorbed in her grief."

One may say to the honor of Charles X. that he
went out poor from his kingdom. He had saved
nothing for himself from his civil list. Everything
had been expended in public displays, in good works,
and in charity. The ministers so little suspected the
importance of the movement in Paris that no one
had thought of providing money; the King's treasury
contained nothing; at Rambouillet His Majesty had
sold his silver plate to pay for the small quantity of
provisions that could be found for the troops, and at
Dreux the receiver had been able to give the commissioners only four thousand francs — all that was in his
safe.

Marshal Marmont mentions this embarrassment
for money. "I was," he says, "the sole intermediary
between the King and the commissioners. I sought
to conciliate dispositions frequently opposed, and
above all to lessen the sufferings of such a journey.

The commissioners had acquainted me with their powers to pay the troops all that was due to them. Those who had been sent to Chartres and were to return to their garrisons were first attended to. At Verneuil payments were made on account to the body-guards and staff officers, who were reduced to pressing need.

" The commissioners charged me to offer the King all the money he desired, declaring that a million awaited his disposal at Cherbourg. I repeated this to the King, who ordered me to acquaint them with his refusal. He required, on the other hand, that an exact account should be kept of the expenses of his journey, so that he could repay them later on."

Even the partisans of the Revolution could not avoid admiring the piety, the delicacy, the disinterestedness of the sovereign who possessed the triple majesty of rank, of age, and of misfortune.

No remarkable incident occurred at Verneuil. The people were tranquil, and in the morning of Friday, August 6, the travellers departed in the direction of Laigle, where they were to sleep that night.

XXIII

LAIGLE AND THE MERLERAULT

THE immense convoy proceeded slowly through a double line of people, who had hastened thither from a distance of ten leagues around to contemplate the unique spectacle of the exodus of a court and a king. "Our method of travelling," says Marshal Marmont, "was this: an hour or two before the King's departure I sent off the baggage and attendants with a detachment of gendarmes; Charles X. heard Mass, never dispensing himself from it even when he started at four in the morning. Two companies of body-guards opened the march. After them, the carriages of the children, the princesses, Monsieur the Dauphin, and that of the King, who had with him the Duke de Polignac, chief equerry, and the Duke de Luxembourg, captain on duty. Then followed the two other companies of body-guards and the gendarmes. I marched on horseback at a short distance from the King's carriage."

Since leaving Rambouillet the ranks of the court-iers of misfortune had been well thinned out. There might still be distinguished on the route, in the suite of the fugitive royal family, Prince de Croï-Solre, captain of the guards; General Count de Trogoff, King's aide-de-camp, governor of the château of Saint-Cloud; General Count de la Lassalle, King's aide-de-camp, governor of the château of Compiègne; Marquis de Courbon-Blenac, major of the body-guards; Baron de Gressot and Marquis de Choiseul-Beaupré, major-generals, adjutant-generals of the royal guard; two other major-generals: Count Auguste de Larochejacquelein and Baron de Crossard; Marquis de Maisonfort, adjutant of the body-guards; Marquis de la Roche-Fontenilles, colonel of the first regiment of mounted grenadiers of the guard; Baron Weyler de Navas, deputy commissary of the military household.

The civil household of the King was barely represented in this cortège of the departure into exile. Besides Duke Armand de Polignac, first equerry, there were Count O'Hegerty, equerry commandant, and Viscount Hocquart, chamberlain and steward.

With the Dauphin were the Duke de Guiche, his first gentleman, and the Duke de Levis; the Duke of Bordeaux and his governor, Baron de Damas, and his two under-governors, Marquis de Barbançois and Count de Maupas.

With the Dauphiness were the Marquise de Sainte-Maure, lady-in-waiting, and M. O'Hegerty, junior, equerry. With the Duchess of Berry, Count de Brissac, knight of honor; Count de Mesnard, first equerry; and Countess de Bouillé, lady-in-waiting.

With Mademoiselle, her governess, the Duchess de Gontaut and Baroness de Charette.

To this cortège of fidelity were adjoined Count de Chateaubriand, colonel of the fourth hussars, and a few officers of the royal guard; among others, MM. Jules and Amedée d'Espenay Saint-Luc, captains of the second mounted grenadiers; d'Offémont, sub-lieutenant of the same regiment; de Bouillé, sub-lieutenant of chasseurs.

They journeyed by short stages. This was a consequence entailed by the method of travelling adopted by Charles X., who desired to be surrounded by his body-guard as long as he should be in France. Hence it was necessary to consider the men, some of whom were on foot, and the horses, which were not relayed. According to Chateaubriand, "sometimes Charles X. and his family halted at wretched stations for wagoners in order to take a repast at the end of a dirty table where cartmen had dined before them. Henri V. and his sister amused themselves in the courtyard with the hens and pigeons of the inn." The author of the *Mémoires d'Outre-Tombe* adds: "As I have said, the monarchy was going away, and people went to the window to see it pass."

They arrived at Laigle during Friday, August 6, and rested there until the next morning.

The King lodged at the chateau. At Laigle they commenced to billet the body-guards. Up to then they had always bivouacked; even now only six billets to a platoon of thirty men could be delivered, to show that this *favor* would not be repeated too often during the journey. Some disturbance was feared at Laigle, a manufacturing town, peopled almost entirely by workmen; but not a word, not a cry, was uttered, and the calm that had reigned there until then was not interrupted.

From Laigle M. Odilon Barrot wrote to Louis-Philippe: " We have made known to the King the steps taken by Your Royal Highness to provide His Majesty with a sum of six hundred thousand francs in Spanish doubloons. He has not yet explained himself on the question of accepting or rejecting it; but, in any case, he has declared that his acceptance would be subject to the condition of repayment of this sum through a third party possessing his confidence, and that this would be effected at Paris. The King has recommended his troops, that is, the body-guards, a few mounted grenadiers, gunners, and two batteries of cannon, to our solicitude; these men belong to France; their fidelity to a fallen power makes them all the more worthy of the solicitude of those who represent her. . . . The King has spoken to us of the rights of the Duke of Bordeaux. He has insisted on the danger arising to peoples from a departure from constitutionality and choosing a sovereign for themselves. Your Royal Highness will feel that we could not discuss such a question in presence of Charles X. Respect for misfortune would have prevented us from professing our veritable principles."

Lamartine has said: "The faithful servitors by whom the King was surrounded, maintained towards him and the royal family, at every halt on the road and in the humblest of the houses which lent him the shelter of its roof, the ceremonial and the etiquette of the Tuileries. The court of the princes was restricted, but decorous and loyal in adversity as in grandeur. Names are found there to which history must record the rare glory of fulfilled duty and gratitude." A little incident that occurred at Laigle shows the respect preserved for the royal family. The King of France never takes his meals at a round table, because the place of honor cannot be made sufficiently prominent. As no table conformable to etiquette could be found in the chateau of Laigle, a round table was sawed off and converted into a square one.

They left Laigle on Saturday morning, August 9, and rested that night at Merlerault, the fifth station from Rambouillet.

There a former body-guard, M. de la Roque, had solicited and obtained the honor of receiving the King in his house. The house was not spacious, but the hospitality was full of forethought and respect. The apartment of the King was composed of but a single room on the ground-floor. The usher on duty, dressed as if at Saint Cloud, remained at the door in order to introduce those members of the suite of Charles X. who were admitted to this favor. On the first floor was a chamber for the Dauphin and

Dauphiness, one for the Duchess of Berry and Mademoiselle, another for the Duke of Bordeaux and his
governor. A squadron of body-guards bivouacked
on the grass at the end of the house.

The royal family dined in the King's chamber.
When the dinner was over, Charles X. and the
princes were obliged to leave the house and go to
walk in the bivouac so as to give the domestics a
chance to clear away the dishes. The King spoke
to several body-guards. He asked them if they were
not too fatigued, if their horses stood travelling well,
and he thanked them for their noble fidelity. At
this moment two travelling-carriages belonging to
the Dauphiness came up. They had been stopped
at Tonnerre when the Princess was returning from
Vichy, and the government was sending them back.
"I am very pleased at the arrival of these carriages,"
said the daughter of Louis XVI. to M. O'Hegerty,
her equerry, "not for the sake of the carriages themselves, for they are heavy and roll with difficulty,
but at all events now I shall have some clean
chemises."

Listen to a body-guard, M. Théodore Anne: "The
weather had been fine ever since our departure from
Saint-Cloud. We arrived in the towns covered with
dust, but at least the rain had spared us. In the
night of August 7-8, it took a notable revenge; but
I was so tired that I felt nothing; and when my
comrades awoke me to go and seek shelter under a
tree, my mantle, a bivouac blouse, my coat, were all

drenched, which did not prevent me from continuing the few hours of sleep that we were allowed, for at daybreak we had to go on guard again."

Sunday morning, August 8, they set out again, and slept that night at Argentan.

XXIV

SHORT as his journey was, Charles X. found it
too rapid none the less. He was unwilling to
believe that his cousin would seize the crown, and he
maintained hopes, if not for himself, at least for his
grandson. At Merlerault he had received Colonel
Cradock, a military attaché of the English embassy,
who had been sent by the ambassador, Lord Stuart,
to say to him that as the Duke of Bordeaux still had
some chances of ascending the throne, it would be
better to retard his progress than to accelerate it.

Misled by memories of his official journeys, the old
King saw or thought he saw marks of sympathy and
sorrow on the countenances of all the peasants who
beheld him passing by. When one of the commissioners inquired after his health, "I am physically
well," he replied, "but I suffer from the grief of these
good people."

There was something sad and solemn in this long
and silent cortège, advancing with the slowness of a
funeral procession, which impressed the commissioners themselves. They found it impossible to contemplate the daughter of Louis XVI., who on her part

was thinking incessantly of the journey to Varennes. "It happened frequently," says M. Barrot, "that the Duchess of Angoulême, fatigued by the carriage, alighted and walked on the high road, silent and absorbed in her grief. Silence fell whenever we caught sight of her. We kept at a distance, moved with respect and compassion by the aspect of this living monument of the greatest vicissitudes and most cruel trials that any human being has ever been called on to endure. Extreme and unmerited misfortune sanctified her as it were in the eyes of this people, so admirable for its delicacy and the sureness of its instincts. For my part, whenever the details of the service caused me to meet her accidentally, I made haste to get away as soon as possible, finding no other means but this respectful reserve to testify to her my profound sympathy for her afflictions."

Baron Schonen, who had not shown the same discretion, and had risked addressing some remarks to the Princess, heard her exclaim: "Am I then condemned to have this man's face always before me?" "This speech was severe and undeserved," adds M. Barrot, "for it was a kindly sentiment which induced M. Schonen to offer his services and his consolations. Only, in this circumstance, his heart had not sufficient intelligence."

On arriving, on Sunday evening, August 8, at Argentan, whence they did not depart until Tuesday morning, August 10, they read a proclamation in which the mayor, M. de Latour, spoke of Charles X. with the respect rightfully inspired by his misfortunes, and adjured his fellow-citizens to abstain from all insulting cries, warning them that to behave otherwise would be a cowardly action, which would dishonor the city.

On Monday, August 9, Charles X. was present at Mass, in the Cathedral of Argentan. A large number of the inhabitants had hastened thither and prayed devoutly. After Mass there was an alarm. In spite of the stay settled on, there was question of starting. The order to do so, given thrice during the morning, was thrice revoked. Some malevolent persons had spread a report in the surrounding country places that the city was given over to fire and sword, and that the body-guards were fighting with the citizens. At this news the peasants had seized their scythes and pitchforks, and had run to assist their fellow-citizens. But on their arrival they perceived that everything was tranquil, and, calmed down by the commissioners, they returned peaceably to their occupations. Apropos of this M. Théodore Anne has made the following reflections : " Throughout the whole distance we had passed over, the inhabitants had been described to us as excited, terrible, and ready at any moment to rise and oppose our progress. We arrived, and instead of enemies we found only friends. On the other hand, the citizens were told that we pillaged everywhere, that we carried off all we needed and all that could tempt our cupidity without paying for it; and when on our arrival they saw the order in which the column marched and the discipline that we observed, they easily perceived that all these reports emanated from those who wished to create trouble and disorder, and, under cover of this commotion, perhaps dishonor France by cowardly assassinations."

Meanwhile, the Revolution did not feel itself at ease so long as Charles X. was on French territory. The commissioners came to Marshal Marmont daily, complaining of the slowness of the march and the anxieties that were felt at Paris. They showed him the sharp, almost severe letters sent them, and the accusations of which they were the butt. "A thousand stories were manufactured at Paris about this journey," says the marshal, "and a curious circumstance had given occasion for them. A report by the commissioners, sent from Verneuil, had been put in the post without an address and had not reached the Minister of the Interior. Another report, intrusted to a courier, had been delayed for thirty-six hours. For two days they had been without tidings, and had been greatly alarmed on that account. The rumor had got about that Charles X. had considerable forces with him, that the commissioners had been arrested and detained as hostages, and that it was the King's intention to gain the country of the Chouans and begin a civil war. When these rumors got back to us, I could not help laughing at them. What Chouans we would have been with this file of carriages and this multitude of cooks and scullions!"

What is certain is that the anxieties of the new government were at their height. One can judge of them from this letter, dated August 8, addressed to the three commissioners by M. Guizot, then charged with the Ministry of the Interior: "Gentlemen, His Royal Highness learns with amazement that the march of King Charles X. becomes slower from day to day, that he proposes to make a halt in certain cities, and that he does not permit you to wear the tricolored cockade. These facts, which are known to the inhabitants of a multitude of departments, increase his irritation and mistrust. The safety of King Charles X. and his family may be seriously compromised by them, and as for you, gentlemen, you will soon find yourselves unable to guarantee it. . . . His Royal Highness determines to send Colonel Jacqueminot as a commissioner, that he may again insist to Charles X. on the necessity of repairing promptly and speedily to the place of embarkation, and thus escape the popular movements which may be manifested around him. . . . His Royal Highness requests you to wear constantly the tricolored cockade, which is that of France, and he thinks that His Majesty King Charles X. can see nothing in this measure but a new token of the ardent desire of His Royal Highness that the safety of King Charles X. shall never be threatened. If King Charles X. refuses to yield to these representations, His Royal Highness orders you to suspend the payments you have been charged to provide for the King's suite, a suite whose numbers and composition seems to His Royal Highness better calculated to compromise the King's safety than to guarantee it."

The commissioners, who were in direct contact with the populations as well as with the persons surrounding Charles X., were much more confident than were those at the Palais-Royal. They were somewhat wounded by M. Guizot's indirect reproaches. M. Odilon Barrot replied to him from Argentan: "My dear friend, I think that the object of your official despatches is to facilitate the efforts we are making to expedite a journey which is too much prolonged. I so explain them to my colleagues, who find them wounding enough, especially Marshal Maison, who regards the announcement of Jacqueminot's coming as a personal insult, inasmuch as it seems to condemn his insufficiency and weakness. You know what the character of our mission is; that it is entirely one of deference and humanity; the private recommendations of the Prince and Princess have, in this respect, made our prudence more necessary. How is it then that you want us to act brutally to the King, an unhappy old man, and to women, by affecting in their presence to flaunt ostentatiously tokens which wound them deeply? A sentiment of deference and propriety has made us hide our colors every time we have approached the King and the princesses; but in so doing we have merely followed the impulse of our hearts; no menace has been made to us, and, as you may well believe, any such would have been powerless. For the rest, in public and before the King's suite, we have never laid aside our colors."

In a letter which he wrote from Argentan to General Lafayette, M. Odilon Barrot recurred to the same subject: "General, this is the first day on which I have found time enough to write you two words about our journey, or rather, our long agony, which the patient takes pleasure in prolonging. Outside of the King's cabinet, in presence of the people and the King's suite, we have always worn our badges. It must not be forgotten, General, that we are not jailers, and that our mission is altogether one of humanity and deference. I think that our cause will be more honored by this generosity than by a brutality which, exercised toward women and old men, might well be taken for something else than patriotism."

In spite of this sentiment of deference for a fugitive and vanquished King, the commissioners thought themselves obliged by their instructions to make more active attempts to induce Charles X. to accelerate his march and to send back the two pieces of artillery that figured in his escort. At Paris a legitimist rising was feared in Brittany, La Vendée, and several departments in the south. As happens in all troublous times, a host of false rumors were in circulation: sometimes it was Charles X. who, escaping from the vigilance of the three commissioners, had withdrawn into the Bocage to give a signal there for

a resort to arms; sometimes it was the safety of
the commissioners themselves, who, so it was said,
were menaced by those composing the suite of the
King. A special cause of alarm was found in that
military display and those two terrible cannons, in
which people thought they saw the nucleus of an
army. These are M. Barrot's reflections concerning
these alarms of the new government: "The government of July, hardly born as yet, was afraid of its
origin and dreamed of disguising its principles; it
was on the material fact of the vacancy of the throne
that they wished to base the advent of the new
branch; it may be imagined therefore with what
impatience they awaited the moment when Charles X.
should have actually left the territory. Coolness and
patience are qualities rare enough among men who
find themselves engaged in a revolution; they are
naturally impatient for denouements; they seldom
have sufficient confidence in the justice of their cause
to have enough in time."

In order to induce Charles X. to send back the
two pieces of artillery, the commissioners were
obliged to exercise a real pressure on his mind;
Marshal Marmont, charged by them with the expression of their request, encountered an active
resistance. Charles X. invoked the dignity of his
ill-fortune, the respect due to his white hairs. The
commissioners then acquainted him with their unal-
terable resolution by a writing which terminated in
these words: "Let the King choose between the

moral protection assured to him by our mission, and
the guarantees he believes himself to find in the
cannons he is dragging behind him. If he places his
confidence in this material force, our mission near
him is useless, and we shall retire."

Charles X. ended by yielding. "This resolution
cost the King a great deal," says the Duke of Ragusa.
"I do not know why the commissioners required it;
it was a matter of parade rather than one of real
utility. Yet, under some given circumstance, these
pieces might have saved us, although the real guarantee of the success of our journey was the presence
of the commissioners and not our forces. We were
about to enter among an ill-disposed population,
exasperated by the recent memory of the incendiary
fires that had ravaged their territory and which the
priests and Jesuits were accused by the multitude
of causing. The whole country is full of manufac-
tories, and such populations are the most mutinous
and difficult to control in times of revolution."

It was on this very day, Monday, August 9, 1830,
that the two cannons were taken away from Charles
X. at Argentan, and at Paris the crown of King of
France and Navarre. The Chambers had assembled
at the Palais-Bourbon to proclaim there the new
sovereign. There were not more than ninety peers
present. Among these were remarked Prince Talleyrand, General Duke de Mortemart, Duke Decazes,
Count Portalis, Count Roy, Duke de Broglie, Marquis de Semonville. Three camp-stools had been

prepared in front of the throne, which was arranged
as for the usual opening sessions; but the lilies had
vanished from the curtains, and four tricolored flags
hung at the two sides of the throne.

At two o'clock Louis-Philippe, who was still merely
lieutenant-general of the realm, but who, in a few
minutes, was to bear the title of king, made his entry
accompanied by his two sons, the Duke of Chartres
and the Duke of Nemours. He sat down on the
middle camp-stool, and his sons on the two others.
Behind the empty throne were ranged Marshals
Mortier, Duke of Treviso; Macdonald, Duke of Tar-
ento; Oudinot, Duke of Reggio, and Marshal Count
Molitor, bearing the insignia of royalty on cushions:
the crown, sceptre, glaive, and hand of justice.
Louis-Philippe having signed the declaration which
modified the charter and which established a contract
between him and the Chambers, the foot-stool in the
middle was taken away, and the new sovereign sat
down on the throne, amidst the shouts of the Assembly.

"The 9th of August," says Duke Victor de Broglie in his *Souvenirs*, "ended in a splendid dinner
and a very uproarious reception on a scale which
was hardly of the first rank. I went away early,
thinking that, having assisted in the morning to
make a king and found a dynasty, I had had business and amusement enough for one day."

After the session, M. Guizot, who was still intrusted with the Ministry of the Interior, wrote to

the three commissioners: "Gentlemen, we have received no tidings from you this morning; it seems that communications are momentarily interrupted. The agitation of the people of Paris and the neighboring departments is becoming great; they talk of taking the road to Normandy *en masse* until they shall come up to King Charles X., and of raising up the people along the way. If this movement should once break out, it would be absolutely impossible to repress it or prevent its consequences. Bring it immediately and in most positive terms to the knowledge of King Charles X., so that he may not perceive too late the perils attaching to the slowness which has thus far marked his journey. The two chambers assembled this morning. Monseigneur the lieutenant-general of the realm has accepted the propositions made to him, and after having sworn to observe the clauses faithfully, he was immediately proclaimed King, amidst universal acclamations. We forward you the *procès-verbal* of this memorable session and a copy of the acts read there. They have produced the greatest effect at Paris. King Charles X. will doubtless be acquainted with it. We do not know how to recommend you too strongly to make every effort to persuade him that a departure by post, as we have said in our last letters, is at present a necessary resolve and the surest guarantee."

M. Odilon Barrot thought it his duty to explain the conduct of the commissioners to the new sovereign, and before leaving Argentan, he wrote to him: "If,

on entering the cabinet of King Charles X., we have
avoided wounding him by useless demonstrations, it
was through a sentiment of deference for misfortune,
and in nowise in consequence of menaces which we
would have set at defiance. In a word, we cannot
reproach ourselves for the respect we have shown to
women and an old man who have been made sacred
by so great a misfortune; we have been sent to protect them, not to insult them, and we hope that it is
not at men who long since risked their heads to bring
about the revolution just accomplished that any one
will cast the reproach of disavowing it. We leave
to-morrow at four o'clock in the morning, and shall
pass the night at Condé-sur-Noireau. We shall
cover fifteen leagues; the succeeding journeys will
be pretty nearly as long. As to the plan of going
by post, the King and his family would never agree
to it, unless we employed violence; they would all
think themselves ruined."

The new government ended by calming down a
little, and even gave up the plan of sending Colonel
Jacqueminot to stimulate the zeal of the commissioners. The dethroned old monarch was almost at
Cherbourg. His successor had nothing more to fear.

XXV

CONDÉ-SUR-NOIREAU AND VIRE

IT was the 10th of August, 1830, the anniversary
of the day when, thirty-eight years before, royalty
had perished. On the road from Argentan to Condé-
sur-Noireau, where he was to sleep that night, Charles
X. perhaps thought of this date while continuing the
journey whose goal was the commencement of his
exile. At every station, he went away in a carriage
from the town where he had passed the night. Half
a league further on a halt was made. The King
mounted a horse, and descended from it a little before
reaching the next station. Then he got into his carriage again to enter the town. "As we advanced,"
says M. Théodore Anne, "Normandy, that noble and
rich province, spread out before us, resplendent with
its harvests and beautiful from its admirable points of
view; one might have called it a new diorama for
each day. At the aspect of this wealth, these smiling
fields, what thoughts doubtless assailed the mind of
Charles X. and what regrets they must have caused
him." Any Frenchman who goes into exile must
lament bitterly, but when this exile is a sovereign,
when on beholding the most magnificent land on

274

earth he says to himself: "I have been king of all that," his anguish must be especially keen.

Towards four o'clock in the afternoon, they arrived in sight of Condé-sur-Noireau, a little manufacturing town said to be very ill-disposed toward the royal family. The body-guards, the *gendarmes des chasses*, and the volunteer officers who followed Charles X., declared they would allow themselves to be killed to the very last man rather than suffer the least insult to their master. The commissioners bore this declaration to the inhabitants of the town, who quieted down; they simply made a condition that the National Guards should not pay the King military honors, to which an officer in the body-guards who had accompanied the commissioners haughtily replied that the King so intended. "His Majesty," he added, "has his guard; he receives the military salute whenever he appears before it, and he considers that sufficient."

Charles X. lodged at Condé-sur-Noireau, in a beautiful house, where hospitality was very courteously offered him by a proprietor belonging to the reformed religion. The latter, fearing that he might not be agreeable to the sovereign on this account, said to him: "Sire, I ought not to leave you in ignorance that I am a Protestant." — "But, sir," replied Charles X., "so was Henri IV."

At Condé-sur-Noireau Marshal Marmont specially excited popular animadversion. He had to change his quarters secretly to escape the violence of persons who talked of inflicting on him the fate of Marshal Brune. At this town began for him the very great dangers which he continued to incur throughout the remainder of this painful journey.

Wednesday morning, August 11, they turned towards Vire, whose population of artisans was considered threatening. According to the account of the Duke of Ragusa, several superior officers of the body-guards, who had been sent ahead to find lodging, came to meet him on the road, and told him they were certain that a plot had been formed to abduct him. Well-disposed persons had warned them that if the marshal crossed the town alone, or feebly accompanied, he would be assassinated or else seized and cast into some den. The Duke of Ragusa profited by this advice, and no longer marched unsurrounded by a good number of officers. The costume of the marshal had been described even to the four stars he wore; and in order to be unrecognized he took off three of them, and retained only one on his uniform.

At Vire Charles X. was received at the château of Cotin, whose proprietor, M. Roger, did him the honors of his house with the greatest respect. The same day M. Odilon Barrot wrote to King Louis-Philippe: "Vire, August 11, 1830, 2 P.M. Sire, we arrived in this town about eleven o'clock, and have found this Bocage, so renowned in our civil dissensions. The passage of Charles X., which had been announced several days before, had brought the whole population out on the road; but we have

CONDÉ-SUR-NOIREAU AND VIRE

remarked not a single demonstration which could give us the least uneasiness. The tricolored flag was hoisted on the steeple of the smallest village. . . . We leave to-morrow. We shall refresh ourselves at Thorigny and sleep at Saint-Lo. Nine leagues. . . . We have been promised the journals every day; we have none. Yet it is important that we should be perfectly *au courant*, if it were merely for the sake of giving the proper impulse to those around us."

Charles X. remained very calm. At Vire he talked with the commissioners about his personal possessions, which, for that matter, did not amount to much. There was no question of depriving him of the savings he had deposited with a banker in Paris at the time of his accession to the throne. It was also recognized that the châteaux of Villeneuve-l'Étang and Rosny, bought under the Restoration, one by the Duchess of Angoulême, and the other by the Duchess of Berry, were the private property of these princesses. Charles X. exacted that an exact account of the expenses of his journey should be kept, so that he might repay it in full later on. Meanwhile, the commissioners desired that the sums he needed should be advanced to him. M. Odilon Barrot has said on this subject in his Memoirs: "Our insistence with our government to induce it to give a large indemnification to the interests of Charles X. did not arise solely from justice and humanity; it was good policy as well. King Louis-Philippe felt this on his part, and had no need of our incitations.

He was only too glad of this diversion; therefore he did not haggle about it, and not merely recognized all that was legitimate in the claims of Charles X., but even advanced him, on his funds, the sum of six hundred thousand francs, which Charles X. needed, and which were sent to him at Cherbourg. I have not verified whether this sum was repaid him by the Treasury. Charles X. was touched by this eagerness, and charged us to express his gratitude to his cousin ; but the Duchess of Berry, more severe and franker, could not refrain from a sarcastic shot. ' Yes,' said she, ' Louis-Philippe is only anxious about our clothes, and takes away our crown.' "

XXVI

SAINT-LO

THURSDAY morning, August 12, Charles X., followed by his family and his escort, went from Vire towards Saint-Lo. On leaving the department of Calvados he found, at the boundary of the department of La Manche, Count Joseph d'Estourmel, who came to meet him in an open carriage, in which were also seated General Count de Bourbon-Busset, Prince de Léon, and Prince de Bauffremont. Count d'Estourmel is the author of a very curious volume entitled: *Souvenirs de France et d'Italie dans les années 1830, 1831, et 1832.* He has related in a very interesting manner the incidents of the journey of Charles X. from August 12 to August 16, the day when the King and his family embarked at Cherbourg.

Counsellor of State, gentleman of the Chamber, prefect of La Manche, Count Joseph d'Estourmel was a devoted but liberal royalist. He had blamed the Ordinances, and when the news of them reached him he had at first desired to send in his resignation. But seeing the throne in danger, he remained at his post.

The Duke of Ragusa says: "At the frontier of the department of La Manche, we found its prefect, Count Joseph d'Estourmel, who had come at ordinary times to receive the King's orders, wearing the habit of a gentleman of the Chamber and a white cockade, when we had found the revolution an accomplished fact all along our road. He had declared himself against the Ordinances, and gave proof of courage and loyalty to the end. We lodged in his prefecture at Saint-Lo, and he accompanied the King as far as the ship."

Let us leave M. d'Estourmel to explain his honorable conduct for himself: "I had announced," he says, "my intention to go and join the King as soon as I knew he was about to enter the department whose administration he had confided to me. Not long since I might have regretted the complete lack of instructions in which I had been left; but at present, relieved of the responsibility which weighed upon me, and of the duties of a public man, I felt myself quite at liberty; and I had no need of ministerial instructions to follow the impulse of my heart, which inclined me to sympathize with and associate myself to great misfortunes. Nevertheless, I was far from blaming those who believed it their duty to act otherwise, for I find this thought strikingly true in its application: 'In times of revolution the most difficult thing is not to do one's duty, but to know what it is.' And independently of absolute duties, that noble chain which links man to the Divinity, there are relative ones which vary according to each one's situation. Without walking in parallel lines, we can each attain equally an honorable end, and we cannot be too suspicious of that disposition we have to judge the opinions of others by bringing them back to our exclusive point of view, nor, above all, can we guard ourselves too well from importing into political differences the hatred which should be inspired by vice only."

On arriving at the limit of the department, between Thorigny and Vire, M. d'Estourmel met Charles X. there. He respectfully approached the sovereign's carriage, asked for his orders, and gave him an account of the state of the department. The King, completely surprised that his prefect should have been allowed to come to him like this, manifested his satisfaction.

General Count de Bourbon-Busset, who accompanied M. d'Estourmel, was commander of the camp of Lunéville. He had married a daughter of the Duchess de Gontaut. Charles X. gave him an affectionate welcome. "At present," said he, "acquaint me with the details which are possibly unknown to me of the movements of the camp of Lunéville." A halt was made hereupon in the middle of a field. The Duchess of Angoulême and the Duchess of Berry sat down on the grass, having the Duke of Bordeaux and his sister beside them. The escort and the horses rested in the shadow of large trees. General Bourbon-Busset thus began his story: —

" On receiving a letter from my mother-in-law, written from Saint-Cloud, July 26, apprising me of the Ordinances, I immediately took measures so as to be able to start at the first summons, which I hoped soon to receive from Your Majesty. This order, through M. de Polignac's forgetfulness, was delayed for three mortal and precious days."

Here the King said with an impatient movement: " I know all that; go on."

The general continued his account: " Afterwards it was M. de Parazza who was enabled to come to me in disguise and with much difficulty. The camp, animated with the most ardent enthusiasm and hoping to save the King's cause, took up its march at once. The brigade of the advance-guard was already at the rising ground of Verdun and that of the centre, with which I was, at Saint-Mihiel, when I received a despatch from Baron de Damas, who enjoined me, without the King's signature, to obey the orders of the lieutenant-general of the realm. These orders were to return to Lunéville with all the troops of my command. Several confidential officers whom I had taken the precaution of sending to receive verbal orders from Your Majesty came at the same time to confirm this in the most positive manner. What was left for me to do? Could I refuse to obey the might of right and the might of fact, which in this unique circumstance were at one? No, doubtless; I must reject the suspicions and the voice of my heart which cried to me not to stop."

The King, painfully affected, and after a moment of profound silence, said to M. Bourbon-Busset: "What did you do then?" He answered: "I assembled the general officers and heads of divisions, and after making known to them the orders of Your Majesty and of the lieutenant-general of the realm, to make a retrograde movement on Lunéville with all the regiments of the camp, I prescribed the immediate execution of this movement, but with a particular recommendation to maintain the most rigorous discipline throughout the march, and to make their flags and cockades respected everywhere as far as Lunéville, where they would then find new leaders and new orders."

After this account — related in the Memoirs of the Duchess de Gontaut, who heard her son-in-law give it — Charles X., seeming painfully preoccupied, went away alone and pensive. The Duchess of Angoulême afterwards talked at length with General de Bourbon-Busset. She was weeping.

They set out again and went to dine at Thorigny, in the house of the mayor, M. de la Varignière. Charles X. took Count d'Estourmel aside, and said to him: "I have abdicated. Everything must now be reported to the Duke of Bordeaux. If people muster anywhere in his name, I will return at once." The prefect was tempted to reply: "If you think of coming back, why do you go away?" He saw the King's forehead flush when he confessed to him that he had started to send in his resignation on the reception of the Ordinances. " I did not see," he added, " the possibility of their execution." — " And yet," returned Charles X., " there was no way of doing otherwise." They went down into the dining-room of M. de la Varignière, where the royal family breakfasted, with the exception of the Dauphiness, who had walked on ahead. M d'Estourmel found her afterwards, seated beside a ditch with Madame de Saint-Maur and M. de Bourbon-Busset. She would not meet the commissioners.

After breakfast Charles X. went on from Thorigny to Saint-Lo, where he arrived the same day, Thursday, August 12. He lodged with his family at the prefecture. " Amidst circumstances so painful," says Count d'Estourmel, " it was a lively satisfaction to me to receive him there. Charles X. had consented to it because he knew he would find there no hearts not keenly affected by his ill-fortune, and that nothing would offend his eyes. In fact, I had obtained, when the flag was taken down, that it should not be replaced."

M. d'Estourmel adds to his recital : "August 12, evening. After dinner they walked in the garden, into which a few curious persons had made their way. The King is always noble, affectionate, and polished ; the Dauphin inexplicable. In looking at the Dauphiness, a saying of Tacitus recurred to me : *Experti invicem sumus ego et fortuna.* She is strong and resigned. The Duchess of Berry, agitated and courageous. The poor children are charming. The

demeanor of all who accompany the King is appro-
priate. It is painful to behold the Duke of Ragusa.
His fatality is written on his forehead. He commands the troop forming the escort, but one may say
the King guards him rather than that he guards the
King. Partiality, let us say injustice rather, is very
great towards him. I could never have believed in
the scene at Saint-Cloud between him and the Dauphin, if he had not just now assured me of its reality.
He gives me curious details of the three days: his
interview with MM. Laffitte and Périer, his urgency
with Charles X. I shall repeat none of this story,
because the marshal has told me he means to publish
it as soon as he leaves France. It seems that nothing
can equal the indecision, disorder, and carelessness
which have presided over all resolutions ever since
the Ordinances."

Count d'Estourmel remarks that they were prepared
neither for combat nor for flight. He says: "The
Duchess of Berry is without chemises. At Rambouillet she had preferred to wear men's clothes.
Always energetic, she dreamed of nothing but the
Vendée, of rides and musket-shots; perhaps she flattered herself that some one would come to deliver
her on the road, and she wanted to be ready to run
all risks. All that would have been excellent in the
Middle Ages. The King was surprised and displeased to see her in this costume, and at Saint-Lo
she was persuaded to put on women's clothes again;
but she had brought only men's shirts, and thence

arose the necessity of borrowing others from my
wife."

Charles X. slept tranquilly at the prefecture as if
he were still reigning, and without the tricolored flag,
which was odious to him, floating above his head.
But, just as he was taking a little repose before continuing his sorrowful journey, alarming news reached
Saint-Lo and caused the prefect and the commissioners keen anxieties.

XXVII

THIS was the night of Thursday–Friday, August 12–13. The commissioners had just gone to bed at Saint-Lo, when they received from Generals Hulot and Proteau some despatches which alarmed them seriously. The first commanded the department of La Manche. The second had been charged to keep the road clear along which Charles X. was journeying, especially on the Brittany side, and to march parallel with him, but so as to disguise his movements and not show his soldiers. The two generals announced that at Carentan there was a great gathering of troops and national guards. General Hulot had received an order from Paris to advance to meet Charles X., as much to hasten the march of the convoy as to safeguard it. These instructions had been given by the new government under the influence of the anxiety produced in official circles by the delays of the journey, and those false terrors which the commissioners had so much ado to dispel. "What proves it," says M. Odilon Barrot, "is a passage in the letter sent us by General Hulot, August 11, in which he commands us to write to him *if we were free*.

General Proteau acquainted us, on his side, with the movement of General Hulot at the head of six battalions of the line, national guards from various cities, and six pieces of cannon: he was himself ordered to go to the junction of the roads from Carentan to Saint-Lo and Bayeux. What disquieted us most in these despatches was the excitement of the national guards and their refusal to obey the orders of the general who had commanded them to retire. The body-guards would not voluntarily yield up their post. A conflict would become inevitable."

A gendarmerie report augmented the uneasiness of the commissioners. This report, dated from Carentan, at eleven o'clock at night, August 12, announced that the town was thronged with national guards from Cherbourg and its environs, whose intention it was to force the King's escort to retreat. The commissioners received this report at three in the morning, and they were not to set out again until three hours later. They sent a liberal deputy from Calvados, M. de la Pommeraie, to Carentan to prevent a mishap. M. de la Pommeraie induced General Hulot to withdraw with his troops. But very excited groups of national guards remained at Carentan.

Friday, August 13, they left Saint-Lo at five in the morning. The weather was rainy and dark. The commissioners preceded the escort. By eight o'clock in the morning, they were at Carentan. The convoy, whose rate of speed they had recommended to be lessened, were not to arrive until towards noon.

They found groups of national guards posted along the road, inspecting all passing carriages, and declaring loudly that they would do the same with those of the royal family, under the pretext that they might contain Prince de Polignac, the object of popular hatred. A bishop who was on his way to meet Charles X. had just been arrested. The commissioners had him released, and made efforts to tranquillize the people. "These worthy people had been persuaded," says M. Théodore Anne, body-guard of the Noailles company, "that the King was arriving with the Swiss, without us. Hence they had come with the intention of respecting the safe-conduct Charles X. held from the government, but determined to serve as his *sole* escort to his vessel, not being willing that the Swiss should go any further; and I even think they would have been very glad if we had been stopped there. In case the King would not accede to this proposition, they had determined to prevent our passage and defend themselves in Carentan, a little town, once fortified, being all the better able to defend themselves from an attack since we were only cavalry, and they had cannon, while we had none."

The commissioners succeeded in soothing this disquieting agitation. They took care to remain among the people, who formed a double line through which passed the royal family. Mingled with the curious crowd, M. Odilon Barrot, on foot, beheld this sad and solemn march which came forward slowly, amid pro-

found silence, through this barely tranquillized crowd.
Listen to his story of it: "The first carriages that
appeared were those containing the Duke. of Bordeaux and his sister. These children had been taught
in their days of grandeur to smile and salute the
crowd whenever they appeared in public. They had
not been told to abandon this practice since their sad
dethronement, and when people saw these two charming little blond heads appearing at the carriage doors
and waving kisses to right and left, there was a general movement of compassion. Men muttered below
their breath in their simple way: 'They are very
pretty all the same, these poor innocents!' and women
wept. Hostility had given way in an instant to a
lively and universal interest. That is the way the
people are made. They have the naïveté and fluc-
tuating impressions of childhood. A few hours
earlier they would not have hesitated to fling themselves into a bloody conflict, and now they were
ready to bow before this ill-fortune which assumed
before their eyes the shape of infancy with its innocence and grace."

It had been decided the previous day, to sleep at
Carentan; but after the threatening news transmitted
during the night, it was resolved not to stop in this
town, but to go on to Valognes. The distance was
fourteen leagues; Charles X. had consented this time
to impose a somewhat greater fatigue on his escort in
order to avoid Carentan.

During the journey to Valognes the populations,

which had been described in advance as very hostile
to the King and anxious to impede his progress by
force, under pretext that he was going to Cherbourg
to deliver that port to the English, showed, on the
contrary, the most lively sympathy for the royal
family. The cortège made a halt between Sainte-
Mère-Église and Montebourg. Charles X. appeared
particularly affected by the welcome he received in
this part of his dolorous journey. The thought of
going into exile when they were still receiving so
many proofs of devotion and fidelity caused profound
emotion in the Duchess of Angoulême and the
Duchess of Berry. The daughter of Louis XVI.
was greatly agitated. She frequently left the carriage, walked a few paces, stopped, sat down by the
roadside, entered the carriage anew, and then again
alighted. Nor could the Duchess of Berry, naturally
ardent and courageous, reconcile herself more easily
to the King's speedy abandonment of the struggle.
The spectacle that presented itself at Montebourg,
two leagues on the hither side of Valognes, increased
the regret of the two Princesses. A great many
peasants from the surrounding country had come to
meet the King. As soon as the escort appeared, all
hats were doffed. The royal family was asked to
stop for an instant and alight from the carriages.
They consented. Acclamations resounded. Some
of the peasants said: " They have forbidden us to
shout; but we defy the prohibition. Long live the
King! Long live the Bourbons! Long live the Duke

of Bordeaux!" The women shed torrents of tears.
One of them said to the young Prince: "Come back,
my beautiful child, come back soon; we are waiting
for you; you will find us faithful." The little Prince
held out his hand. It was covered with kisses. The
emotion of the peasants won the Duchess of Berry.
She was unwilling to part from these honest people
whose fidelity consoled her for so many griefs. "Let
us stay here," she cried; "let us cling fast to a tree,
to a post, but for God's sake let us not go any further."
Nevertheless they started on again, and that evening
reached Valognes, the last station before Cherbourg,
— Cherbourg, where the exile was to begin.

XXVIII

VALOGNES

CHARLES X. and his escort reached Valognes on Friday, August 13, towards six o'clock in the evening. At the entrance of the town, the convoy passed slowly through the long street which in 1827 had been carpeted with flowers and foliage for the coming of the Dauphiness, each of whose journeys was then a triumph. This pleasing souvenir in a day of evil fortune returned to the memory of the Orphan of the Temple, and alighting from the carriage she wept.

The town was full of people and of animation. The whole population had come out to meet the King, some drawn by sympathy, others by curiosity; there was no disorder, no shouting, not a hostile word.

The royal family lodged in the beautiful house of M. de Mesnildot, an ancient dwelling whose souvenirs are historic. It was there that the Empress Marie Louise had alighted, in August, 1813, when she went to Cherbourg to preside at the opening of the great dock. James II. had passed the first night of his exile in France at this house, and it was under the same roof that Charles X., the French James II., reposed for the last time in his kingdom before commencing his eternal exile.

It was known that the King would take ship at Cherbourg, but the place of his debarkation was not yet fixed. Charles X. had at first designated Ostend. On the formal interdiction of this port by the French government, he chose Amsterdam. A new despatch from Paris having extended its interdiction to all ports of Belgium and Holland, he fell back on Hamburg. This also was prohibited, and he was then induced to consent to a landing at Portsmouth.

There remained another question to be settled. Was Charles X. to be transported by French vessels or by foreign ones? He had made known to the British government his desire to sail in English vessels; but that government had refused, fearing to displease the new power in France. As to French ships, the King would not hear of them, the notion of sailing under a tricolored flag being so odious to him. A compromise was adopted. It was decided that Charles X. and his suite should embark on American vessels chartered by the French government. The captains and crew would be subject to French authority, but the vessels would not carry the tricolored flag. In the view of Charles X. this was the only essential matter.

Finally, it was necessary to determine the number of persons who would embark with the royal family and follow them into exile. Charles X. had talked of two or three hundred persons, exclusive of domestics. At Valognes, these courtiers of misfortune were reduced to sixty or seventy, and at Cherbourg their number was to diminish still further. As has been remarked by M. Odilon Barrot, only a few of those friendships, always rare, which are impervious to all shocks, were about to brave the sorrows of exile.

Duke Victor de Broglie remarks in his *Souvenirs*, concerning the events of 1830: "When one has taken service under a government, and has faithfully, loyally, fulfilled his duties toward it up to the last, if this government falls, either by its own fault, or by accident, he is at quits with it; he is free to contract a new engagement, and the best way, in such a case, is to do so openly and at once; delays, transitions, are affairs of personal prudence, and, perhaps, smack of hypocrisy rather than of honor and probity." The noble duke concludes thus: "As a general proposition, in politics there is doubtless nothing better, nothing more important, than to remain faithful to one's principles, one's cause, and one's friends; but nothing is more stupid than to sacrifice good sense to Mrs. Grundy. 'Madame,' said a waiting-maid of much good sense to her mistress, who was in despair and refused all nourishment, 'if you must eat one of these days, why not to-day?'"

We do not defend this thesis, but in 1830 it certainly had numerous adherents. As always happens, those whose protestations of fidelity to Charles X., during the prosperous period of his reign, had been loudest and most enthusiastic, were the first to abandon him in misfortune.

The old King might have made sad reflections on human nature, but he would not admit that he had erred in publishing the fatal Ordinances. "Don't you see," he said to General de Bourbon-Busset, "that there was nothing else to do? We should have to come to that anyway; the blow of the revolutionists was aimed." — "But, Sire," replied the general, "it could have been parried." — "No; don't believe that; this comes from the notions of your journals and salons."

Count Joseph d'Estourmel vainly asked from Charles X. a written testimonial of satisfaction. "I render justice to your conduct," said the King to him; "it is honorable; but you committed a serious fault when, in the proclamations you published on resigning your functions, you laid blame on the Ordinances, calling them fatal, and, above all, illegal; possibly they were extra-legal, but I cannot admit that they were illegal." — "Sire," returned Count d'Estourmel, "I said that the Ordinances were fatal; what could I adduce in support of that assertion? The facts speak for themselves; as to illegality, if I permitted myself to qualify thus the act of the King, it is because I adhere to the principle of ministerial responsibility, as Your Majesty has been able to see in my letter of August 3, written, I may say, under the enemy's fire." "It is all the same; it should not have been said." — "But, Sire,

such is my opinion, and it is above all to the manner
in which I expressed it that I owe the regard with
which I am still surrounded and the influence I have
retained, the effects of which the King has been able
to remark since he has been in the department. If I
had supported the ministerial system, do you think,
Sire, that on this 14th of August I should be near
your person, and that I should have been allowed to
go with my white cockade, and my coat embroidered
with lilies, to meet Your Majesty at the boundary of
this department, and escort you as I have done now
that the Revolution has been accomplished for a fort-
night? My devotion has been respected on account
of my having made known my opinion of the Ordinances." — "I know that you are doing all that you
can; I see that all goes well along the route. If
everywhere in France people had the same affection
for me that was displayed at Montebourg, I would
not be obliged to embark. But you should not have
found fault with the Ordinances. There were not
two roads for me to take. The event has proved it,
and it would have come to that a little later on; I
say to you just what I think." — "Sire, I have also
said what I thought, and the three lines of approbation which I flattered myself I might obtain would
have satisfied my heart, which is afflicted by such a
refusal."

Count d'Estourmel, after having related this conversation between the King and himself, adjoins the
following reflection: "So it was that a functionary

whose conduct, I may say, had been so honest, who
had been the last of this party to make the royal
authority respected in France, who had hastened to
meet Charles X. when so many men were flying from
him, and who, at this moment, as prefect, as council-
lor of State, and as gentleman of the Chamber, found
himself by force of circumstances almost the sole
person of his robe who was near him, could not obtain a voluntary testimonial of satisfaction, because
he had described as fatal and illegal the Ordinances
which had ruined the dynasty."

M. d'Estourmel went to the Duchess de Gontaut
to hide his chagrin. In order to console him, she
told him that, a few days before, the King, at the
close of a very animated political discussion, grew
angry with her, and said she deserved " to be sent
into exile." — " If I could only go there alone now !"
added the Duchess, with a sigh.

Charles X. was permitted to remain at Valognes
until August 16, the day when he was to embark at
Cherbourg. Meanwhile, the commissioners went to
that city to satisfy themselves as to the measures
taken in view of the departure. After this inspection
they returned to Valognes, where the King had completed all his preparations. They found him less sad
and more expansive than on the preceding days,
either because he now felt himself delivered from the
apprehensions he had entertained during his journey,
or because the religious resignation which sustained
him in this rude trial was receiving a new strength
as it approached its dénouement.

In his relations with the commissioners Charles X. had always shown a benevolent and dignified, yet cold and reserved, politeness. "Perhaps," M. Odilon Barrot has said, "his speech with me had a little more freedom and familiarity, on account of my youth, and especially because, having never been attached to his government by any link whatever, I seemed to him, with his ideas of fidelity and loyalty, less burdened than my colleagues with the reproach of treason. Sometimes he had even carried this freedom so far as to talk with me about the Revolution, a subject on which he generally declined all conversation. 'I had no choice,' he said to me; 'the Ordinances were an imperious and absolute necessity. Once started on the declivity of concessions, and there is no stopping. I had my brother's example before my eyes; I like better to mount a horse than a tumbrel. Besides, I knew all the threads of the conspiracy that had been contrived, and as to which I merely took the initiative; I could name to you the banker who paid for all this popular movement.'"

M. Barrot made some respectful objections. He sought to prove that but for the Ordinances the throne would not have been shaken. But, even while he listened with indulgent attention, the commissioner could see well enough by Charles X.'s half smile, and the liftings of his head, that the lessons given to the King by events had profited him so little that he would be all ready to begin anew.

"And yet," adds M. Barrot, "it was in one of these

effusive moments, and when we had just acquainted
him with the measures we had taken to secure for
him and his suite all the security and ease he could
desire, that he addressed us in these words: 'We
are soon to part, gentlemen. I experience the need
of thanking you for the cares with which you have
surrounded me in circumstances at once so painful
and so perilous.'"

Marshal Maison thought this a favorable moment
for risking a sort of personal apology. "Be assured,
Sire," said he to Charles X., "that I would not have
assumed the mission I have fulfilled near Your
Majesty if I had not seen in it the occasion to prove
to you my devotion and my gratitude." — "We will
not speak of that," returned Charles X. drily, and he
turned away.

"The word 'gratitude,'" says M. Barrot, "had just
reminded the old King that Marshal Maison had
received the baton of a marshal of France from his
hand, and it was painful to see him among his adversaries, even and perhaps especially in the character
of a protector. Strange and singular coincidence!
In 1814 it was General Maison who, as commander
of the military division of the North, had given his
hand to Louis XVIII., when he landed at Calais.
It was the same man, now become a marshal, who
was to give his hand to Charles X., embarking at
Cherbourg. It is comprehensible that all these souvenirs should throw some coolness, and even severity,
over the relations of Charles X. with Marshal Maison,

who, on his part, felt this himself and avoided these relations as far as was compatible with the require-' ments of his duties."

The King seemed to have nothing more to fear until his embarkation, but it was otherwise with Marshal Marmont. It was said that if he were not massacred on the way, he would fall at Cherbourg. "These rumors acquired great strength at Valognes," he has written in his Memoirs. "They said I was the price of the King's liberty, and that he would not be allowed to embark until he had surrendered me. I could not suppose any ulterior design in the deposi- taries of power, but I might fear a popular movement. A former body-guard, a proprietor in the environs, offered to assure my safety. I thanked him. It was proposed to me, and the commissioners themselves, as on a previous occasion, tried to induce me to lay aside my uniform and not show myself. . . . I declared that, as I was commander, I could remain at my post with the guards and not put off my uniform until I was on board ship."

The commissioners had at first decided that the body-guards should leave Charles X. at Valognes. Marshal Marmont represented to them in lively fash- ion that the King owed it to his military household not to separate from them until the moment when the earth should fail under his feet. After the conduct of the body-guards this was a deserved testimony of esteem and affection, and for them a question of honor. Moreover, in passing through Cherbourg with

a simple escort, nothing guaranteed him from an
insult or some attack, while six hundred determined
men, well armed and marching in serried ranks, would
impose a salutary fear on the population. " The
body-guards," says M. Odilon Barrot, "entreated us,
through their leaders, to permit them to accompany
the King up to the moment of the embarkation. We
did not think it our duty to prevent them from giving
their master this last proof of a fidelity we could not
but honor. Simply, we had to take some measures
to prevent any conflict between the seafaring population, the warmth of whose opinions was well known
to us and the guards." It was decreed that the
enclosure of the military port of Cherbourg should be
rigorously closed, that only Charles X., his suite, and
the four companies of body-guards should enter it,
and that the guards should return to Valognes
immediately after the embarkation. The moment
of farewells was approaching. A touching ceremony
was in preparation for Sunday, August 15, feast of
the Assumption.

XXIX

AUGUST FIFTEENTH

CHARLES X., in spite of his afflictions, still enjoyed the happiness of being in France. Each day he passed there was a day stolen from that exile which was to endure as long as his life. With a soul tranquil and free from remorse, he found an efficacious consolation in prayer, and submitted with resignation to the decrees of Providence. On Sunday, August 15, 1830, the royal family, who were to depart for a foreign land the next day, thanked God who had granted them the grace of celebrating once more on French soil the feast of the Mother of the Saviour.

"August 15, at six o'clock in the morning," says Count Joseph d'Estourmel, "I entered the church at Valognes. A woman was kneeling on the altar steps in the attitude of most fervent prayer, wholly absorbed in God whom she had just received. When she returned to her place I recognized the Dauphiness. Poor daughter of Saint Louis! on the next day she was to be led for the third time into a land of exile; but the recompense cannot fail her, and whatever happens, Marie Thérèse has chosen the better part."

An hour later, the Duchess of Berry came to kneel in
the same place. Both the daughter of Louis XVI.
and the widow of the assassinated Prince had great
need of prayer. The one left behind her in France
the ashes of her father and her mother; the other,
the remains of her husband and the cradle of her
children.

Charles X., who did not go out during his sojourn
at Valognes, heard Mass at the house of M. de Mesnildot, whose dining-room was transformed into a
chapel after breakfast. The Duchess of Angoulême
made the Latin responses to the priest when he came
to the *Exaudiat.*

It is eleven o'clock in the morning. The trumpets
are sounding. One might say they are those of the
funeral of the ancient monarchy. When they become
silent, the measured tramp of men under arms re-
sounds like iron on the pavement. These are the
brave body-guards who are coming to deliver up
their standards to the unfortunate King. The gendarmes *de chasse*, on duty at the outer gate, unfasten
the wicket besieged by a curious crowd, and admit the
column of body-guards, who march four abreast, the
officers and the standards in front, and in as trim
array as on the days when they crossed the court
of the Carrousel to enter the King's apartments in
the Tuileries.

The Duke de Luxembourg and Prince de Croï were
in advance, the commander's baton in hand. Here

in the group of superior officers are MM. de Bon-
neval, du Roure, de Sainte-Aldegonde, Ducosquer,
de Naylico, de La Maisonfort, de Fraguier, de Bize-
mont, de Lucinge. Here is the venerable Count de
Pellan, who, in spite of his great age, has determined
to accomplish his duty to the very end. Each of the
four companies — companies de Croï, de Gramont, de
Noailles, de Luxembourg — is introduced according
to its seniority of rank into the salon where Charles
X. and the royal family are. The standard of the de
Croï company is carried by M. Dumesnil, that of the
de Gramont by M. de Brancion, that of de Noailles
by M. de Chabrignac, that of de Luxembourg by M.
de Suze. Each standard is escorted by the six oldest
guards of each company.

Charles X. has left off the uniform in which they
have seen him for so long   He wears a blue frock
coat with metal buttons, without star or decoration.
He holds his grandson by the hand. At his right is
the Duchess of Angoulême.

Tears were flowing from every eye. "Come, my
friends," says the old King; "calm yourselves; must
it be I that shall console you?"

Every standard comes forward in its turn.

"Gentlemen," exclaims the King, "I take these
standards; you have known how to preserve them
spotless; I hope that one day my grandson may have
the happiness to return them to you."

An eye-witness of this scene, which, according to the
remark of Count d'Estourmel, recalls, due proportion

being observed, the heroic adieux of Fontainebleau,—
M. Mazas, has said: "As soon as the return of the
standards had been effected, the ranks broke up; the
princes found themselves surrounded on all sides; in
the twinkling of an eye there prevailed a confusion
round them which, certainly, they did not find dis-
pleasing. Voices rose; one could hear an exchange
of testimonies of devotion, and of congratulation on
the splendid conduct of the body-guards up to the
present. What a touching spectacle, to see that
child, the heir of so many kings, passing from hand
to hand and receiving the embrace of arms so faithful! The Duke of Bordeaux will never lose the
memory of a day like that, for his young mind was
already too formed to leave him insensible to such
transports. The King, the Dauphin, the two princesses, found for each of the guards an affectionate
word stamped with feeling. I heard Mademoiselle
say to an officer of the body-guards whom I did not
know, and who bent down to listen to her: ' Are you
coming with us? ' This question contracted the
countenance of the officer. He remained dumb-
founded. I could not catch the words he murmured."

Charles X. exclaimed: "I cannot tell you how
much I am affected; your conduct has been very
fine, very devoted; I shall never forget you; I know
all of you. Tell your comrades that I should like to
bid each of them adieu by name. Do you undertake
to do this for me. We must let the storm pass over;
but we shall see each other again." Similar words

were addressed to the remnant of the royal guard and
to the *gendarmes des chasses,* worthily commanded
by Baron d'André (who since died marquis, senator,
and general of division). Count d'Estourmel, who
also witnessed this scene, thus expresses himself:
"The old soldiers wept; it was a universal sobbing;
they kissed the King's hands and those of the Duke
of Bordeaux. Charles X. observed me in the crowd;
I was very much affected. He saw it, and held out
his hand to me, which I laid on my heart. 'People
show themselves very well disposed in your department,' said he; 'I was touched with the reception
given me at Saint-Lo. Here it is wonderful, as it
was at Montebourg.'"

In the evening there was sent to each of the body-
guards, by order of Charles X., a copy of the following document: —

"Order of the day: —
"The King, on quitting French territory, would
like to be able to give each of the body-guards and
each of the officers and soldiers who have accompanied him as far as his vessel, a proof of his attachment and his remembrance. But the circumstances
which afflict the King do not permit him to listen to
the voice of his heart. Deprived of the means of
recognizing a fidelity so touching, His Majesty has
had sent to him the muster-rolls of the companies of
his body-guards, also those of the staff of the general
officers, and those of the subaltern officers and soldiers who have followed him. Their names, pre-

served by the Duke of Bordeaux, will remain inscribed in the archives of the royal family, to attest forever both the misfortunes of the King and the consolations he found in so disinterested a devotion.

"CHARLES.

"VALOGNES, August 15, 1830.

　"*The Major-General,*
　　"Marshal DUKE OF RAGUSA.

　"For copy conformable to the original:
　"*The Captain of the Guards,* etc."

And lower down:

　"By order of the King,
　"*To M. . . . body-guard of the company of* . . . ."

Marshal Marmont, Duke of Ragusa, has thus appraised this document: "The order of the day, a certified copy of which was given to every individual present, became by the circumstance a title of family. Never had a corps manifested a more admirable spirit. Order, respect, and devotedness reigned to the very end. No unreasonable demands had been urged. When, at the opening of this sad campaign, rations and money had been insufficient, the body-guards refused to be served before the troops, whose needs, said they, were still more pressing than their own. I wish I were able to express to each body-guard of the four companies all my admiration for their noble conduct."

After the distribution of the order of the day, Charles X. wrote to the King of England and the

Emperor of Austria, to ask their hospitality. M.
Mazas, as secretary to Baron de Damas, was charged
with re-copying the two letters. "An antique simplicity," says he, "reigned in every expression.
There was in them neither a complaint against fortune nor a regret for the past. In his letter addressed
to William IV., the King asked a temporary asylum
for himself and his family. He spoke of his *poor
grandchildren* in such a touching manner that I was
most profoundly affected, so that my tears dropped
on the original from which I was copying. I dried
the paper as best I could, but was not wholly success-
ful, so that when the King of Great Britain opened
the letter of his brother, the King of France, he
might still have seen the marks of the tears of a
faithful Frenchman."

At Valognes, Charles X. and the royal family felt
themselves enveloped in an atmosphere of sympathy,
compassion, and respect. The windows and roofs of
the houses neighboring that of M. de Mesnildot were
thronged with curious persons anxious to catch a
glimpse of the princes. The Duke of Bordeaux and
his sister showed themselves several times at the
window. Their graces allured the crowd. Little
Mademoiselle was charming with her fair locks neg-
ligently knotted on top of her head, and her summer
dress striped in white and pink. The Duchess of
Berry often came to look at her son and daughter
and embraced them with transports of tenderness.

During the day the two children were heard chatting: "I am sure," said Mademoiselle, "that we shall come back in two years." Then some one would exclaim: "In two years! I do not doubt, Mademoiselle, that we shall have the happiness of seeing you again at the end of six months."

At this moment a smile of incredulity appeared upon the lips of the Duke of Bordeaux. His under-tutor, M. de Barande noticed it, and said: "And you, little lord, what is your opinion? Will you bind yourself to return at the end of the Olympiad?" — "The Olympiad!" responded the young Prince after a moment's reflection. "Ah! I know, four years! Eh! well, yes; nobody could be better satisfied than I if I were sure we were to return in four years!"

In the evening, Count d'Estourmel came to see the daughter of the Duchess of Berry. The pretty child gave him some of her hair, which she cut off for that express purpose, and then some of her brother's, adding a flower for Madame d'Estourmel. Viscount Hocquart, who acted as chief steward, said to the little Princess: "You will return to France, Mademoiselle, you will dine here again, and I swear on my honor that I will serve you with your first breakfast."

XXX

CHERBOURG

ON Monday, August 16, the royal family rose at
five o'clock in the morning. They were to
start for Cherbourg and had but a few minutes longer
to spend upon the soil of France. On awaking, the
Duke of Bordeaux went down on his knees. "I have
been present many a time when the Prince was at his
prayers in the Tuileries or at Saint-Cloud," says M.
Alexandre Mazas, "but never did I join with such
fervor in the petitions of those who were present at
these pious exercises. How affected was my heart
at seeing the young Henri praying God for the last
time on the soil of his native land!"

The prayer was ended when an officer of the body-
guards came to announce to Baron de Damas that
Charles X. desired the presence of the Duke of Bordeaux in order that he might assist at the presenta-
tion of the *gendarmerie des chasses*, which was about
to take place. This body, designated also as *gendarmerie d'élite*, was then composed of a total of one
hundred and seventy-seven gendarmes, forty-three
subaltern officers, and eight officers, commanded by
Colonel d'André. It had acted as rear guard in

every march since leaving Rambouillet, and had
bivouacked every night around the lodging of the
King. Wishing to give this select body a testimonial
of his satisfaction, he had ordered Colonel d'André
to present to him not merely the officers, but also
the subalterns, and, placing himself in the midst of
the circle, with the Dauphin, the Dauphiness, the
Duchess of Berry, and the Duke of Bordeaux, he thus
expressed himself: "I wished to see you, my friends;
I am grateful for your devotion. You have fulfilled
to the end and faithfully a very painful service."
Then he took the hand of each of these brave soldiers
without excepting one. Listen once more to M.
Mazas, a witness of this scene: "One of the subalterns who seemed most affected was Quartermaster
Cleret, a veteran of the Empire; he was present
at Napoleon's farewells at Fontainebleau and followed
the great man to the island of Elba. His fidelity
to his masters obtained him much celebrity. What
reflections he must have made within himself on
comparing the two events of which fate had made
him an eye-witness! In his retirement, Cleret could
tell his children whether thrones are fragile."

The royal family left Valognes toward ten o'clock
in the morning. The courtyard of the house was
filled with spectators; the wicket, thronged with a
mass of villagers, could hardly be opened; all countenances wore an expression not simply of curiosity,
but of sympathy; the neighboring windows and roofs
were packed. Charles X. found M. de Mesnildot at

the foot of the grand staircase. "Ah, sir," he said to him, "I have been looking for you this long time." And he thanked him warmly for the hospitality he had received.

"This was the most painful day of all," says M. Théodore Anne. "We were about to attain the end of our journey; a few hours more and our task would be completed. The farther we advanced in the days of this dolorous escort, the less could I persuade myself of the reality of our position. It seemed to me that all that was passing was a dream. It was impossible for me to get it into my head that the monarchy was destroyed, that Paris had been for three days at the mercy of fire and sword, and that the Bourbons were once more leaving France. When the King passed in front of us, his costume recalled me to the truth. Until then His Majesty had marched in the uniform he had worn since his accession to the throne : a blue coat, cut military fashion, with two big gold epaulettes surmounted by the royal crown, the cross of an officer of the Legion of Honor, that of Saint Louis, and the star of the Order of the Holy Ghost. To-day the King had laid aside these badges and put on a citizen's coat. It was the same with Monsieur the Dauphin, who had merely a red ribbon in his button-hole. The King had none.

"On the steps Charles X. stopped for a moment and looked kindly at the crowd. The Duchess of Berry was leaning on the arm of M. de Brissac, a veritable *chevalier* of honor, with whom loyalty was

even a religion. Great tears were flowing from the
eyes of the Duchess of Angoulême. The body-
guards marched four abreast. The King's carriage,
into which the Dauphin and the Duke of Bordeaux
had entered, was placed between two sections of the
guards. The Duke de Luxembourg, Prince de Croï,
a lieutenant of guards, and Colonel d'André were on
horseback at the carriage doors. The four companies of body-guards marched in their order of seniority. That of Croï was at the head of the column,
and that of Luxembourg on the left. A detachment
of *gendarmes d'élite* cleared the way, and the remainder of the two squadrons acted as rear guards.
Marshal Marmont was in the centre of a group of
officers of all arms; the population of the town and
the neighboring villages continued to salute the
exiles with respect.

When they were nearly half-way, a short halt was
made. The King, the Dauphin, the Duchess of
Berry, the Duke of Bordeaux and his sister alighted
to chat a moment. Presently the call "to horse!"
was sounded. Those who had alighted returned to
their ranks. Charles X. and the princes re-entered
their carriages, and they were about to set off when
the Dauphiness, who had walked a little in advance,
and had stopped in a farmhouse with Madame de Saint-
Maur, regained the cortège. The body-guards thought
the Princess was about to enter her carriage. They
had already ranged their horses so as to give her place
when she exclaimed: "No! no! I am going to enter

the King's carriage." She wished to be near her uncle and to share the danger he might incur if, as they had room to suppose, they found threatening dispositions at Cherbourg. The carriage step was let down, and the royal family found themselves all together.

At the summit of the hill which must be descended to arrive at Cherbourg they caught sight of the sea on the horizon. At the foot of the hill, at the entrance of the city, a movement of hesitation was noted at the head of the column. The guards of the de Croï company halted. Marquis de Courbon, major of guards, hastened to the door of the King's carriage. "Well, what is the matter?" exclaimed the King.—"Sire, a rather large crowd has assembled at the foot of the hill, but no hostile intentions are manifested." — "Keep on marching," replied the King.

A deputation of the National Guard had just come up to the advance guard, assuring them that if they did not put on the tricolored cockade before entering, they would not be responsible for the consequences. "The die was cast," Marshal Marmont has said in his Memoirs. "To go on was the only thing to do, and we continued our march. I believed in a catastrophe, and that this proceeding was the prelude and pretext for it; but the noble bearing of the body-guards awed them. They saw it would be unsafe to meddle with such men. . . . I was very glad I had insisted on bringing the King's whole household to the place

of embarkation. To this caution alone we owe our
having ended our journey fortunately."

At the entrance of Cherbourg they met a captain
of the 64th line, who was not on duty. The officer,
seeing the King pass by, took off his shako by a sudden movement and put it behind him, so as to hide
the tricolored cockade he was wearing from Charles X.

It takes nearly three-quarters of an hour to go from
the city barrier to the port, skirting along the sea-
shore. During this passage, the crowd bordering the
roadsides made no disagreeable manifestations. The
only thing was that certain individuals shouted:
"Down with the white cockade!" At every little
distance detachments of the 64th line were drawn up
in battle array. Officers were seen to lower their
swords and put their points to the ground in sign of
mourning. Before reaching the port, the cortège
passed within fifty paces of a little obelisk raised in
memory of the disembarkation of the Duke of Berry,
in 1814.

The nearer they came to the military port, the larger
grew the groups of people. The crowd, in which,
along with the marine workingmen, were many com-
mercial travellers and persons foreign to Normandy,
became noisy and excited. Nevertheless they succeeded in passing without accidents through the grat-
ing that separates the city from the military port.
The 64th line facilitated the passage of the royal family and the escort, and closed the wicket brusquely as
soon as the last platoon had entered.

The four companies of body-guards then drew up in line, facing the sea. The carriages stopped in front of a little bridge covered with some blue material, and the royal family alighted. The weather was magnificent, and the sun illuminated this doleful scene with all its splendors. The commissioners had just made a final inspection of the vessels, and standing with uncovered heads, they awaited the exiles, to assist them to embark. "That was a moment of universal emotion," says M. Odilon Barrot, "when we beheld descending this old man, upon whom so many misfortunes had weighed without taking away the graces of his youth, and without troubling that serenity of soul given him, amidst his most cruel trials, by his sincere and profound beliefs. Emotion was redoubled, and the sobbing broke out again all around us, when the Duchess of Angoulême alighted after him, clothed in those mourning robes which she had never laid aside, — that holy woman to whom Providence had not spared a single affliction. Then came a young child, and at sight of him, a shudder made itself felt in the midst of this crowd of exiles.

"The body-guards," continues M. Odilon Barrot, "discharged their weapons, yet without uttering a cry. M. de Clermont-Tonnerre seized this child with a sort of exaltation, and showed him to the spectators before carrying him to the ship. The Duchess of Berry came next. We followed them, ourselves profoundly moved by this scene which the genius of some great artist should transmit to pos-

terity, if only as a striking lesson for peoples and
for kings."

The departure of Charles X. had been calculated
in the morning on the tidal hour. All the baggage
had been taken aboard the previous day. As soon
as he descended from his carriage, the King could
go on board the *Great Britain.* The installation was
accomplished. The Dauphin followed, holding the
Duke of Bordeaux by the hand; the Duchess de
Gontaut led Mademoiselle; the Duchess of Berry
leaned on the arm of M. de Charette, the Duchess
of Angoulême on that of M. de La Rochejaquelein.
Afterwards came: the Duke de Luxembourg, Marshal Duke de Ragusa, Baron de Damas, governor of
the Duke of Bordeaux, the two under-governors, and
the tutor of the young Prince, all of whom were to
sail on the *Great Britain.* The second ship, the
Charles Carroll, received the other members of the
suite, notably, Duke Armand de Polignac, M.
Ogherty, Madame de Bouillé, M. Alfred de Damas,
M. Emmanuel de Brissac.

The new government had desired that Marshal
Maison should follow the King until he landed on
English territory. It had so written to the commissioners; but the latter thought it impossible to obey
this injunction, and responded by the following despatch: "Impossible to embark Marshal Maison.
Engagement made with the King: no national cockade on his ship. The marshal cannot leave it off,
representing his sovereign and France before a foreign

crew. Moreover, the presence of the marshal could
no longer be classed under the title of *safeguard*, but
of *keeper*. Now, this is not our mission. We accepted
no rôle but that of *safeguards*. We presented ourselves to Charles X. in no other character. The
vessel is a place of asylum and of liberty; a foreign
one has been chosen: as such, the King should be
entirely free in it."

On the question of the cockade, Charles X. had
been inflexible. He would not look at the colors of
the Revolution. The crews of the *Great Britain*
and the *Charles Carroll* carried the American flag.
Although belonging to the French military marine,
Commander Dumont-d'Urville had to wear citizen's
dress on board, so as to spare the King the unpleasing
sight of a tricolored cockade. This officer, for the
sake of additional security, asked for two convoy ships.
Two little vessels belonging to the State, the *Seine*
and the *Rôdeur*, were put at his disposal. But this
proceeding was carefully concealed from Charles X.

Before giving the signal for departure, the commissioners came on board to take leave of the royal
family and to ask if they had no recommendations
to transmit to their government. It was then the
King gave them these lines written with his own
hand: "At the moment when I am about to embark,
I ought to testify to you, gentlemen, that, in the
commission with which you were charged near me,
I have nothing but praise for the cares and attentions
you have shown to me personally, to my family, and

the persons who have accompanied me. I owe you
this justice, and I render it to you, as you have testified your wish for it."

Charles X. afterwards spoke to the commissioners
of the interests he was leaving behind him in France.
He had it especially at heart to continue the pen-
sions he had been making to some poor old émigrés,
to whom he felt himself personally bound. "Only,"
adds M. Odilon Barrot, "even while recommending
to us this debt, which he described as a debt of honor,
he was quite unwilling to owe its acquittal to the
government of the Revolution, and this is the way
he reasoned: 'You know, gentlemen, that a considerable treasure was found in the *Casauba* of Algiers.
It is needless for me to remind you of the principles
of our public right. This treasure came to me by
right of conquest; I dispose of it in favor of my
unfortunate pensioners.' At such a moment, any
discussion would have been a sovereign impropriety
and a useless brutality. We bowed, and confined
ourselves to saying we would refer the matter to our
government."

Is not this mention of the conquest of Algiers,
made at the very hour when the exile was commencing, a striking thing? "Heaven was pleased at
this moment," the author of the *Mémoires d' Outre-
Tombe* has said, "to insult both the victor and the
vanquished. Just while people were saying that *all
France* had been made indignant by the Ordinances,
addresses from the provinces reached King Louis-

Philippe which had been sent to King Charles X., congratulating him upon the *salutary measures he had taken and which would save the monarchy*. The Bey of Tittery, on his part, forwarded to the dethroned monarch, then on his way to Cherbourg, the following submission: 'In the name of God, etc., etc., . . . I recognize for sovereign and absolute master the great Charles X., the victorious; I will pay him the tribute, etc. . . .' Neither fortune could have been sported with more ironically. Revolutions are made nowadays by machinery; they are made so fast that a monarch who is still King on the frontier of his dominions is already a mere banished man in his capital."

Charles X. had at least this privilege of departing as a sovereign, escorted by his body-guards up to the hour when he took ship for exile. Seventeen years and a half later, Louis-Philippe will be obliged to quit France in disguise and with scarcely an attendant to follow him.

The ship which was to carry Charles X. and his family toward the shores of England had but a few moments longer to remain in the French roadstead. The King wished to speak for the last time to Marshal Maison. He had him enter his cabin. On coming out, the marshal exclaimed: " What a beautiful character that man has! It is impossible to be better or nobler!"

The moment was approaching when leave must be taken of the persons who were not going, but who

had come aboard to bid the exiles a last farewell.
" Madame the Dauphiness remained on the deck of
the vessel," says Count Joseph d'Estourmel; "she
kept the two children pressed close against her, and
extended her hands over them.   I looked at her
through my tears; her attitude was sublime.   The
Queen's sorrow and the mother's, the most moving
spectacle, in a word, that earth can show to heaven:
the strife between virtue and misfortune. The appearance presented by the ship at this moment would be
difficult to describe.   We were all mixed up together,
the royal family, the commissioners, sailors of every
grade, and we courtiers of the exile. . . .   Marshal
Maison made the most respectful of reverences to
Mademoiselle; one might have said he was still saluting the future Duchess of Chartres.   I have been
assured, but I did not hear it myself, that one of the
three commissioners said to Charles X., pointing to
the Duke of Bordeaux: ' Bring him up well; he may
be very useful one day.'   I received a last adieu and
acknowledgment of gratitude from the King.   I
ascended the ladder, which was drawn up after us,
and the royal family remained, delivered over to M.
Dumont-d'Urville, whose death has been too disastrous
to permit one to disturb his ashes."

The commissioners were withdrawing, when a
woman belonging to the suite of Madame the Duchess
of Angoulême approached M. Odilon Barrot and delivered to him, on the part of the Princess, an unsealed
letter, apprising him at the same time that after some

time a confidential person would come to take it from his hands; it was a blank signature which was to be used in the administration of the affairs of that Princess. "I was all the more touched by this mark of confidence on her part," says M. Barrot, "because, through respect, I had constantly kept away from her and had never once addressed a remark to her. It seemed as if she had divined the lively and profound sympathy with which she inspired me. I confess that, in the whole course of my life, no distinction has seemed more valuable to me." Is not this a significant remark from the man who had advised the march of the Parisians on Rambouillet?

The embarkation of Charles X. at Cherbourg will leave in history a pathetic souvenir. One of the writers most devoted to the Orleans family, M. Jules Janin, has thus expressed himself in his work entitled *La Normandie:* "With a firm step the King of France, grandson of that Philip Augustus who had retaken Normandy, of that Charles VII. who had saved it, of that King Louis XII. who had so much loved it, goes up into the ship which takes him and his family away. Along the shore the peoples cease talking, the Christians are praying with fervor; the body-guards, last companions of a prince so good, present arms, weeping. . . . And that is how the greatest monarchy of the universe may end!"

At half-past two the gang-plank was raised, the signal of departure was given, and the two ships began to move. Before they had cleared the last channel of the roadstead, the Duchess of Angoulême approached the captain and reminded him, as she looked at the Artois dock, that it was in her presence, two years before, that the waters of the sea had flooded it for the first time. Then her eyes sought among the different vessels lying at anchor, that which bore the name of the Duke of Bordeaux. M. Dumont-d'Urville pointed it out to her, but added that its name had been changed to *Friedland* the day before. According to the captain, consternation was depicted on the countenance of every member of the suite. Marshal Marmont's face changed, and his whole bearing betrayed a profound dejection. The Duke of Bordeaux and his sister were the only ones who occupied themselves wholly with the spectacle, a new one for them, of the ship and its rigging. The two ships moved out into the open sea. The shores of France were about to disappear in the distance. Sad, but resigned, Charles X. cast a final glance on that dear country which Providence had condemned him nevermore to see. As to the Duchess of Berry, nothing in her attitude indicated discouragement. She wore a riding-cap on her head. Her physiognomy had a nameless confidence and audacity, and while beholding the land of France on the horizon, she seemed to be saying: I shall return.

INDEX

Abdication of Charles X., 201, 211, 220.

Address of the Two Hundred, 20; read to the King, 22.

Algiers, war declared against, by France, 18; taking of, 50, 53, 55; French forces at, 51; the Dey of, informed of the attack by the opposition journals, 52; quotation from the *Journal des Débats* on, 54.

Angoulême, Duke of. See Dauphin.

Angoulême, Duchess of, ignorant of the Ordinances, 78; not informed of the King's intentions, 177; her journey to Vichy, 178 *et seq.*; at Autun, 180; learns of the Ordinances at Mâcon, 181; reception prepared for her at Tonnerre, 183; meets the Duke of Chartres, 185; at Fontainebleau, 186; reaches Rambouillet, 187; and the abdication, 202; greatly agitated at the prospect of exile, 291; her grief, 263, 314; demeanor of, on the ship, 322; sends a letter by M. Barrot touching her private affairs, 322.

Anne, M. Théodore, describes the departure from Saint-Cloud, 158; on the departure from Valognes, 313.

Argentan, alarm at, during the stay of the King, 264.

Barrot, M. Odilon, sent by the Duke of Orleans to escort Charles X., 197; brings back the answer of Charles X. to Louis-Philippe's message, 212; interview of, with Charles X., 227; letter of, to Louis-Philippe, 233; memoirs of, quoted, 250; letter of, to Louis-Philippe, 258; letter of, to Guizot respecting the King's protracted journey, 267; letter of, to Lafayette on the slowness of the King's march, 268; letter of, to Louis-Philippe respecting the conduct of the commissioners, 272, 276; tells of the passage through Carentan, 290; his conversations with Charles X. on the Ordinances, 299.

Bazaine, Marshal, 165.

Berry, Duchess of, her soirées at the Tuileries, 7; ball given by, to the King and Queen of Naples, 38; her devotion to her husband's memory, 65; ignorant of the Ordinances, 78; invites the Duchess of Orleans to be her guest at Dieppe, 79; courage of, during the insurrection, 111; sees the tricolored flag on the Louvre, 131; does not approve the King's policy, 145; forbidden by the King to leave Saint-Cloud, 147; goes with the King to Versailles, 157; departs for Rambouillet, 163; wears a man's costume, 167, 285; does not approve of the King's decision to entrust Bordeaux to the Duke of Orleans, 205; not permitted to plead her cause, 207; her courage, 285; her unwillingness to go into exile, 291.

Norwood Press:
J. S. Cushing & Co. — Berwick & Smith.
Boston, Mass., U.S.A.

Made in the USA
Lexington, KY
30 August 2010